Daniel Silander & Mats Öhlén (editors)

Sweden and the European Union

An Assessment of the Influence of EU-membership on Eleven Policy Areas in Sweden

Santérus
Academic Press
Sweden

www.santerus.se

ISBN 978-91-7335-056-3

Cover art: Composition IX. Painting by Wassily Kandinsky 1936. (Musée National d'Art Moderne, Centre Georges Pompidou, Paris).

Cover profile: Sven Bylander

Typefaces used: Indigo Antiqua Pro by Fontanova Ström AB; Anziano Pro by Stefan Hattenbach, MAC Rhino Fonts

Santérus Academic Press is an imprint of Santérus Förlag, Stockholm, Sweden

info@santerus.se

Printed by BOD, Germany 2020

Contents

Preface

This book on Swedish politics and the European Union (EU) has been produced in a time characterised by a democratic deficit in Swedish citizens' knowledge about the EU at home. On 17 July 2014, the Government decided to initiate an inquiry into the possibilities of improving transparency, participation and influence concerning policy issues within the EU and to investigate the level of knowledge Swedes have about the EU and how this knowledge level could be impacted by Swedish actors. Furthermore, the inquiry was to identify potential measures to improve transparency and participation of Swedish citizens in policy issues (Ju 2014:20). The main purpose was to 'contribute to democratic development in line with the democracy policy goal of strengthening the individual's capacity for influence' (SOU 2016:9).

Based on the premise that a well-functioning Swedish democracy requires transparency, knowledge and the capacity for civic influence, the inquiry emphasises that while more and more issues are being discussed and decided at the European level and within the EU's institutions, the conditions required for Swedish citizens to be informed on and influence policy issues decided on at the EU level have worsened. There are several reasons for this growing Swedish democratic deficit. One such reason is that the EU is a complex political project that can be difficult to understand and exert influence over from within. The inquiry, however, also points to deteriorating conditions in Sweden for transparency and participation insofar as national channels for demos are not sufficiently open, that the Swedish public conversation is too limited in its depiction of policy at the European level, and that the general knowledge among social groups regarding EU institutions and policy issues at the European level is too low.

The inquiry points in particular to an extensive lack of knowledge in Swedish society regarding the relationship between Swedish policy and the EU. This lack of knowledge is identified in those groups whose public assignment is to act as channels for and disseminate knowledge about democracy. The inquiry emphasises, inter alia, how politicians and civil servants in Swedish municipalities have limited knowledge of how municipal policy is linked to policy at the EU level, how journalists need to expand their knowledge of how the EU is structured and functions, and how the Swedish school system exhibits limited knowledge about how Swedish democracy and the EU are interconnected. Unfortunately, even political scientists at Swedish universities and university colleges demonstrate insufficient knowledge in this regard.

This lack of knowledge among Swedish people concerning Swedish policy and the EU is also affected by shifts of power and new functions for the political institutions. Among other things, it is emphasised that while the Swedish Government, at the expense of the Riksdag, has gained increased legislative power in the areas decided on at the EU level, information to the citizens has been limited, which has obstructed transparency, influence and support for the legislative work. This also applies to policy at the municipal level where the inquiry points to the absence of debate and discussions with citizens about how municipalities should act in matters that link the local to the European. Another problem in terms of the democratic deficit is the absence of a public conversation about Sweden, Swedish policy and the EU.

It is emphasised that neither the media nor Swedish political parties highlight how Swedish and European policies are intertwined or how Swedish institutions and EU institutions are interconnected in a common political system. Furthermore, there is no public conversation about the actual political parties and divisions that exist within the EU, but rather the picture provided is simplified in terms of Sweden and the EU without informing the citizen of the fact that there are major divisions within Sweden regarding how policy should be designed at the EU level.

This book is an attempt to contribute to a public conversation about Swedish policy and the EU. It is our hope that this type of book will fulfil an important function at schools and universities, but also for politicians, civil servants and the media with regard to how Sweden and Europe in general, and Swedish policy and the EU in particular, are interwoven in one political system.

References

Official Government Inquiry, SOU 2016. *EU på hemmaplan [EU on the home field]*. Stockholm.

1. Swedish Politics and the EU

An Introduction

Daniel Silander & Mats Öhlén

Studies on international dependency in the 1960s, the comprehensive globalization literature of the 1990s and research on networks in the 2000s show that social sciences for a long time have focused on how international politics influence national politics. This study uses this tradition of studies as a basis on which to define how the European Union (EU) has impacted Sweden and Swedish politics. Sweden joined the EU on 1 January 1995. The Swedish Government with Ingvar Carlsson as prime minister applied for membership in the union on 1 July 1991. An agreement developed in March 1994 under Carl Bildt's government, and the outcome of the advisory referendum on 13 November 1994 made way for membership. For a long time after the formal accession in 1995, political discussions continued among both politicians and citizens as to whether it was right or wrong to become a member and how membership could affect Sweden. However, a more active Swedish disposition towards the EU was realised when Sweden officially took over the presidency of the EU Council of Ministers in the first half of 2001 (see Johansson 2002, Tallberg 2001). Today, about 25 years after accession, Swedish participation is strongly rooted in the political establishment and among the majority of citizens (Standard Eurobarometer 2014).

The aim of this anthology is to analyse what being a member of the EU since 1995 means for Swedish politics. The purpose is to study what changes to the organisation (form) and content (substance) of Swedish policy have resulted from a more deeply ingrained membership. Based on the assumption that Swedish policy is a part of multilevel governance at a local, regional, national and European level, the focus is on the interaction between Swedish national policy and the EU. The study therefore partly analyses how Swedish policy is governed and shaped, and partly how the content of the policy has changed in the interplay between Swedish political institutions and the EU.

To understand how Swedish policy is affected, the concepts of Europeanisation, governance and policy processes are introduced (see Chapter 2). The use of this conceptual framework allows for a deeper understanding of how and why Swedish policy has changed. Swedish policy refers to the following eleven 'policy areas': economic policy, agricultural policy, environmental policy, social policy, education policy, gender equality policy, asylum and migration policy, crime prevention policy, foreign and security policy, neighbourhood policy and development and aid policy. Every policy area has been scrutinised over time, from the moment of EU membership until today.

Further discussion in this chapter provides a brief, overall picture of what it means for Sweden to be part of the EU. Chapter 2 presents the theoretical point of departure of the study, with a particular focus on Europeanisation, governance and policy processes. These concepts provide guidance in the individual analyses of policy areas that are subsequently presented in Chapters 3–13. It is important to point out that the various chapters take on an outside-in perspective, which means that the organisation and content of the change to Swedish policy is of interest. Sweden is also treated as a homogeneous actor in relation to the EU, which means that the primary focus is on the nation/state of Sweden rather than, for example, on regional or local actors. Each chapter can be read separately and provides insight into a specific policy area, but comparisons with other policy areas provide a more comprehensive picture of the change to Swedish policy. In conclusion, Chapter 14 therefore discusses the overall change to Swedish policy that has resulted from EU membership.

Sweden, the EU and Competencies

The policy change of recent decades has shown strong tendencies towards increased international cooperation. On the one hand, according to the historically prevalent intergovernmental cooperation, two or more states have agreed, by written treaty or verbally, to work together within one or more policy areas but with retained sovereignty. On the other hand, supranational cooperation has also emerged, which means that the states have partially abandoned their sovereignty to a supranational power and have become federal states with autonomy within specific areas. In a global comparison of regional development, these patterns have been most evident in Europe and throughout the EU.

The EU wields real power within Swedish, European and global policy. However, the EU is a complex project that constitutes a mix of international and supranational cooperation. In a number of areas, the EU has sovereignty over the member states, but in other areas, the member states assume this sovereignty. In addition, some policy areas are of no concern to the EU. The EU has therefore come to consist of institutions representing various interests in Europe. It is a hybrid, where some EU institutions represent the Union's interests (Commission), whereas others represent the member states (Council of Ministers) and the individual citizens of the Union (European Parliament).

In short, it should be emphasised that the Commission's right of initiative represents the Union's interests and is a driving force in the Union's work. The Commission enforces and monitors EU law, the budget and policy decisions that the Council of Ministers and the European Parliament make. The Commission is also the Union's face to the rest of the world and is responsible for the establishment of international agreements. The Council of Ministers is the decision-making body and the legislative body of the Union, but it shares responsibility with the European Parliament within a number of areas, which have increased over time. In addition to adopting European regulations and directives together with the Council of Ministers, the European Parliament also approves the EU budget and controls the Commission by approving or rejecting Commissioners during elections to the Commission. Furthermore, the Court of Justice is responsible for monitoring compliance with community law, but it also provides interpretations of the law and settles legal disputes among member states, institutions, companies and citizens of the Union (Nugent 2010, Tallberg 2013).

For a long time, from the Maastricht Treaty in 1993 to the Lisbon Treaty in 2009, the EU organisation could be described using a metaphor of three pillars of cooperation areas. *The first pillar* was the European Communities (EC); it constituted the old cooperation in place since the 1950s but with the new addition of the Economic and Monetary Union (EMU). *The second pillar* was the Common Foreign and Security Policy (CFSP), which was an attempt to coordinate a common foreign and security policy within the Union's member states. *The third pillar* included police and judicial cooperation in criminal matters, as well as justice and home affairs, but many of these were subsequently moved to the first pillar.

Cooperation in the first pillar was largely supranational, which meant that supranational institutions steered policy by using decisions with a qualified majority, through the Commission's legislative competence and the direct effect of the EC law at the time. Large parts of these areas were developed over decades following the creation of the European Coal and Steel Community in the 1950s, but in the 1990s, new areas were also added to the cooperation within the European Monetary Union (EMU). The other two pillars were intergovernmental, which meant that the member states were formally independent in their decision-making and that different states made and implemented decisions unanimously. These areas were also newer within the Union cooperation or were areas where a deeper integration had historically proved difficult to realise. Therefore, the decision-making mechanism was intergovernmental, and each state retained the right not to participate (Nugent 2010, McCormick 2014).

The supranationality within the former first pillar's policy areas has made the EU a unique international cooperation forum in comparison with other regional organisations/cooperations. This supranationality means that membership entails the transfer of decision-making rights to the supranational institutions of the EU. Membership also entails limited sovereignty insofar as membership has required the implementation of the EU's regulations, particularly EU law. EU law is directly applicable to the member states and has constituted a part of the national law in each member state. In the event of conflicting EU law and national law, the former takes precedence, and Swedish courts are required to apply EU law. For citizens and organised actors, this entails the right to appeal to the Court of Justice to examine the rulings of national courts. The previous cooperation areas within pillars two and three lacked these supranational mechanisms. No legal obligation existed regarding the transfer of decision-making authority. Furthermore, member states (within the cooperation areas in pillars two and three) were not required to implement legal rules (Hettne & Bergström 2014, Gröning & Zetterquist 2010). On 13 December 2007, the EU's heads of state and government signed the Lisbon Treaty in Lisbon, Portugal. The treaty officially entered into effect on 1 December 2009 and modified the aforementioned pillar structure of policy areas and responsibilities. Some important examples of changes are that the former intergovernmental cooperation in pillar two that concerned foreign and security policy was intensified between the member states via the Union, creating the position of high representative of the Union for foreign affairs and security policy, and through the establishment of the European External Action Service. Furthermore, the previous rotating presidency of the European Council was replaced with a permanent presidency for 2.5 years. Additional important reforms included a strengthening of the European Parliament's power in legislative processes, giving it the same status as the Council of Ministers within an increasing number of areas. Another major transformation that the Lisbon Treaty sparked is that the pillar structure discussed above was replaced when the EU became a single legal entity. Previously, after the Maastricht Treaty, each pillar constituted its own legal entity with the right to ratify new international agreements. Through the new treaty, the Union's powers were clarified in Articles 2 to 6 of the Treaty, by way of a division into three categories of decision-making competencies. These categories highlighted the party under whose responsibility a policy area falls, be it the individual member state or the Union. Within Sweden's so-called competence catalogue, the policy areas were divided into three categories for the *EU: exclusive competence, shared competence* and *supporting competence* (Gröning & Zetterquist 2010, McCormick 2014).

The first category of *exclusive competence* (or assigned power) refers to the Union's exclusive right to legislate and institutionalise legally binding acts, in which the role of the individual member state is only to implement the Union's decisions. The member states assign this exclusive competence to the Union, which means that the Union's laws and regulations come into being after the member states have jointly decided to give exclusive competence to the Union. The exclusive competence gives the Union the right to initiate and implement legislation for all of the member states, but the Commission must have a basis in one or more articles of the treaty to institute any binding legislation. The European Parliament and the Council of Ministers scrutinize the Commission's legislative work, which ensures that the Commission's legislative work is, in fact, based on the treaties. It is also the role of the Court of Justice to examine whether acts are based on the treaties, and if not, to annul them.

The second category of *shared competence* emphasises that each individual member state has the right to institutionalise legislation if the Union has not previously done so within the area. This means, in practice, that both the individual member state and the Union have the right to legislate and institutionalise binding legal agreements. If the individual member state has regulations within an area, the Union must not legislate in a manner that undermines or prevents the country's act from being applied.

The third category of *supporting competence* emphasises that the Union has only a supporting role in relation to individual member states' legislative processes through providing advice and coordination. The Union may not act in a way that forces member states to harmonise laws and regulations, as such an influence would imply that the Union is restricting the competence of the individual member state (regarding competencies, see European Commission, European Union).

These three categories of competencies illustrate how different policy areas can be included under various types of competencies, thus regulating the extent to which the individual member state or the Union has the main power to formulate regulations and directives. However, it should be emphasised that the policy areas that are not explicitly regulated in the EU treaties are entirely beyond the EU's decision-making power, and if new policy areas fall under the EU's competencies, all member states must approve this by ratifying amendments to the existing treaties, which requires unanimity. A single exception to this is the so-called Flexibility Clause (Article 352 of TFEU), which allows the EU to make decisions within a policy area where the treaty does not confer power on the EU. However, this is done only in cases where such action is required to achieve the overall objectives that the treaty sets for the specific policy area. However, the Council of Ministers must agree on such a necessary action of the EU, and the European Parliament must approve it.

The above division of competencies is the official design of the EU's structure as it exists today. However, it should be emphasised that Swedish policy and that of the EU are rarely entirely designed based on the competence under which the issue formally resides. *First*, even if the EU has exclusive competencies within an area, member states are involved in the legislative process, as they have ministers on the Council of Ministers approving regulations and directives. In addition, the European Parliament has members from each country, who together with the Council of Ministers make proposals, amendments and decisions. In addition, the various member states should implement the Commission's initiated proposals, following a decision to do so. Legislation is therefore often broad in the form of directives concerning targets to be achieved. Each member state is subsequently required to respond to it and shape it to implement nationally.

Second, even if the EU does not have competencies regarding a member state's policy area development, it has been found that new Swedish laws and ordinances have increasingly come to refer to regulations and directives at the EU level. Furthermore, it has been emphasised that the EU's adopted legislation is largely implemented at the regional and local levels in Sweden and that the EU influences an extensive number of policy issues raised at the municipal council's table in Swedish policy, either in temporary projects or via EU legislation and rules (Sveriges riksdag, Swedish Parliament 2009).

As the complexity of the political process has increased with EU membership, Swedish political control and governance have been hampered. For Sweden, this has meant that it has become increasingly important to identify a national position at an early stage in the preparation and decision-making process, to demonstrate a uniform and well-organised policy and to find allies at the negotiating table so as to leave Sweden's mark on the political agenda. In addition to this formal structure, a very important informal structure of lobbying consists of negotiations and pressure from the member states' governments, parliaments and committees of institutions and politicians. These informal structures may also comprise contact with Commissioners and members of the European Parliament to influence what proposals are put forward and how these are formulated. Thus, in all decision-making processes within the EU are a formal and informal path of influence, where the formal pathways are visible, whereas hierarchical structures and the informal ones are more invisible and network based (Tallberg 2013, Blomgren & Berggren 2005).

Today, 1,200 Swedes are estimated to work within the EU, including politicians as well as civil servants. In addition to around 120 employees at the EU Representation in Brussels and an EU ambassador, an extensive staff of civil servants also exist within the Commission. Furthermore, there are politicians and/or civil servants within the European Council, the Commission, the Council of Ministers, the Court of Justice, the European Parliament, the Court of Auditors, the European Committee of the Regions and the European Economic and Social Committee. Our foremost Swedish representative vis-à-vis the EU is, of course, our prime minister, and under the prime minister are all of the Swedish ministers responsible for managing the EU issues within each policy area, which means interpreting and following the applicable EU regulations in the area, as well as coordinating the policy area in relation to Swedish structures. These ministers also represent Sweden within their particular affair areas before the Council of Ministers (Sveriges riksdag, Swedish Parliament a, b).

The prime minister's state secretary is the chairman of the coordinating group for EU relations, which consists of all state secretaries. The coordinating group is responsible for the coordination of EU matters within the government offices and is the channel to the ministries. The ministries have their own EU-coordination functions for the internal organisation and for cooperation with other relevant ministries. Many EU matters naturally also concern multiple ministries, which requires a committee in consultation with all of the relevant ministries (Blomgren & Berggren 2005). EU membership saw the establishment of the Committee on European Union Affairs, which represents all parliamentary parties. The Committee has an advisory function and is an information channel between the Riksdag and the coordinating group for EU relations in the government offices. The coordinating group is required to consult the committee on EU matters. The coordinating group informs the committee of what matters should be discussed in the Council of Ministers, and a joint discussion is had on the government's proposed position. The Committee on European Union Affairs can also convene a meeting to influence what issues should end up on the EU agenda and be discussed within the Council of Ministers (Blomgren & Berggren 2005).

Against this background, the next chapter introduces the theoretical departure points of the anthology. These then form the basis of the book's analysis of changes to the Swedish policy areas from 1995 until today.

References

Blomgren, M & T Berggren (ed.) 2005. *EU och Sverige – ett sammanlänkat statsskick [EU and Sweden – an interlinked form of government]*. Stockholm: Liber.

European Commission 20150228. *The European Citizens' Initiative, official register*. http://ec.europa.eu/citizens-initiative/public/competencies/faq?lg=en

European Union 20150228. *Treaty Establishing a Constitution for Europe*. https://europa.eu/european-union/sites/europaeu/files/docs/body/treaty_establishing_a_constitution_for_europe_en.pdf

Gröning, L & O Zetterquist 2010. *Konstitution, institution och jurisdiktion [Constitution, Institution and Jurisdiction]* Stockholm: Liber.

Hettne, J & C F Bergström 2014. *Introduktion till EU-rätten [Introduction to EU law]*. Lund: Studentlitteratur.

Johansson, K-M (ed.) 2002. *Sverige i EU – dilemman, institutioner, politikområden [Sweden in the EU – dilemma, institutions, policy areas]*. Stockholm: SNS förlag.

McCormick, J 2014. *Understanding the European Union – A Concise Introduction*. London: Palgrave MacMillan.

Nugent, N 2010. *The Government and Politics of the European Union*. London: Palgrave Macmillan.

Standard Eurobarometer 82 autumn 2014. *Public Opinion in the European Union – First Results*. Brussels: European Commission.

Sveriges riksdag, Swedish Parliament 2009. Svensk lagstiftning som härrör från EU [Swedish legislation deriving from the EU]. Utredningstjänsten [Parliamentary Investigative Service] Ref. 2009:791.

Sveriges riksdag, Swedish Parliament, a 20150228.
EU Information Services. EU-lagar gäller före svenska lagar [EU laws before Swedish laws]. http://www.
eu-upplysningen.se/Sverige-i-eu/eu-lagar-galler-framfor-svenska-lagar/ (in Swedish)

Sveriges riksdag, Swedish Parliament, b 20150215. *EU Information Services. Mer än 1000 svenskar arbetar inom EU [More than 1000 Swedes work within the EU]*. http://www.
eu-upplysningen.se/Sverige-i-eu/Svenskar-i-eu/ (in Swedish)

Tallberg, J 2013. *EU:s politiska system [The EU political system]*. Lund: Studentlitteratur.

— (ed.) 2001. *När Europa kom till Sverige – Ordförandeskapet i EU 2001 [When Europe came to Sweden – Presidency of the EU in 2001]*. Stockholm: SNS.

2. Europeanisation, Governance and Policy Processes

Mats Öhlén & Daniel Silander

There is no doubt that EU membership has influenced Sweden's political system. Three examples may suffice to illustrate this. First, the full set of EU regulations (*acquis communautaire*) was incorporated into Swedish legislation once membership was in place. Second, Swedish actors on various levels became potential receivers of European Union (EU) funds. Third, Sweden's external relations were either completely subordinated to the EU (as in the area of trade) or coordinated by it (as in foreign and security policy). The relevant question, however, is *in what way* the country's political system has been influenced, and *to what extent*.

What does it mean to say that Sweden's political system has been influenced by EU membership? A clarification is necessary here. In political science, it is customary to differentiate between politics, policy, and the polity. Politics involves what is usually referred to as the political game, which mostly relates to party politics and party organisations. Policy concerns the making of concrete political decisions and their implementation. The polity, finally, comprises the organisation of the state in terms of government and public administration. The focus of this book is on the second and third of these: policy and the polity. Thus, we are interested in how EU membership has affected the Swedish political system in terms of its content (*i.e.*, its outcomes), and in terms of its form (*i.e.*, its organisation). This book is *not* concerned, however, with how the country's party system and political parties have been influenced in terms of organisation, strategy, or cleavages.

In this chapter, we introduce two central concepts for our book – Europeanisation and governance – before concluding with a section on policy processes. These concepts are vital for understanding how and why a member state of the EU – in this case Sweden – is influenced by its membership therein. Influence of a more technical type (*e.g.*, a new regulatory framework for farmers) is relatively easy to identify, but gradual and subtle changes in terms of organisation and policy content are more difficult to pinpoint. We need more precise concepts if we are to understand the dynamics in the relationship between Sweden and the EU. By utilizing these concepts, we can add a theoretical aspect to the discussion on the consequences of EU membership. We hope thereby to provide a starting point from which various policy areas can be compared, and to contribute to a wider discussion on the consequences of EU membership for Swedish politics.

Europeanisation

Europeanisation relates specifically to a process whereby EU institutions and political arrangements, both formally and informally, influence their counterparts at the national level within the member states. Studies on this question emerged already in the 1970s, but it was in the 1990s that the theme became popular among academics. This likely reflected the creation of a political union in 1993, with the Treaty of Maastricht, and the intense integration process that followed. The main focus of studies in this area has been on explaining the processes involved, and on tracing significant variations amongst member states and amongst policy areas when it comes to the consequences of Europeanisation (Pollack 2010: 37). One central claim made in the literature is that the level of Europeanisation is likely the product of two factors: (1) how well demands from the Union mesh with existing institutions, rules, norms, and practices at the national level; and (2) how strongly different variables at the national level – such as the number of veto points or the resistance of national institutions to change – intervene (Cowles *et al.* 2001). The pressure to change will be weaker when there is a good fit between the EU level and the national level with regard to rules and institutions. Conversely, the pressure for change at the national level will be stronger when national institutions differ significantly from their counterparts at the level of the Union. However, the match between the two levels is not a constant. On the contrary, it varies over time and (especially) between different policy areas. Our aim in this book is to clarify this variation in the case of one particular member state: Sweden.

Demands and expectations for national adaptation as a consequence of EU membership take various forms (Tallberg *et al.* 2010: 17). On the one hand they may be formal, as when legislation and guidelines result in juridical demands for the adaptation of national rules and institutions. When a country joins the Union, for example, it must adopt the full framework of EU rules (*acquis communautaire*). The EU also adopts new treaties, new rules, and new targets over time, which in turn creates new demands and expectations for national adaptation. On the other hand, the pressure for national change has a more informal character when norms, ideas, and practices established at the Union level slowly influence national political systems. An example of this can be seen in the increasingly strong position of the governments of the member states, reflecting the role that they play in representing the latter in EU negotiations. Another example of such informal pressure is evident in the changes which national governments have made in their administrative organisation.

In the theoretical literature, the division into formal and informal demands for national change has been linked to two different logics of Europeanisation: the logic of consequences, and the logic of appropriateness (March & Olsen 1989, Börzel & Risse 2007). The logic of consequences is based on the assumption that actors are rational and that their preferences are fixed. In the context of the EU, this may apply to situations where actors try to link new proposals to the most suitable (from their perspective) paragraph in the treaties. For example, the European Commission might formulate a proposal in such a way as to link it clearly to a treaty paragraph, thereby positioning the proposal within a policy area over which the member states have limited influence once the proposal is approved. The logic of appropriateness, by contrast, involves an entirely different view on actors, opening up for a broader view on their preferences. Rooted in the social-constructivist tradition, it portrays the ideas, interests, and aims of actors as dynamic rather than static – as changing over time and according to context. Compared to the rationalist tradition, moreover, this approach entails a broader view on institutions – as involving rules and routines that define which actions are appropriate in each specific situation (March & Olsen 1989: 21). In this tradition, furthermore, rules, norms, and values are viewed as independent variables. Thus, through the behavioural expectations that they bear, institutions exert influence over the actors involved. They reward behaviour seen as appropriate, and they punish behaviour seen as inappropriate. In this way, they influence both actors and decisions.

Thus, the Europeanisation of national politics and policy may be both direct and indirect (see Vink & Graziano 2007). Direct effects are the result of specific demands from the EU – *e.g.*, for new regulations in the area of agriculture. Indirect effects, by contrast, do not derive directly from EU decisions, but they still arise as a consequence of Union membership. Organisational changes in the public administration of member states – for the sake of a better fit with official EU policy areas – are an example. The Swedish constitution mentions nothing about EU influence on the country's public administration, but pressures to adapt are in fact heavy. Ministries are continually reviewing how to coordinate their management of EU-related issues with various interest groups and with other agencies. They usually do this during an early phase of the decision-making process, thereby simplifying the formulation of Swedish opinions before negotiations are conducted in the Council, as well as – at a later stage – before the EU's directives are implemented in Sweden (Beckman & Johansson 2002). Furthermore, public administration in Sweden is linked – as it is in all member states – to the policy process at the Union level. This generates further informal pressures to adapt. Most notably, Swedish public servants participate in various expert groups and in the so-called 'comitology committees'. The role of the expert groups is primarily to provide advice as the Commission prepares new proposals. The task of the 'comitology committees' is to assist the Commission in implementing new EU legislation – in other words, to help it ensure that all of the member states enforce the new rules. Taken together, these elements point to an informal and indirect Europeanisation of Swedish public administration, at both the organisational and the individual level.

Some clarifications are in order where informal and indirect Europeanisation is concerned. For one thing, Europeanisation does not necessarily mean convergence, *i.e.*, the shaping of all member states along the same lines by EU legislation and institutions. The relevant thing is the response of the actors – how they adapt to changes in the political context in which they work. Their adaptive responses may take different forms in different member states, as well as in different policy areas within a single member state. It is furthermore often difficult, methodologically speaking, to assess the impact of the Union on national political systems – whether for change or for continuity. Europeanisation is only one of several factors influencing political processes at the national level. Economic globalisation, intensified urbanisation, an ageing population, a transformed media landscape, a transformation in the values of the population – these are just a few of the factors that may strongly influence national political development.

Governance and Multilevel Governance

Governance can be described as a distinctive form of government. It is carried out through organised networks of public and private actors, which steer public policy towards common aims (Rhodes 1996: 660). In fact, governance can be regarded as the opposite of 'government', inasmuch as it lacks a clear single power centre.

It is in the EU, without any doubt, that we find the most visible instance of governance today. As compared with traditional international organisations, the EU involves cooperation of more advanced and institutionalised kind, for its member states have delegated their sovereignty to joint institutions in several areas. Yet the EU is far from being a traditional state, inasmuch as its member states have kept their sovereignty in many areas; moreover, they exert influence in areas which fall under the Union's own competence, through their involvement in the Council and in the various bodies that support the Commission. The EU is thus a unique hybrid – part state, part international organisation (see chapter 1). This demands a new theoretical framework. Earlier accounts of the EU have tended to use models and concepts from established theories. Neofunctionalism and liberal intergovernmentalism, for example, theorize integration in terms of concepts within international relations. Theories of the EU as a political system proceed on the basis of models from comparative politics. The governance perspective, by contrast, portrays the EU as a unique fusion between a state-like system and an international organisation, in which 'governing without government' takes place.

The governance perspective is not one single theory about the EU or European integration, but rather a cluster of theories with the same general focus. According to Hix (1998), it has four characteristics. *First*, it portrays the Union's governing processes as non-hierarchical, wherein public and private actors operating in networks devote substantial time and energy to deliberation and problem-solving. These actors are expected to abide by both formal and informal norms and rules. *Second*, according to this viewpoint, the governing processes of the Union are so unusual that traditional concepts do not suffice for analysing them. A new set of terms and concepts is thus essential. *Third*, scholars in this vein devote special attention to a specific type of policy process – one with a heavy stress on 'deliberation' and 'persuasion' – which is thought to characterise the EU in particular. In this model, actors adapt their goals and preferences to the needs of the process, and they put a stronger stress on good argument than on negotiating strength. *Fourth*, there is a tendency among these researchers to pay considerable attention to normative issues, such as the Union's democratic deficit or its less than complete legitimacy. According to the governance perspective, then, the EU holds the potential for a new model of democracy which does not copy the national type. This new model is built instead on discussion and persuasion, along lines envisioned in theories of deliberative democracy (see Joerges 2001, for example).

Our focus so far has been on the broad governance perspective, and on the view of EU politics that it entails. A more specific view zeroes in on the built-in multilevel logic of the EU system. Traditional research on the Union has tended to focus on its central institutions in Brussels, Luxembourg, and Strasbourg; however, these institutions do not exist in a vacuum. Most of the actors that prepare and administer EU legislation are actually situated in the member states. For them, the European dimension is just another policy level, not a separate activity. In fact, a large portion of EU policy is prepared and implemented by national officials who spend hardly any time in Brussels. They are politicians, civil servants, or experts who spend most of their time as national decision-makers. They spend a great deal of their time trying to assess how the EU influences their primary activities at home, and how they can apply its legislation in their daily work. At a reasonable guess, some 80 percent of their daily work on EU matters is coloured by domestic concerns (Wallace *et al.* 2010: 9). This may seem paradoxical. On the face of it, it seems unreasonable that 80 percent of national legislation should derive from the Union, even as 80 percent of the political context in which national decision-makers carry out their work reflects domestic problems and demands. But this is exactly how the Union works. For this reason, the EU is best portrayed as a kind of fusion or amalgam between the two levels of governance. Decisions and competencies sought at the national level get compiled into European rules, which are then implemented nationally.

While the main focus of this book is on the European and national levels, it must be stressed that there are additional levels as well. All of the member states have various local and regional sub-levels, the competence of which is conditioned in varying degrees by EU rules and decisions. Many decision-makers at these levels have direct contact from time to time with the institutions of the Union. In Sweden, moreover, a decentralisation process took place in the 1980s and 1990s, which had significant consequences for the relationship between the state and the municipalities. Traditionally, the central government in Sweden directed the doings of the municipalities by issuing formal mandates to them; now, however, it generally seeks dialogue and coordination with them. This process began in the 1990s, with the explicit goal of strengthening the link between political institutions and the various actors associated with them. One example of this can be seen in the 'region reform' carried out in two prominent regions in the south of Sweden: Skåne and Västra Götaland. In these two regions, so-called 'growth agreements' were concluded. In consultation with local and regional business groups, political bodies in each region prepared plans for the economic development of the region and its municipalities (Pierre 2010: 263). A parallel tendency is the broad globalisation trend of recent decades, which has further weakened the role of the

Swedish state. In several policy areas, including those where the EU is active, there are broad transnational consultations and agreements. These processes vary greatly in both range and significance, but they form part of a continuum of decision-making which includes several levels: local, regional, national, European (EU), and global (see Figure 2.1.). Many actors, moreover, are active on several different levels, and the way in which a given political issue develops often reflects a choice between these levels.

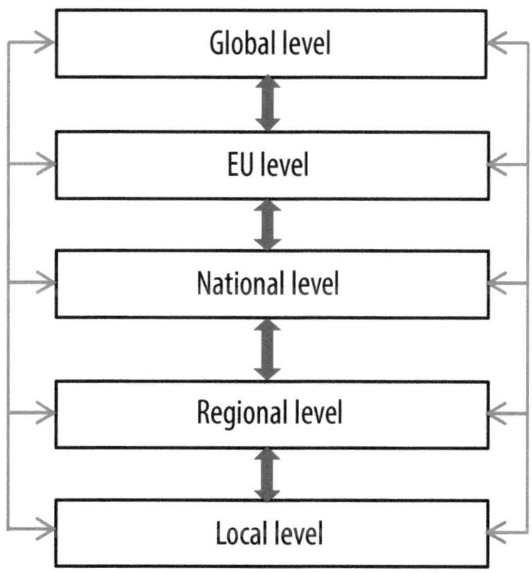

Figure 2.1: The different layers of government within the multilevel system of governance

Today, the governance perspective has established itself in the academic literature to the extent that its main assumptions about how politics works – especially at the level of the Union – are generally accepted. However, this new model is not uncontroversial or without critics. In its treatment of political accountability, for instance, it may be less than clear. Blomgren & Bergman (2005) argue there is something modern and seductive about this new trend, with its concepts of governance, policy networks, multilevel governance, and the like. But it has an aura of being so complex and advanced as to render traditional methods for measuring democratic aspects like openness and accountability unusable. The authors of this book agree with this critique. If we proceed on the assumption that policy is increasingly shaped in processes without transparency or a clear power centre, then it is obvious that power is becoming blurrier and less visible. This in turn leads to difficulties when it comes to holding those in power accountable. The lobbyists and network actors involved in EU policy-making are generally unknown to the public, both in Sweden and in other member states. Accordingly, Blomgren & Bergman argue, the legitimacy of political processes within systems marked by governance is insufficient for handling politically delicate matters (like the redistribution of resources). This reminds us of the vital role that traditional institutions play in guaranteeing democracy and transparency. They are central for promoting social trust, and they set out clear frameworks for the exercise of political power (Pierre 2010: 263). When we analyse the impact of EU membership on Sweden, therefore, we must confront the problems of weak accountability and insufficient transparency head on.

Policy Processes in the EU

The term 'policy' has no direct equivalent in the Swedish language, and as in several other countries it has been integrated into the Swedish conceptual toolbox. To simplify the matter somewhat, a policy can be defined as a broad political goal within a certain area. Rather than being a single decision, it consists of a package of strategies and decisions on various levels (Hill 2005: 6–7). A policy process, in turn, comprises the whole pattern whereby policy is created, implemented, and evaluated. To a great extent, the research on policy processes is about understanding the dynamics in the different phases of the policy process, and how these are linked together. The traditional distinction between the sphere of politics and that of public administration is not so prominent here. In the research on policy processes, actors from both the political domain and the civil service feature explicitly. Our aim in this book is to advance the discussion on the consequences of EU membership for the organisation and content of politics in Sweden.

What are the different phases of a policy process? The research on this point is not unequivocal, but in broad terms they can be described as: (1) agenda-setting; (2) policy formulation; (3) decision-making; (4) implementation; and (5) evaluation (Buonnano & Nugent 2013: 101; Young 2010: 47).

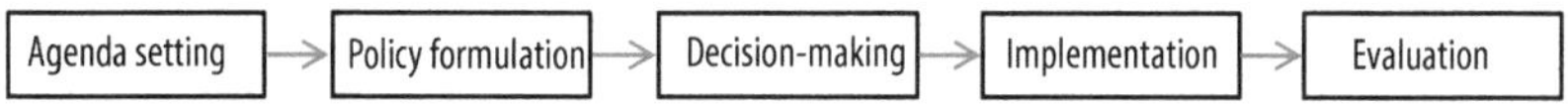

Figure 2.2: A Linear Model of the Policy Process

Such 'sequence-thinking' around the policy process (see Figure 2.2) has been criticised for picturing it according to an abstract model of how the process *should* work, instead of how it works in reality. More specifically, researchers have criticised the approach for giving the impression of a rational process with a clear starting and ending point, in which each phase causes the next. In reality, the different phases often overlap or even melt together (Hill 2005: 135, Sabatier 1999: 7). Instead, therefore, the metaphor of a 'cycle' has become increasingly common among analysts of policy processes (see, *e.g.*, Howlet *et al.* 2009; Parsons 1995). This tackles the critique mentioned above, since it portrays the policy process as a dynamic circular flow without a clear starting or ending point (see Figure 2.3). However, the critique regarding an overlap or fusion between different phases remains (see Kingdon 2003: 205). Nevertheless, the latter critique does not rule out the model as an analytical point of departure. Instead it cautions against relying on the model too heavily, due to the excessively simple and cut-and-dried way it portrays the policy process.

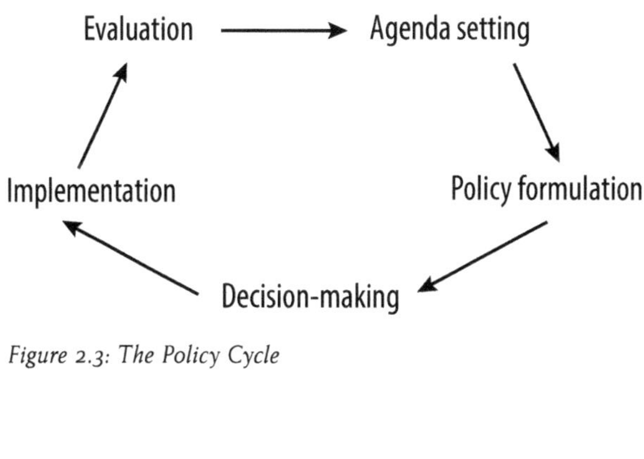

Figure 2.3: The Policy Cycle

A short presentation of each phase of the policy process now follows. Note that the EU provides the point of departure here, as our main focus is on the institutions of the Union in conjunction with the member states. Agenda-setting is primarily about putting a certain issue on the political agenda. In this phase, there is considerable scope for various actors or 'policy entrepreneurs' to exercise influence. These may be interest groups, political parties, administrative agencies, or individual politicians. The type of actors involved depends on the issue, inasmuch as the Union has different competencies in different policy areas. On issues where the EU has exclusive or shared competence, the European Commission plays a prominent role, in view of its exclusive right to formulate proposals for new legislation. Here the efforts of policy entrepreneurs are focused mainly on getting the Commission to pay more attention to their specific issue, or on persuading it to view their issue in a particular way. By contrast, on issues where the EU has merely a coordinating role – as in relation to the common foreign and security policy – it is domestic policy entrepreneurs that have the key role.

When an issue is finally on the agenda, the phase of *policy formulation* begins. Realistic options are identified, and concrete proposals prepared. This phase is integrated with the agenda-setting phase in part, since the actors that seek to put an issue on the agenda usually have a concrete proposal for addressing it. At this stage of the process, however, the central actors are clearly fewer in number, being limited to a quite narrow circle of key actors around the Commission (Buonanno & Nugent 2013: 105).

Then, once a proposal has been presented, the *decision-making* phase begins. Now the matter is less complicated: the proposal is either accepted or rejected. As mentioned in chapter 1, there is great variation between different policy areas when it comes to procedures for decision-making. All decisions on the common foreign and security policy, for example, require unanimity in the Council. By contrast, a majority in both the Council and the European Parliament suffices for market regulation and environmental issues (a qualified majority in the Council, a simple one in the Parliament). There are also various combinations, where the procedures employed fall somewhere between these two extremes.

In the *implementation* phase, the object is mainly to make sure the new legislation is realised in the member states. This phase is particularly important in the EU, because the difficulty of reaching agreement in the decision-making phase often has the consequence that vaguely worded compromises are adopted. This in turn results in many situations where different interpretations are possible about how the legislation is to be implemented. Formally speaking, the Commission is responsible for ensuring that all legislation is implemented; however, the concrete enforcement of new rules and directives lies in the hands of the administration of each member state. Moreover, the implementation process is prepared through the so-called 'comitology system', in which representatives from the member states keep a watchful eye on the Commission, in order to ensure that the process does not exceed the boundaries set out in the legislation. As a result, civil servants at the national level have a stronger role in the phase of implementation than they do in that of agenda-setting or of policy formulation (Young 2010: 50).

In the last phase, finally, the effectiveness of the policy is evaluated. If the policy implemented does not solve the problems it was created to address, there is usually pressure for further action, or for an altogether different strategy. The evaluation of policies is especially problematic at the level of the Union. There are two main explanations for this. First, the distance between the body which formulates proposals (the Commission) and the actors that implement them (primarily the administrative agencies of the member states) is huge. Second, the feedback often taken for granted at the national level – from political parties, interest groups, critical citizens, and above all scrutinising media – is weak or non-existent at the EU level. The first problem has been solved to a degree through the comitology system, but the second can only be addressed over a long period – perhaps a *very* long period – during which the requisite institutions are built up.

It should be noted that the policy process within the EU takes different forms in different policy areas. In part this is a consequence of certain differences between the member states that existed earlier, and which to some degree persist. In this regard, political actors have shown impressive creativity in adapting working procedures, decision-making processes, and constellations of actors to the needs of the different policy areas. Over time, then, five different models for policy-making have evolved. Their unique traits are displayed in Table 2.1 below.

Table 2.1: Models of Different Modes of Policy-Making in the EU

	Community method	***Regulatory model***	***Distributional model***	***Policy coordination***	***Transgovernmentalism***
Prominent examples	Agriculture, external trade	The single market, environment	Structural funds	Education	Foreign and security policy
Degree of centralisation	High	Varies	High	Low	Low
Role of member states	Subordinate, implementation of common policy	Implementation	Contributor/recipient	Participation in a learning process	Central
Role of the European Council	Rare	Rare	Sets the framework for broad agreements	Limited	Sets the guidelines
Role of the Commission	Extensive in agenda-setting and implementation	Agenda-setting and supervision	Agenda-setting and implementation	Initiator of various networks	Marginal
Role of the Council	Decision-making, qualified majority	One of several legislators	Decision-making: primarily through unanimity	Forum for deliberation	Agenda-setting and decision-making
Role of the European Parliament	Limited, consultative	One of several legislators	Originally weak, but increasingly equal to the Council's	Limited dialogue	Excluded
Role of the Court of Justice of the European Union	Irregular but relevant	Relevant	Marginal	Excluded	Excluded

Source: Wallace 2010: 92–93 (modified)

The first model for how EU-based policy should be formulated was the so-called *community method*, for which the common agricultural policy became a kind of template. The most notable feature of this model is the dominant position of the Commission throughout the process. The main logic consists in 'locking-in' the agricultural interest groups, by offering them better conditions through Union policies. This in turn guarantees support for the dominant position of the Commission. Nationally based organs then serve as subordinate agents for the common policy. The role of elected politicians – whether at the national level or in the European Parliament – is marginal in this policy model. However, the Court of Justice of the European Union may intervene occasionally, primarily to strengthen the legitimacy of the policy regime.[1]

The *regulatory model* evolved during the 1980s, in step with the establishment of the single market. To some degree, it emerged as a response to external pressures on the member states – from international markets – for enhanced competitiveness in an increasingly globalised economy. The new policy model, modern and flexible as it seemed, was thought to be suitable. It also freed national governments from difficult tasks. The role of the Union in this model is to develop transnational standards, adjusted to national variations. The typical policy process here starts with the formulation of goals and rules by the Commission, 'in consultation' with experts and interest groups. It is this consultation procedure that allows for a certain flexibility. The Council has a rather modest role in this regard, but it may serve as a forum for reaching agreement on harmonisation and minimum standards. The Court of Justice, on the other hand, plays a key role as a supervisor here, its function being to ensure that rules are followed and applied uniformly throughout the Union. EU agencies and bureaus are also important actors, due to their role in mediating between the Commission and national authorities. The strength of the regulatory model lies in its function as a forum for technical

1 To a great extent, this model overlaps with the initial plan for the entire project of European integration: the Coal and Steel Community. Jean Monnet, the architect of this scheme and the president of its High Authority, saw it as a more realistic option than the creation of a federal Europe. If small steps were taken, he believed, the long-term result would be a 'silent revolution' in men's minds. Interest groups would shift their loyalty to the European institutions, thereby endowing them with legitimacy from below (Rosamund 2002: 52–53).

cooperation. The strong legal process also frees national politicians from slow decision-making processes.

The third model – *the distributional model* – arose to some extent as a reaction against the strong market focus of the 1980s. The heavy stress on markets resulted in the marginalisation of certain groups and regions, leading in turn to a stronger focus on economically weak regions within the Union. This latter development must also be viewed in light of the accession to the Union of several poorer countries: Spain, Portugal, Greece, and (to some degree) Ireland. This model highlights the importance of social cohesion. It also puts a heavy emphasis on the Union's different regions – an emphasis which has stamped the whole policy model. The policy process here typically takes a certain course, whereby the Commission designs various programmes for social cohesion in consultation with local and regional authorities. The Council then approves the proposals, under intense pressure from the local and regional authorities which took part in the consultation. The European Parliament is involved as well, through the additional pressure which its members – primarily those from the regions in question – put on the Council to approve the programmes. The Committee of the Regions is also important here, even if its role is only consultative. The multilevel logic inherent in this process has furnished a template for theories of multilevel governance. Yet it bears noting that, while the pressure on the Council is often intense, the member states have the last say when it comes to financing far-reaching EU projects. And especially since the financial crisis of 2008, national governments have grown more restrictive in this regard. In this sense, the distributional model has receded in some degree. At the same time, however, the financial crisis has opened up for a new type of redistribution – through massive loans to specific member states. On the other hand, this type of redistribution does not follow the pattern of this model.

The fourth model – *policy coordination* – was at first seen as a strategy for bringing an issue within the EU's remit.[2] Since the 1990s,

2 Environmental issues were an example. In this policy area, the EU had no formal competence. During the 1970s, however, the Commission campaigned for greater consultation between member states on these questions. This led eventually to the inclusion of environmental issues within the formal competence of the Union.

however, it has been seen as an established policy model in its own right. It usually goes by the name of the 'open method of coordination'. This method was especially evident in the Lisbon Strategy of 2000, in which recommendations rather than binding laws were used to influence the policies of the member states. In the course typically taken in this model, the Commission starts the process by presenting, with the aid of a network of experts and/or related actors, some technical arguments for a common policy on a certain issue. Independent experts are then involved as supporters of the ideas or techniques recommended. Finally, meetings are arranged between groups of national experts, sometimes with the participation of ministers from various member states. The idea is that such meetings should have a 'brain-storming' rather than a negotiating character. This model of decision-making clearly differs from those above, as it entails no binding decisions. Instead, it is about creating networks and dynamic discussions. At its best, this method offers an opportunity to combine the experiences of experts and to devise better solutions. The inspiration for this model clearly comes from Habermas' concept of a deliberative democracy, wherein the better argument – not superior bargaining power – determines the final decision. But this model has a crucial weakness. Citizens who are dissatisfied with the decisions that result find it difficult to pinpoint who is responsible for them: in other words, the procedures for ensuring political accountability are weak. The Lisbon Strategy was an example hereof. Hardly any of its goals were reached in practice (see Wyplosz 2010), and no specific individual or group could be held accountable for the failure.

Transgovernmentalism, finally, differs quite substantially from the other policy models, as it does not necessarily refer to the EU. In this model, cooperation begins between politicians from different member states (often no more than two or three), without any involvement from the EU. This collaboration may then 'spill over' into the sphere of the Union, and become a formal area of EU competence. This model recalls 'classical intergovernmentalism' in some measure (Rosamund 2002: 75–77); but it is more intense and more institutionalised, and as mentioned the resulting cooperation often spills over into the EU. The European Parliament and the Court of Justice are completely excluded in this policy model, and the role of the Commission is limited. The collaboration achieved, moreover, is rooted only weakly in national parliaments or among citizens. It is instead the Council and the European Council that have the key roles: the former through its steering and consolidation of the process; the latter through the general goals it sets out for it. A specific network of national politicians and experts also plays a key role here. The Council Secretariat is central in this regard, through the special forms of cooperation it sets up on the basis of the demands articulated by these various bodies and networks. This policy model is quite elitist in character, as indicated, but it is also highly results-oriented. The common currency is a result of such a spill-over process, as is the common foreign and security policy. In other instances, however, the cooperative scheme has remained separate from the EU, as in the case of NATO or the Schengen Agreement.

Conclusion

The primary purpose in this chapter has been to contribute to a nuanced understanding of how and why politics in the member states (in our case Sweden) is affected by EU membership. We have sought to do this with the aid of certain theoretical concepts and models – of Europeanisation, governance, and policy processes. Without these concepts and models, even an analysis which appears to yield clear results runs a risk of lacking depth. Our focus in this book, simply put, is on how specific Swedish policy areas have changed – in terms of both organisation and content – as a consequence of EU membership. Of course it is no simple matter, methodologically speaking, to distinguish changes due to EU membership from those that arise from other causes. Identifying causal chains in social science is always problematic. All the same, we hope this chapter has developed a specific framework for addressing this question, and served as a starting point for analysis in the different policy areas. The specific area chapters that follow will problematize how and why the organisation and content of politics and policy in Sweden have changed. The object of the conceptual framework set out in this chapter is to advance our understanding of the Europeanisation process in Sweden, and to furnish the basis for more sophisticated comparison between the various policy areas.

References

Andersson, T. & T. Bergman 2005. 'Unionens byråkrater: Kommissionen och de svenska statstjänstemännen', In: Blomgren, M. & T. Bergman (eds.) *EU och Sverige – ett sammanlänkat statsskick*. Stockholm: Liber.

Blomgren, M. & T. Bergman 2005. 'Ett sammanlänkat statsskick', In: T. Bergman & M. Blomgren (eds.) *EU och Sverige – ett sammanlänkat statsskick*. Stockholm: Liber.

Börzel, T. A. & T. Risse 2007. 'Europeanization: The domestic impact of EU politics', In: K. E. Joergensen, M. A. Pollack & B. Rosamund (eds.) *The Handbook of European Union Politics*. London: Sage.

Cowles, M. Green, J. Caporaso & T. Risse (eds). 2001. *Transforming Europe: Europeanization and Domestic Change*. Ithaca, NY: Cornell University Press.

Hill, M. 2005. *The Public Policy Process,* 4th ed. Harlow: Pearson Longman.

Hix, S. 1998. 'The Study of the European Union II: The New Governance Agenda and its Rivals'. *Journal of European Public Policy* 5(1).

Howlett, M., M Ramesh & A. Perl 2009. *Studying Public Policy: Policy Cycles and Policy Subsystems, third edition*. Oxford: Oxford University Press.

Joerges, C. 2001. 'Deliberative Supranationalism: A Defence'. *European Integration Online Papers*, 5/8. Available at http://eiop.or.at/eiop/pdf/2001-008.pdf (retrieved 2019-02-26).

Jönsson, C. 2010. 'Organisering och förvaltning i globaliseringens tid', In: B Rothstein (ed.) *Politik som organisation: Förvaltningens grundproblem*, 4th ed. Stockholm: SNS.

Marsh, J. G. & J. P. Olsen 1989. *Rediscovering institutions: the organizational basis of politics*. New York: Free Press.

Pollack, M. A. 2010. 'Theorizing EU Policy-Making', In: Helen Wallace, Mark A. Pollack and Alasdair R. Young (eds.) *Policy-Making in the European Union, sixth edition*. Oxford: Oxford University Press.

Rhodes, R. A. W. 1996. 'The New Governance: Governing without government'. *Political Studies*, 44/3.

Rosamund, B. 2002. *Theories of European Integration*. New York: Palgrave.

Sabatier, P. A. 1999. 'The need for better theories'. In: P. A. Sabatier (ed.) *Theories of the Policy Process*. Boulder: Westview.

Tallberg, J., N. Aylott, C. F. Bergström, Å. Casula Vifell & J. Palme 2010. *Europeiseringen av Sverige*. Demokratirådets Rapport, Stockholm: SNS.

Vink, M. P. & P. Graziano 2007. 'Challenges of a New Research Agenda', In: M. P. Vink & P. Graziano (eds.) *Europeanization: New Research Agendas*. Basingstoke: Palgrave.

Wallace, H., M. A. Pollack & A. R. Young 2010. 'An Overview', In: H. Wallace, M. A. Pollack & A. R. Young (eds.) *Policy-Making in the European Union*. Oxford: Oxford University Press.

Wyplosz, C. 2010. 'The failure of the Lisbon strategy'. Voxeu.org, 12 January 2010. Available at https://voxeu.org/article/failure-lisbon-strategy (retrieved 26 February 2019).

Young, A. R. 2010. 'The European Policy Process in a Comparative Perspective', In: H. Wallace, M. A. Pollack & A. R. Young (eds.) *Policy-Making in the European Union*. Oxford: Oxford University Press.

3. Economic Policy

Changed Conditions for Entrepreneurship and Competition in Sweden

Tobias Bromander

> 'Economic policy is about creating the conditions for economic growth and employment.' (The Ministry of Enterprise and Innovation 2015).

Economic policy is extremely important to a country's economic development. Sweden is a small country and therefor extremely export dependent' (SOU 2007:55). In 2016 export of goods and services were 45 percent of the Swedish GDP (OECD 2017) and approximately 60 percent of Sweden's exports go to the EU (the National Board of Trade 2017). The EU membership have had a positive impact on the growth in trade between Sweden and its member states (Erixon and Fölster 2014). Of the ten countries that Sweden exports the most goods and services to, eight are members of the EU. Sweden's smallness means that innovations and exports are necessary to maintain the welfare state. Moreover, for it to be able to finance its welfare society, Swedish companies must be successful on the global market.

In 2014, the Social Democratic government set a goal for Sweden to have the lowest unemployment rate in Europe by 2020. A successful economic policy is necessary to meet this goal. New companies need to be created, existing companies need to grow, and competitiveness must be strengthened. Simply put, people need to be employed in order for the Swedish welfare model to survive. Within the European Union (EU), similar beliefs have been voiced. The focus is on the economy, employment and growth. What most clearly governs European cooperation on economic policy is the need to be able to meet prevailing global competition.

Economic policy is one of the areas where the EU holds fairly strong power over individual Member States. That is why EU membership has had such an impact on Swedish economic policy. For example, the Union has exclusive authority over competition regulations while within the internal market, the EU and Member States share the authority. Decisions that are made within these two areas have consequences on how Sweden is able to formulate its economic policy.

The object of the following chapter is to report on Swedish economic policy and the impact that EU membership has had in shaping national policy. The chapter is divided into three time periods. The first part (1980–1994) has its beginning in the economic policy considerations that were taken during the 1980s by the Swedish Government and the decisions that paved the way for Swedish EU membership. The second part (1995–2015) focuses on the EU's direct effect on Sweden's economic policies, while the last part of the chapter (2016–2020) focuses on future challenges that Sweden and the European cooperation face.

Path to Swedish EU Membership (1980–1994)

During the 1980s, Swedish economic policy was confronted with several tests. To some extent, the previous decade had been shaped by an international oil crisis. Decreases in productivity and reduced demand for Swedish goods created crises within the shipbuilding, textile and steel industries. To help the industries out of the economic turbulence, the Swedish Government decided to implement two measures. First, in 1975, then Minister for Industry, Nils Gunnar Åslin, established an 'industrial emergency aid' that offered economic support to affected branches and, to a certain extent, the takeover of the company by the State.[1] Second, on several occasions the government chose to devaluate the Swedish krona against the German mark (Riksbanken 2011). It became apparent that the goal of the government's 1981 proposition on Swedish industrial policy was to:

1 For example, SSAB.

> ... stimulate and facilitate the transfer of production resources to the profitable and competitive parts of the industry and thereby promote the industry's international competitiveness.

The economic difficulties that arose during the 1970s continued throughout the 1980s. The devaluation policy continued in step with the decline in industrial growth. In 1981, the Swedish krona was devalued by 10 percent, only to be further devalued by 16 percent the following year (Riksbanken 2011). The previously established industrial emergency aid, which continued up until the mid-1980s, was unable to prevent the forced restructuring of the industry due to the high costs and low demand for goods (SOU 2000:7). Three characteristics can be attributed to the industrial policy from the 1980s:

1. Support targeted industrial policy;
2. Expansion of infrastructure and
3. Deregulations.

1. Support targeted industrial policy: The Swedish industrial policy focused on larger companies. In the 1968 election, former Minister for Finance Gunnar Sträng, made a pithy statement when he said that 'What is good for Volvo is good for Sweden'. This approach to industry was also characteristic of the Swedish Government during the 1980s. Essentially, the largest industrial companies were prioritised and one of the political goals was to strengthen the competitiveness of selected branches, and thereby ensure Swedish jobs.[2] Small and medium-sized businesses were not prioritised and industry support for companies and branches was selectively targeted. For a very long time, big business had been considered to be of such great significance to Sweden that it was described as the backbone of the Swedish economy.

Despite industrial policy primarily focusing on large Swedish businesses, the issue was also raised for small and medium-sized companies. One example was the problem of company financing. To simplify the possibility of obtaining financing for smaller companies, an OTC

2 This policy was, to a certain extent, justified. Of the total Swedish exports for 1985, ten Swedish companies made up one third of the exports (Fredriksson 1988:10).

list was established on the Stockholm Stock Exchange in 1982. The decision not only meant that share trading was enabled for smaller companies; but it was also a step towards admitting the significance of smaller companies' socio-economic impact.

2. *Expansion of infrastructure:* One of the economic policy's tasks is to provide conditions for companies to be able to conduct business on a competitive international market. A condition that is often highlighted is access to infrastructure. During the 1980s, significant investments were made in Swedish infrastructure (SOU 2006:106). These included the expansion of nuclear power. Altogether, six new reactors were put into operation in the first half of the 1980s. One objective of the expansion was to ensure access to inexpensive electricity for energy intensive sectors, such as the mining, steel, pulp and paper industries. Expansion of the transport network and telecommunications also contributed to improved conditions for Swedish companies to be able to compete on global markets. From having been an industrial society, Sweden increasingly transitioned into an information and knowledge-based society, during the first half of the 1980s (Svenskt Näringsliv (Confederation of Swedish Enterprise) 2009).

3. *Deregulations:* Along with much of Western Europe in the 1980s, Sweden began to successively deregulate markets that had previously been viewed as being particularly important to the country. By being open to competition, trade between countries was to improve. This Swedish development was, in part an adaptation to the European Communities' (EC's) work to establish an internal market. The goal was to eliminate trade barriers between the countries. The first market that was deregulated was the financial market. In 1985, the credit market was deregulated, which meant that previous limits on bank loans was eliminated. Riksbanken's decision to deregulate the credit market was followed by a deregulation of the foreign exchange in 1989. Even if these reforms were not the direct result of active economic policies, Swedish industry and the business climate were affected to a great extent. One effect was that loans to companies increased dramatically and that international financial markets slowly

began to be integrated after previously having been nearly completely closed to foreign actors.[3]

From industrial policy to broad economic policy

At the end of the 1980s, Swedish industrial policy changed. Instead of prioritizing targeted support aimed at specific industries, government political leaders began to formulate economic policy reforms that were adapted to a broader array of company groups than previous ones. The new perspective came to be known as a 'broad economic policy'. A broad economic policy refers to political decisions that aim to create equal competition conditions for all companies, regardless of industry or technology (Svenskt Näringsliv 2008). The political tools most often used are strengthened competition laws, changes in tax laws, investments in research and education policies, continued privatization and deregulation as well as simplification of regulations for businesses.

The idea of a broader economic policy made a major breakthrough in connection with the financial crisis Sweden experienced at the beginning of the 1990s. During the first three years of the decade, Sweden showed negative economic growth (Svenskt Näringsliv 2001). Many politicians and social commentators argued that small business growth was a vital factor for Sweden's economic recovery. To achieve this, a more inclusive economic policy than the previous one was needed. One result of this new mindset was that traditional economic policy was replaced with a more modern economic policy. The Swedish Department of Trade and Industry, which was first established in 1961, was replaced after 30 years by the Ministry of Enterprise and Innovation in 1991. By merging authorities, including the Statens Industriverk (SIND), the Swedish National Board for Industrial and Technical Development (NUTEK) was established. NUTEK became a symbol of the change from an industrial policy to an economic policy.

Another result of the political ambitions for a broader economic

3 For example, the opportunity for foreign companies to acquire Swedish companies was regulated by law (Swedish Companies Act 1982:617).

policy was a strengthening of competition laws. Increased globalization and strengthened international competition had made Swedish law outdated. Moreover, reforms were made in other areas to erase trade barriers and increase competition between companies. For example, restrictions on foreign company acquisitions were removed in 1992. One of the arguments for the decision was the aligning of legislation to the EC's regulations on the free movement of capital and the freedom of establishment (Proposition 1991/92:71). Several State activities would also be privatized. At the beginning of 1991, the Riksdag decided to fully or partially privatize 35 companies (Munkhammar 2009: 11). The economic policy and monetary reforms that were carried out in the beginning of the 1990s were intended to do more than simply strengthen the free movement of goods, services and capital. They were also carried out with the idea of eventual EU membership in mind. Many of the policy decisions that were made contributed to a lowering of the EU threshold and simplification of the transition to a possible membership. Thus, it should be emphasized that Swedish economic policy reforms should be viewed as a result of an ongoing European cooperation that had a direct impact on Swedish economic policy long before Sweden became a Member in 1995. This indirect impact was identifiable in part from increased globalization and an international trend toward free trade and increased competition, which is difficult to abstain from, as well as in part from an internal desire to become a Member of the EU and thus initiate an alignment process through conscious reforms.

European Cooperation on Economic Policy (1995–2015)

Prior to the general election on Swedish EU membership, economic policy was often at the forefront of political debates. Proponents of membership felt that membership was an opportunity to secure Swedish jobs and safeguard welfare. In connection with membership, Sweden would be tied to European regulations, which to a large extent, impacted the opportunities to formulate economic policy. The EU's treaties and policy papers created the framework for Swedish economic policy. For example, the European competition law is binding for all Members. Within this area, the EU has exclusive discretionary powers. The European competition commissioner is tasked with, among other things, the responsibility of ensuring that all regulations in the area are followed.[4] The EU impacts Sweden and Swedish economic policy through such things as 1) competition laws and 2) rules on state aid. One of the fundamental principles of the European cooperation is free competition between companies. Together, the EU Member States have developed binding competition regulations for both businesses and States, which has had a direct impact on Sweden's Swedish economic policy. Several such tangible direct consequences on Swedish economic policy, which appeared in Swedish political and media debates, should be mentioned.

First, no contract can be entered into that reduces competition. This can be an agreement on pricing or other attempts to divide a market between actors. For example, in 2013, six banks in Europe were sentenced to pay 1.5 billion euro in penalties for having intentionally manipulated the European internal bank rate, Libor (TT-Reuters 2013).

Second, no company can abuse a dominant position by impeding the ability of competitors to enter into contracts or conduct business. In part, the objective is to strengthen the protection of smaller companies. During spring 2015, Competition Commissioner Margerethe Vestage accused the American IT company Google of abusing its dominant position regarding Internet searches. Companies cannot have an overly dominant position (Andersson 2015). With concentrations between undertakings, it is important that new companies do not gain too strong a position and thus eliminate competition. The European Commission is tasked with stopping company buyouts whenever necessary, if competition on the market is expected to significantly decline.

Third, the authorities must use public tendering when making larger purchases. Competition must not be distorted by the favoring of domestic companies or local actors on the common European market. In 2010, the Federal Republic of Germany was found guilty of breaching the coordination of procedures for the award of public service contracts (Case C-160/08).

4 Margrethe Vestage is the EU competition commissioner for the 2014–2019 term.

Fourth individual States cannot provide aid to affected industries or companies. Within the framework of the current EU rules, the earlier Swedish industrial emergency aid from the 1970s and 1980s would not have been possible. However, there are exceptions to the basic rule that state aid is forbidden within the EU. Prior to Swedish membership in the EU, Sveriges riksdag adopted a law on the application of the EU's state aid rules. The law regulates, among other things, Sweden's disclosure requirements. Following notification from the Member States, it is up to the European Commission to approve any state aid. In 2011, the Government launched an investigation into illegal state aid. The investigation was tasked with reviewing the disclosure requirements of municipalities and county councils. The report from the Official Government Report on Illegal State Aid (SOU 2011:69) resulted in a new law on the application of the EU's state aid rules, which was added in 2013. The EU rules on state aid are included in three articles (107–109) in the Treaty on the Functioning of the European Union. In Article 107:1 it appears that:

> Save as otherwise provided in the Treaties, any aid granted by a Member State or through State resources in any form whatsoever which distorts or threatens to distort competition by favouring certain undertakings or the production of certain goods shall, in so far as it affects trade between Member States, be incompatible with the internal market.

According to the Swedish Competition Authority (2015), state aid is that which 'can be attributed to a state, municipal or county council activity that is typically carried out on a market'. State aid often occurs in different forms of subsidies or tax relief for companies. All economic support measures that a government, county council or municipality decides on, should not, however, be considered to be state aid. State aid requires the fulfilment of four criteria (Eklund & Pedersen 2013).

1. That an advantage is granted by a Member State or with the help of government funds.
2. The advantage must favour certain undertakings or certain productions.

3. The advantage distorts or threatens to distort competition.
4. The advantage impacts trade between Member States. Article 108:3, stipulates that the European Commission must be notified in cases where Member States provide aid to undertakings or industries. It is the Commission who decides whether or not Member States' aid complies with the EU's treaty.

Despite the thought that state business support is negative to competition, it is not completely forbidden for the States to provide aid to certain affected industries. For example, the EU Commission approved state aid to Västerås Airport (EU Commission Memo/14/544). The aid that was paid out between 2000–2010 was not considered to have distorted the competition. The EU rules give the Member States the right to give aid to airports if, for example, it leads to improved accessibility in the region (EU Commission 2014/C 99/03). During economic crises that affect Europe, the Commission also has temporarily introduced more generous rules for the Member States to be able to provide state aid to save affected industries or support essential institutions.

Economic policy in crisis

Numerous times the economic policy has been strongly tested in connection with national and international crises. In connection with the global financial crisis of 2008, the EU Commission introduced temporary dispensation for aid to banks. The rules made it possible for Sweden to, among other things, give direct aid to systemically important institutions in the financial sector. In the wake of the American Lehman Brothers bank bankruptcy in 2008, it came to light that many banks worldwide had major credit losses and liquidation problems. To minimize the spreading of the financial crisis, several banks were judged to be 'too big to fail', which in reality meant that they needed to be saved at any cost.

A global financial crisis turned into a global industrial policy crisis. In the case of Sweden, more stringent demands and expectations were made on Swedish economic policy to mitigate the impact of a drastically reduced Swedish export. For small export-dependent country like Sweden, the global reduction in demand had major economic consequences. This was particularly true for the automotive industry and its subcontractors. Almost overnight, production for several big Swedish companies came to a complete or partial standstill. Sweden's then Minister for Enterprise and Energy in the Alliance led government Maud Olofsson (2014), illustrated the extreme situation that arose in a conversation with Volvo's CEO Leif Johansson:

> Just one year later (2008), Volvo's CEO Leif Johansson called from Gothenburg and described the rows of trucks that were standing in the parking lot outside the factory. Polished and read for company logos. The problem was the companies could not pay. Everything had ground to a halt. He sounded shaken.'

To ease the difficult situation, the Swedish Government implemented several support measures. For example, companies were given the opportunity to defer tax payments (Ridderstolpe 2009). The situation carried the issue of state aid to companies to the top of the political agenda. To avoid the collapse of European industries and to lessen the downswing in economic growth, Member States were allowed to give companies up to 500,000 euro in aid as well as loan guarantees. These were extraordinary measures taken to lessen the impact of an extraordinary situation. In the case of Sweden, the question of state aid came to a head in connection with Saab Automobile's liquidity problems in 2008–2011. During discussion between the owner of Saab and the Ministry of Enterprise and Innovation, the possibility of different state support measures was examined. Many assessors realized that withholding economic aid would mean the business would declare bankruptcy. One of the proponents of State involvement was the Swedish Social Democratic Party Leader Mona Sahlin (Andersson 2009). However, the Swedish Minister of Enterprise and Innovation Maud Olofsson was of the opinion that no direct economic aid should be offered to Saab. The Government, on the other hand, gave Saab guarantees for a loan from the European Investment Bank. Despite this, Saab declared bankruptcy in 2011.

Throughout the 2000s, Swedish industry was marked by major cutbacks in personnel. The ever-increasing automation of jobs in connection with austerity measures and rationalizations in the wake of a global financial uncertainty meant that many people were given notice. The restructuring of the industry begun in the 1980s had not stopped. At a meeting of the World Economic Forum in Davos, in 2013, Sweden's then Prime Minister for the Alliance Fredrik Reinfeldt held a noteworthy speech where he said that 'We used to have people in the industry, but they are basically gone'. Even if the statement gave an exaggerated image of Swedish social changes, the trend is clear. Swedish industry jobs will be fewer and fewer over time. The Swedish Alliance Government's (2006–2012) stance on the issue of state aid for affected industries had been to not distort competition. This was also their premise during the crisis that arose in 2010, when an ash cloud from an active volcano on Iceland caused a large part of European air traffic to grind to a halt for a long time. According to the Swedish Aviation Industry Group (SFB), Swedish airline companies lost about 100 million kronor each day (Melén 2010). Demands were being made for the Government to help the affected airline companies, but the Minister for Enterprise and Energy Maud Olofsson motivated the negative decision by stating that any aid would lead to unhealthy competition.

The EU institutions that have an impact Sweden's economic policy

Several EU institutions participate in the formulation of the common economic and competition policies. Economic policy is a broad area that is closely connected to several other policy areas. Common decisions for questions on infrastructure investments, housing construction, research and development and climate and energy issues impact the possibility of European industrial policy reaching its goals. The European Commission has a central role in the creation of a common economic policy. Three of the EU's commissioners impact Swedish economic policy. These are:

- The commissioner with responsibility for Jobs, Growth, and Investments
- The commissioner with responsibility for Competitiveness

- The commissioner with responsibility for Internal Market, Industry, Entrepreneurship and SMES

The commissioner also holds the role of monitor during implementation of common agreements. For example, work with the Lisbon Strategy required each Member State to regularly submit an action plan to the Commission. The Swedish Government submitted an action plan in 2008 for growth and jobs (SKR 2008/09:34). Furthermore, the Commission also administrates the EU's framework program for increased Competitiveness for Small and Medium-sized Enterprises (COSME).

Another institution with major influence on common industrial policy issues is the Council. In the Council, government ministers from each EU country meet on a competitiveness council (COMPET). The Council's goal is to strengthen competitiveness and improve the business climate in order to increase growth within the Union. In 2015, during Luxembourg's time as president of the EU, the issue of competitiveness and economic policy ranked high on the policy agenda. One of the Competition Council's expressed goals has been to help small and medium-sized businesses and newly started businesses to grow in the service sector. Within the EU and Sweden, the service sector has been emphasized as an important sector to develop in order to create new jobs through small and medium-sized businesses.

A third institution that impacts economic policy is the European Parliament. The Parliament participates in the formulation of the Union's industrial policy. The goal of the economic policy is established in Article 173 in the TFEU and reads 'Industrial policy is horizontal in nature and aims at securing framework conditions favourable to industrial competitiveness'.'. In January 2014, the Commission presented views on 'For a European Industrial Renaissance' COM(2014) 14. In a report, the Commission notes, among other things, that a weak domestic demand, low investments in research and development and high energy prices strongly contribute to the European industry losing international competitiveness. A priority for the Commission was to hurry industrial adaptation to structural changes.

The European Council is the fourth institution that formulates EU's economic policy. Several of the visions and goals that Member

States and heads of state negotiated had direct consequences on Swedish economic policy. The Lisbon Strategy, which was adopted in 2000, and the subsequent growth strategy, Europe 2020, are examples of common European goals that clearly influenced Swedish economic policy. The European Council is tasked with identifying the overall guidelines or itinerary for Europe and the EU's Member states and what within the economy has had an impact on EU institutions' and Member States' discussions on the shaping of economic policy in the Union.

EU projects that impact Sweden's economic policy

Simplifying the rules for entrepreneurship and providing opportunities for business growth are two main economic policy points of the EU cooperation. European leaders jump-started this area in the 2000s by unanimously agreeing on two programs that impacted Member State economic policies. These were the *Lisbon Strategy* and a *European Charter for Small Enterprises* (see European Commission 04/06/2010). To varying degrees, both papers aimed to hurry the process of enabling Member States to go from being traditional industrial nations to high-tech knowledge-based nations. The vision was for Europe to be able to compete in knowledge, innovation, and entrepreneurship. In June of 2000, the European Charter for Small Enterprises was approved. Among other things, it was concluded that 'Small businesses are a key source of jobs, business dynamism and innovation' (IP/04/283). Altogether, 99 percent of all businesses in Europe are small and medium-sized businesses. (European Commission 2002).[5] Ten improvement areas were identified and considered to be significant for establishing and growing businesses. Three of the areas were:

- Training in entrepreneurship,
- Simplification of laws and
- Regulation of entrepreneurship, simplification of taxation and financing.

5 Within the EU, the average business has four employees (Svenskt Näringsliv 2010).

The ambition was for the charter to steer the Member States during formulation of their national political reforms. On the other hand, it is emphasized that the paper was not binding for Member States. By using the power of a good example, the architects behind the charter hoped that the EU's Members would learn from each other, and together, find solutions to common problems and challenges.[6] The hope was that discussions, analyses and experience exchanges would be the key to improvements for the Member States.

Parallel to the European Charter for Small Enterprises, a ten-year Lisbon Strategy was adopted that formed a larger program of change within the EU (European Commission 04-06-2010). The background was increased globalization and the increasingly intense competitive situation that Europe's States and heads of state found in their global analyses. The Lisbon Strategy's ambitious goal was for 'Europe to be the most competitive and dynamic knowledge-based economy in the world in 2010'. Once again, the EU emphasized the transition to a knowledge-based economy. To achieve the Lisbon Strategy goal of creating a more resilient and higher rate of growth, and better jobs, the European Commission adopted a so-called 'Small Business Act for Europe' in 2008. This was a broadening of the Charter for Small Enterprises that was adopted in 2000. On numerous occasions the European Parliament had pointed out the great need of new small businesses and that larger investments needed to be done in this area. The goal of the Small Business Act for Europe was the creation of a more favourable business climate in Europe for small and medium-sized businesses. Under the 'Think Small First' principle, a number of principles were identified that were to guide the Member States during the shaping of their economic policies. For example, Union Members shall:

1. Create a climate that favours small and family businesses and rewards entrepreneurship.
2. Help small and medium-sized businesses to better utilize opportunities on internal markets.

6 In 2008, approximately 200 examples of small enterprise policy good practice were presented in the EU (European Commission 2009).

3. Make public administrations responsive to the needs of small and medium-sized businesses.
4. Make it easier for small and medium-sized businesses to access financing.

In 2011, the authorities conducted a Growth Analysis, an Evaluation of the Swedish Government's Implementation of the Small Enterprises Charter. Several areas were identified in the published report where Sweden had not fully achieved the set EU goals. One example was the opportunity for business owners to be given a 'second chance' if their business had undergone bankruptcy. Furthermore, the participation of small businesses in public procurements was also identified as an area for improvement. This was also confirmed in a survey conducted by Företagarna (2012). Only 27 percent of the surveyed businesses responded that they had participated in a public procurement. The primary reasons businesses refrained from public procurements were the complicated rules and over large size of contracts. Providing small businesses with the opportunity to compete and grow was identified as one of the biggest challenges the Swedish economic policy faced.

Despite several challenges, Sweden is at the forefront in terms of European competitiveness and business climate. In the 2015 country report from the European Commission (SWD (2015) 46 final) showed, among other things, that Sweden is characterized by one of the most favourable business climates and has cemented its position as one of the EU's most competitive economies. The report also found that the manufacturing industry was still a vital source of product innovation and export income for Sweden and that small and medium-sized businesses had good access to financing. However, the Commission noted that the processing time for starting a business in Sweden far exceeded the Small Business Act's goal of three days, and thus, was a complicating factor for start-ups in the country. Start-ups of small and medium-sized businesses are an important factor for a favourable and dynamic future economy that can continue to maintain jobs and welfare in Sweden.

Future Goals and Funding for the European Economic Project (2016–2020)

In 2010, the Commission launched *Europe 2020*, a new strategy paper for growth and economic development. After several years of financial crises, the need for a European concentrated effort was clearly presented in the Commission's description of the economy's development.

> The recent economic crisis has no precedent in our generation. The steady gains in economic growth and job creation witnessed over the last decade have been wiped out (COM(2010) 2020 final).

Europe 2020 is a ten-year strategy for growth and should be viewed as a continuation of the Lisbon Strategy. The focus is on *smart growth*, *sustainable growth,* and *inclusive growth*. Different growth goals are linked to the strategy that the EU structural fund program is to work for. Smart growth refers to each Member State working to develop a national economy based on knowledge and innovation. Each Member state is tasked with working on its own national goals' formulation. The Swedish Government has set five national goals. In the annual follow up report published in 2015, it was, however, noted by the Commission that Sweden might not reach the national goals of Europe 2020 (SWD (2015) 46 final). The overall responsibility for Europe 2020 lies with the European Council. Each year, a report is compiled that maps the progress made by the Member States in order to be able to reach the overall goals by 2020, at the latest. As with the Lisbon Strategy, the Europe 2020 Strategy underwent evaluation after five years. Work with part-time monitoring was begun in 2015 and will be phased out in a revised strategy paper. Each year, Sweden presents a national reform program to the European Commission. The report is to include what measures were taken and what measures are intended to be taken to enable Sweden to reach the goals in the Europe 2020 Strategy. One example of Swedish economic policy goal setting has been the work to eliminate obstacles in order to promote cross-border e-commerce (Regeringskansliet 2015 (Government Offices of Sweden)).

In 2014, the Swedish Government set a goal of having Europe's lowest unemployment in 2020. A vision of this sort is an enormous challenge, especially in the area of economic policy. In connection with the presentation of our spring budget in 2015, Social Democratic Prime Minister Stefan Löfven noted that Sweden '... cannot afford to lose any more competitiveness' (Holmqvist 2015). Despite the EU having provided a framework for economic policy, Sweden continues to maintain a large amount of control over the content of its economic policy. In the 2016 budget, the Swedish Government's economic policy priorities are clearly shown. The focus is on entrepreneurship and simplifying enterprise as well as investing in innovation and capitalization (Proposition 2015/16:1).

In January 2016, the Minister for Enterprise and Innovation Mikael Damberg presented a new industrialization strategy for Sweden. The motive behind the strategy was to strengthen Swedish industry competitiveness and make investments more attractive (The Ministry of Enterprise and Innovation 2016). It emphasized that Swedish economy and welfare must be based on new ways of thinking, innovations and export business that create the conditions for changes and adaptations to new global challenges and opportunities for production and products on markets that are under constant reshaping. The new strategy should also be viewed as a result of Europe's (and the world's) financial crisis, which created political and economic challenges within the EU Member States, and the need to be politically active in order to lessen the crisis' economic and social effects in the short term and policy-wise, in the long term, remain stronger during any future crises. This strategy has emphasized being important in order for Sweden to be better prepared to handled increased unemployment by being able to offer short-time work, training, and an improved investment climate, etc. Several critical areas have been identified that are of particular importance for politicians to be able to handle in the future. Two of the areas were resource allocation and competence management. The Swedish industry is not seen as being sufficiently resource-efficient at the same time as many businesses find it too difficult to recruit the competence, they need to be to handle international competition.

In the new industrialization strategy, Sweden places particular emphasis on strengthening businesses' adaptability and competitiveness as well as which stresses can be managed by focusing on four central areas. Sweden shall have:

- Swedish industrial leaders that are able to adapt to and utilize digital developments and their endless possibilities;
- Sustainable production with improved resource efficiency, based on environmental consideration that will to lead to new jobs and increased competitiveness;
- Improvements in the accumulation and quality of industrial knowledge with secure competence management for long term development and competitiveness; as well as
- World leading research in sectors that provide improved opportunities for industrial production of goods and services.

Future Challenges for the Swedish Economy and Welfare Model

Since 2016, three important political events have had effect on Swedish trade and export of goods and services. First, the 2016 referendum held in United Kingdom on whether the country would apply to leave the European Union. Second, the 2016 election of a new president of United States. Third, the 2018 general election in Sweden.

A majority of the British citizens voted for United Kingdom to leave the European Union. On the 29th of March 2019 UK will no longer be a member of the EU. This will have effect on Swedish jobs and trade for a long period. In a report written by members of The Stockholm Chamber of Commerce and Oxford Economics it is stated that the potential cost of a hard Brexit could cost Sweden 18 billion SEK in lost GDP by the end of 2020 (Hatzigeorgiou and Nixon 2018). The amount equals 8 200 jobs. It is difficult to calculate the exact costs since no withdrawal agreement between the UK and the EU is settled. United Kingdom is an important trade partner for Sweden, being the fourth largest export market. Sweden will face economic costs and loss of GDP if United Kingdom is not a full member of the European Union. A future trade agreement between the UK and the EU will eventually give us the answer to the question of Sweden's cost of Brexit.

A second political event that has direct implication on Swedish trade is the American presidential election. During the presidency of Donald Trump, the administration has passed several trade policies that have strengthens protectionism and weakens global free trade.

Leading economic journalists are predicting a possible trade war between USA and China that will have a negative effect on European Union member states. CNBC reports that 'Europe will be the big loser in US trade war with China' (Reid 2018). In March 2018, the American government imposed tariffs on imported steel and aluminium. This was a first step from the Trump administration to fulfil the election campaign promise to secure American jobs. Not long after the policy was implemented the European commission imposed tariffs on several imported goods such as blue jeans, bourbon and Harley-Davidson motorcycles. This was a direct response to the US steel and aluminium tariffs (Erlanger 2018).

The third political event that has direct implication on Swedish trade and export is the general election held in September 2018. On September 25th the general assembly voted a no confident against the current government. The process of forming a new government has been extremely difficult. Still two months after the election there is still no new government in place. Which future trade policy's Sweden will pass depends on the government. Most likely, the future government will continue the path of free trade and export friendly political policies. Not all political parties in Sweden favour the European membership. For example, the Swedish democrats, the third largest party in the general election 2018, are agitating for Sweden to leave the European Union. Many economic scholars argue that a Swexit would weaken the Swedish economy and even threaten the future of the welfare state (Worthington 2018).

Because Sweden is a small country with an export-based economy it is extremely important that they can cope with international competition, which gets tougher every year. In 2017 almost 69 000 new businesses were started in Sweden (Tillväxtanalys 2018). To be able to give these newly started companies the chance to grow there is a need for a national export strategy and governmental policy's for economic growth. The latest Swedish export strategy was decided by the Ministry of Enterprise and Innovation in 2015. There are four main strategic goals:

- increase exports, both in absolute figures and as a proportion of GDP;

- increase Sweden's attractiveness for investments, expertise and tourists;
- increase the proportion of exporting enterprises; and
- increase Swedish enterprises' participation in the global economy.

Historically the success of Swedish export has mostly come from industrial businesses such as Volvo, Electrolux, SCA, Boliden and ABB. In recent years, Sweden has also become world known for its exports in chart music and development of computer games and mobile games (Hoikkala 2017, Swedish Institute 2017). Two examples of Swedish IT-business that have reached all corners of the world are Mojang (developing Minecraft) and King (developing Candy Crush Saga).

A country's economic growth depends on many different events and political decision. The national agency Growth Policy Analysis (2018) has identified several crucial aspects for increasing future economic growth in Sweden:

- competence provision needs to be assured. This means that citizens have their own responsibility to get a proper education. This could also mean that a person with a long working life needs continuously develop his or her skills and competence through education. In 2012 the Swedish Prime Minister Fredrik Reinfeldt was quoted saying that, in the future, more people need to start new careers late in their working life (Stenberg 2012). If no jobs are offered, a person will need to get a re-educate themselves.
- Sweden has to increase its innovation capacity. Many of the biggest export companies in Sweden were established due to innovations made in the late 19th century or in the early 20th century. New knowledge and innovations are crucial for Sweden's export dependent economy and welfare model.
- infrastructure is crucial for businesses in order to grow and attract highly qualified people. For example, physical infrastructure such as housing, communication, public transport, roads, harbours, IT and power distribution grid. The nonphysical

infrastructure is equally important. For example, educational system or rules and laws that set the conditions for private businesses.
- Sweden needs a greener economy. The government should reduce the environmental risks and strive towards an ecological and sustainable development. The importance of combating climate change also brings business opportunities. A government needs to support the transition to a greener economy by supporting research and development.

Conclusion

As stated, the EU sets the framework for Swedish economic policy, to a great extent. However, Sweden has substantial power over the content of the policies. For the most part, Swedish economic policy during the 2000s has been shaped by the European recession that was the result of the global financial crisis and euro crisis that took off in 2008. Despite the crises, the EU's work in improving the conditions of European business has progressed. A major change is that Europe's politicians, today, strongly underscore the need for small and medium-sized businesses. These businesses primarily contribute to increased employment within the Union. During the 1980s, the focus was solely on large businesses. Parallel with Europe's biggest businesses undergoing structural changes and many jobs either moving to other parts of the world or being rationalized away, politicians have begun to target small and medium-sized businesses. Sweden is no exception. Small businesses are becoming an increasingly significant key to continued economic growth. According to the organization Företagarna (2015), four out of five new jobs in Sweden are created in businesses with fewer than 50 employees. It is on entrepreneurship and innovation that Europe's leaders are placing their greatest hope for securing employment and growth in the Union. Over the years, the EU has had a major impact on Swedish economic policy. The shaping of policy is directly impacted by common competition rules and rules on state aid to industries and activities. Economic policy is extremely important to a country's economic development and there is very little evidence to suggest that the current development of an increasingly competitive globalized world will taper off. This will put even higher demands on both national and European economic policy reforms.

References

Andersson, J. 2009. 'Sahlin vill se stort statligt stöd till Saab'. *Sveriges Radio*, 2 December.

— 2015. 'EU: Google utnyttjar sin ställning'. *Sveriges Radio*, 15 April.

Eklund, E. & Pedersen, K. 2013. 'Ny lag om olagligt statligt stöd – hur hanteras de ökade riskerna?' *Ny Juridik* 2:13.

Erixon, F. & Fölster, S. 2014. *Vad har eu gjort för Sverige. Och vad har Sverige gjort för EU?* Stockholm: Samhällsförlaget.

Erlanger, S. 2018. 'Europe Averts a Trade War With Trump. But Can It Trust Him?' *The New York Times*. July 26, 2018.

Europeiska Kommissionen. 2002. 'Europeisk stadga för småföretag.' Europeiska Kommissionen: Näringslivspublikationer.

— 2004. 'Europeiska stadgan för småföretag: förbättringar i miljön för småföretag och medlemsstaterna lär av varandras starka sidor.' Press release IP/04/283.

— 2009. 'Europeiska stadgan för småföretag. 2009 års urval av god praxis.' DOI: 10.2769/92879.

— 2010-06-04. 'Lisbon Strategy for Growth and Jobs.' Http://ec.europa.eu/archives/growthandjobs_2009/

— 2010. Europa 2020. En strategi för smart och hållbar tillväxt för alla. KOM(2010) 2020 slutlig.

— 2014a. Statligt stöd: mer information om kommissionens beslut om offentlig finansiering av flygplatser och flygbolag i Tyskland, Belgien, Italien och Sverige. Memo/14/544.

— 2014b. Riktlinjer för statligt stöd till flygplatser och flygbolag. 2014/C 99/03.

— 2014c. För en industriell renässans i Europa. KOM(2014) 14 final.

— 2015. Landsrapport Sverige 2015. Inklusive en fördjupad granskning av åtgärderna för att förebygga och korrigera makroekonomiska obalanser. SWD(2015) 46 final.

Fördraget om Europeiska unionens funktionssätt. 2012. *Europeiska unionens officiella tidning*, nr C 326, 26 October.

Företagarna. 2012. 'Små företag och offentlig upphandling – hur går det?'

— 2015. Företagarfakta: 'Ni skapar 4 av 5 jobb'. http://www.foretagarna.se/Opinion/Nyhetsarkiv/2015/oktober/foretagarfakta/.

Hatzigeorgiou, A and Nixon, J. 2018. *8,200 Lost Jobs–the Cost of Brexit for Sweden and Stockholm*. The Stockholm Chamber of Commerce and Oxford Economics.

Hoikkala, H. 2017. 'Sweden Beckons for Investors Seeking to Bet on Next Candy Crush'. *Bloomberg News*. June 8th 2017.

Holmqvist, A. 2015. 'Regeringen satsar på näringspolitik för fler jobb.' *Aftonbladet*, 13 April.

Konkurrensverket. 2015. 'Statligt stöd'. Http://www.konkurrensverket.se/konkurrens/om-konkurrensreglerna/transparenslagen/statligt-stod/.

Melén, 2012. 'Ministern: Inget stöd till flygbolag'. *Aftonbladet*, 20 April.

Ministry of Enterprise and Innovation. 2015. 'Sweden's Export Strategy.' Stockholm: Government Offices of Sweden.
Munkhammar, J. 2009. *Försäljning av statliga bolag under tre decennier*. Stockholm: Timbro.
Mål C-160/08. Talan väckt den 16 april 2008 – Europeiska gemenskapernas kommission mot Förbundsrepubliken Tyskland. Http://www.notisum.se/rnp/eu/lag/60890160.htm.
Näringsdepartementet. 2016. 'Smart industri – en ny industrialiseringsstrategi för Sverige.' Näringsdepartementet: N2015:38.
OECD. 2017. 'Sweden. Trade and Investment Statistical Note.'
Olofsson, M. 2014. *Jag är den jag är*. Stockholm: Wahlström & Widstrand.
Pierre, J. 2004. *En samlad tillväxtpolitik?* Institutet för tillväxtanalytiska studier. R2004:014.
Proposition 1980/81:130. *Om industripolitikens inriktning, m.m.*
Proposition 2015/16:1. *Budgetpropositionen för 2016. Förslag till statens budget för 2016, finansplan och skattefrågor.*
Regeringens skrivelse 2008/09:34. *Sveriges handlingsprogram för tillväxt och sysselsättning 2008–2010.*
Regeringskansliet. 2015. *Sveriges nationella reformprogram 2015. Europa 2020 – EU:s strategi för smart och hållbar tillväxt för alla.*
Reid. D. 2018. 'Europe will be the big loser in US trade war with China'. *CNBC*. August 28, 2018.
Ridderstolpe, E. 2009. 'Regeringen lovar företag skatteuppskov'. *Sveriges Radio*. January 22, 2009.
SOU 2007:55. *Betalningstider i näringslivet*. Stockholm: Fritzes.
— 2011:69. *Olagligt statsstöd*. Stockholm: Fritzes.
Stenberg, E. 2012. 'Fler måste kunna byta karriär mitt i livet'. *Dagens Nyheter*. February 7th 2012.
Svenskt Näringsliv. 2001. 'Fakta om Sveriges ekonomi'. Stockholm: Svenskt Näringsliv.
— 2010. 'Smått om små företag'. Stockholm: Svenskt Näringsliv.
Swedish Institute. 2017. 'Swedish pop exports – Sweden – one of the leading pop-music nations today.' Stockholm: Swedish Institute.
The National Board of Trade Sweden. 2017. 'Sveriges utrikeshandel med varor och tjänster samt direktinvesteringar.' Stockholm: The National Board of Trade Sweden.
The Swedish Agency for Growth Policy Analysis. 2018. http://www.tillvaxtanalys.se/in-english/areas-of-study.html.
Tillväxtanalys. 2011. 'Sveriges implementering av Small Business Act for Europe – Hur långt har vi kommit? 'Rapport 2011/194.
— 2013. 'Näringspolitik i kriser – vad kan vi lära av finanskrisen 2008–2009?' Rapport 2013:13.
— 2018. 'Nystartade företag i Sverige 2017.' Rapport 2018:03.
TT-Reuters. 2013. 'Rekordböter från EU mot sex banker.' *TT-Reuters*, December 3.
Worthington, H. 2018. 'The macroeconomic implications of Sweden's departure from the EU.' Stockholm: the Stockholm Chamber of Commerce.

4. Agricultural Policy

From Overproduction to Import Dependency

Camilla Eriksson

Do we need to bother with agricultural policy? The share of the population that earns a livelihood from farming in Sweden is steadily decreasing. Today less than 2% of the population get a share of their income from agricultural activities (Statistics Sweden 2018, 106). In 2017, agricultural production accounted for just 0.28% of Sweden's GDP (Statistics Sweden 2018, 132). Farming, then, is no longer a preoccupation for a large part of the population, and from a political perspective it does not involve many citizens or voters. The situation is similar in most EU member states. Yet, in spite of this, expenditures on the Common Agricultural Policy (CAP) take up roughly 40% of the EU's budget (European Commission 2018) – a figure which indeed has often drawn sharp criticism.

However, the reason why the European Union (EU) expenditures on agriculture are so high is that the larger part of overall spending on agricultural policy is done at EU level. In other areas, such as social or environmental policy, national budgets cover most of the costs; in the case of agriculture, however, the Union accounts for some 75% of public spending. This is due to the fact that the member states are not allowed to conduct their own agricultural policies (the rationale for the CAP being to create fair conditions for trade on the single market for agricultural produce). Therefore, EU spending on the CAP should be compared with the sum total of EU and national spending in other areas. Calculated this way, spending on the CAP only accounts for 1% of public spending in the EU (European Commission 2017, 7).

The CAP should be seen as a European single market project and a food security project. Lessons learned from the two world wars made food security an important policy field. Food security is vital for guaranteeing state sovereignty: any country without a reliable and well-functioning provision of food risks starvation during war, which in turn accelerates social upheaval. Most countries have chosen to guarantee food security by stimulating national self-sufficiency in food. In 1957, when the European Economic Community (EEC) was established through the Treaty of Rome, a common agricultural policy was deemed a *sine qua non* for the creation of a single market in Europe. It was critical, namely, that national food production not be negatively affected. In the case of Sweden, however, EU membership has meant a loss of market shares to imports from member states with lower production costs. As a result, Sweden is now more dependent on food imports than it has ever been. Also, the ambitious contingency plans that Sweden had had since the 1920s – for guaranteeing food security in the event of an embargo or war – were abandoned when the country joined the EU. However, in the wake of an increasingly tense security situation around the Baltic Sea, food security has resurfaced as an important issue in Swedish political debate. Recently, therefore, new contingency plans have been proposed for securing food supplies during a war or major crisis.

In this chapter, I review how Swedish agricultural policy worked before EU accession, and I describe the changes in organisation and content that Union membership subsequently brought. I begin with an overview of the 1990s, a decade during which Swedish agricultural policy changed at its core twice: first in 1990, when the country embarked on a radically neoliberal path of deregulation; then in 1995, when EU membership brought a re-regulation of the agricultural policy field, with direct support to farmers. In the next section, I examine Swedish agricultural policy today, and I describe the policy process involved. I also explain the difference between the two pillars of the CAP, which contain the Single Payment Scheme and the Rural Development Programme respectively. I conclude, finally, with a discussion of policy outcomes in Swedish farming, with a focus – seen through an agricultural-policy lens – on the societal role that farming is perceived to fill.

The 1990s: A Cataclysmic Time for Swedish Agriculture

In 1990, Sweden adopted a radically new agricultural policy. The sector was deregulated; agricultural production would now be steered by market forces. The reform was strongly conditioned by neoliberal ideas of New Public Management (NPM) and minimal state intervention. NPM entailed a marked change in public administration, with governance mechanisms modelled on the private sector. The only other country in the world to have embarked on a similar policy journey was New Zealand (Ingemansson & Olsson 1990). To this day, no other country has carried out a similar reform. The change was radical indeed, and it shook up the entire agricultural sector. The week after the deregulation decision was made, the Federation of Swedish Farmers (Swedish acronym: LRF) came out in favour of membership in the EEC (which in 1993 became the EU – the European Union). The question of EEC membership had split LRF into two camps, with some members strongly defending Sweden's traditional foreign-policy stance, which entailed nonalignment in peacetime aiming at neutrality in war. Adherents of this view took EEC membership to mean that this policy would be abandoned (which indeed it later was, although EU membership might not have been the root cause). In any case, what was the background to the deregulation decision, and how had Swedish agricultural policy looked prior to it?

For a 50-year period, from 1940 to 1990, prices for agricultural produce in Sweden were negotiated between the central actors in the area: *i.e.*, farmers, consumers, and the state. Through import duties and export subsidies, the Swedish market was strictly regulated. The aim of these measures was to reach three overarching targets: one for production, another for consumption, a third for incomes. The purpose of the production target was to secure the country's food supply in the event of armed conflict. The focus of the consumption target was on protecting consumers' right to safe, nutritional, and affordable food. The aim of the incomes target was to ensure that farmers' earnings would match those of industrial workers. These goals were set out in the Agricultural Act of 1947 (SOU 1946:42, 15). Responsibility for implementing the Agricultural Act was assigned at the time to the newly instituted regional Agricultural Boards, the grand mission of which was to rationalise agricultural production. Rationalisation was seen as a means of realising the three goals mentioned above. The regions in which the Boards were instituted were the 26 regions which the Rural Economy and Agricultural Societies (*Hushållningssällskapen*) had established at the end of the 18th century, and on the basis of which they had worked since. With the 1947 Agricultural Act, the state took over portions of the work that had previously been carried out by the Societies, which had played a central role in shaping Swedish agriculture through the advisory services in agricultural science they provided (and which they continue to provide to this day).

The production target turned out to be the easiest to reach. Levels of production consistently exceeded the target, and at times were so high that policymakers saw them as a problem. Already in 1954, a commission was appointed to investigate how these levels could be lowered, by encouraging the conversion of less productive arable lands into forests (see SOU 1966:30, 273). Over subsequent decades, in fact, the production target was more important as a ceiling than as a floor. According to the Agricultural Act of 1967 (SOU 1966:30), production was to be limited to 80–100% of national self-sufficiency. This goal would be achieved through 'concentrated rationalisation' (*koncentrerad rationalisering*; Swedish acronym: KR). KR aimed at consolidating land into a small number of farms in each village, called KR farms. With the support of the Land Acquisition Act (*jordförvärvslagen*), the Agricultural Boards could steer land purchases towards selected KR farms, helping them to grow. The Boards could also stop other farms – those deemed inappropriate for development – from acquiring land. Regional aid was offered in order to ease the social effects of the new policy (Arvidsson 1988). Thus, with the assistance of the Boards, the rational and efficient KR farms would gain access to the best arable lands, thereby attaining the incomes target of the agricultural policy (which had proven the most difficult to reach).

In the 1980s Swedish farming was struck by economic crisis, due to large overproduction that was regarded as unmanageable. The number of farms fell from around 300,000 in the 1930s to a bit over 100,000 in the 1980s. But despite this, and despite the efforts of the Agricultural Boards, production levels continued to rise. Due to rapid technological progress and more effective fertilisers and pesticides, farm efficiency continued to exceed expectations (Wastenson *et al.*

1992). Then, with the help of export subsidies, the resulting overproduction was sold on the international market, at prices below the fixed ones that applied within the country. This entailed large costs for the state. During the 1980s, accordingly, Swedish agricultural policy came under heavy criticism, on the grounds that it resulted in unnecessary surpluses, wasted resources, and unfair trade conditions (see Hedlund & Lundahl 1985; Bohlin *et al.* 1984).

As a direct consequence of the deregulation policy enacted in 1990, a transition programme *(omställning-90)* was introduced. The aim was to reduce the acreage under cereals cultivation, as well as to ameliorate the social effects of the deregulation. The idea was to carry out the deregulation in a number of steps, until its completion in 1996. The most important measures sought to reduce cereals harvests, by turning arable lands to other uses such as forestry or energy production. However, on the very same day the transition programme entered into force – 1 July 1991 – Sweden applied for membership in the EEC. Public agencies started thereupon to prepare the country for membership, by adjusting various policies and regulations (SJV 2011). Thus, the transition programme (and by extension the deregulation policy) was never implemented fully. Since EU accession in 1995, Swedish agriculture has been embraced by the supports and measures of the CAP, which means it is once more subsidised and regulated.

Sweden Joins the Common Agricultural Policy

When Sweden joined the EU, a massive reform of the CAP had just begun. As of 1995, the CAP resembled Swedish agricultural policy as it had been up until 1990. During the 1980s, moreover, the CAP had met with similar criticism. Since its establishment with the Treaty of Rome in 1957, the CAP has had five goals: to stabilise markets, to increase productivity, to ensure farmers a decent standard of living, to guarantee the availability of supplies, and to assure consumers access to food at reasonable prices (European Parliament 2004). These goals, like those of Swedish agricultural policy, have reflected a combination of security and social policy considerations. Europe, the resolve went, would never again allow a situation to develop where political uncertainty resulted in a lack of food; and it would ensure that farmers' incomes increased (Garzon 2006).

As early as in the 1970s, the CAP drew massive criticism from the environmental movement, which expressed grave concern over the effects of agricultural chemicals on birdlife and biodiversity. As in Sweden there were conflicts between policy goals: on the one hand, the object was to keep prices low for consumers; on the other, high incomes for farmers were to be ensured. The result was a situation where fewer and fewer farms were using the land more and more intensively. The agricultural sector was producing more efficiently and bringing in higher revenues, but the consequences for the environment were negative. Then, during the 1980s, the environmental critique was complemented by an economic one. The CAP, the claim went, had a distorting impact on trade, and it hurt producers in the Global South. Neoliberals joined international aid organisations like Oxfam in condemning subsidies and high import duties for penalising countries outside the EEC, and for preventing free trade in agricultural produce. Price supports were criticised for causing overproduction of certain agricultural products; newspaper headlines spoke of beef and butter mountains (Grant 1997).

Despite the massive criticism, the CAP was not reformed at all substantially during the 1970s or 1980s (Garzon 2006). The critique from the environmental movement did not result in any major reforms; in time, however, the economic critique proved more successful. Reforms initiated in the 1990s changed the CAP in a way that the European Parliament has labelled 'radical'. Reforms under Commissioner MacSharry in 1992 introduced income supports tied to production levels, in order to compensate farmers for the deregulation of agricultural markets, for the removal of price supports, and the like. The MacSharry reforms also featured a set-aside scheme resembling the Swedish transition programme. The aim was to reduce cereals harvests, by requiring farmers to take 15% of their land out of production (Kay 2003, 414). When Swedish farmers first started receiving payments from the CAP, these came in the form of income supports tied to production levels, which essentially stimulated increased production.

The Common Agricultural Policy Today

The CAP today has two pillars, known as Pillar I and Pillar II (not to be confused with the EU's three pillars before 2009, when the Lisbon Treaty went into effect). The aim of the first pillar is to hold up production and to support farmers. The purpose of the second is to protect the environment and to promote rural development. The division of the CAP into Pillar I and Pillar II came about in 1999, as a result of the Agenda 2000 reform, which introduced broader objectives for the CAP. Having been focused earlier solely on agricultural production, the CAP was now enjoined to promote rural development as well. The new measures were organised in Pillar II; the previous production-focused ones were organised in Pillar I (Daugbjerg & Swinbank 2007, 8).

The production-tied income supports – which had stimulated high production levels – were discontinued by the Fischler reform of 2003. They were replaced by the Single Payment Scheme (SPS), which was implemented in Sweden in 2005. The SPS decoupled supports from levels of production. Its aim was to make the CAP more compatible with WTO agreements, and to reduce costs and cut bureaucracy in anticipation of the EU's enlargement in 2004 (Daugbjerg & Swinbank 2007, 3). The SPS is paid out as a certain number of euros per hectare, given that the land is managed according to certain specifications. Today the SPS is the largest single support paid out to European farmers, and it takes up almost two thirds of the total CAP budget (Hill 2012, 137). Until 1 January 2015, moreover, it made up the entire content of Pillar I, together with a few less costly market regulations. Following a reform in 2015, furthermore, Pillar I has been complemented by a number of targeted supports, in the application of which the member states are allowed a degree of flexibility. In Sweden, three more targeted supports have been implemented: one for cattle, another for greening, and a third to farmers under 40 years of age. The purpose of these new supports is to tackle some of the structural problems in agriculture that have been discussed in recent years. These include the high average age of farmers, the excessive incidence of monoculture, and the damage to dairy and beef production which has resulted from the particularly severe market fluctuations in that area (see Swinnen 2015 for a rich analysis of the reform at EU level). The reform of the SPS involved levelling out the sum paid out per hectare, so that all arable land receives the same amount. When the SPS was first introduced, more productive land received higher payments than less productive land, in order to ease the consequences of replacing production supports with the decoupled SPS measures. This means, of course, that the SPS was never fully decoupled. By the year 2020, however, the difference in SPS payments will be levelled out completely, and total costs for the programme will be lower (see Ds 2014:6, 12–3). At the EU level, incidentally, the SPS was renamed the Basic Payment Scheme; but the Swedish term (*gårdsstöd*) has remained the same. For the sake of simplicity, I refer to the scheme both before and after the 2015 reform as the SPS.

To sum up, the reform of the CAP since the 1990s has been motivated by the economic critique adumbrated above, rather than the environmental one. But there has been no conflict between environmental considerations and the reforms that have been introduced. On the contrary, the concerns raised by the environmental movement have been incorporated. A different content has been given to agricultural policy: the prior focus on productivity needed to be replaced by something new. This is evident from the introduction of the decoupled SPS, as well as from the more specific supports added to Pillar I over the last few years. It is most evident, finally, from the establishment of Pillar II itself. All member states must follow the rural development policy laid down by the European Commission, which prescribes that national or regional Rural Development Programmes (RDPS) be drawn up for seven-year periods (European Council 2005, 1698).

The first Swedish RDP was launched for the 2000–2006 programme period, and the second for 2007–2013. We are currently at the end of the third (2014–2020). The latest version has a budget of 36.1 billion SEK – a bit over 5 billion SEK per year. Around half of the programme is funded by the EU, the other half by the national budget. The SPS is paid in full by the EU, with a budget of around 5 billion SEK per year for Sweden. The SPS had a larger budget than the RDP previously; the overall goal, however, has been to reduce spending on the SPS in favour of the RDP or more specific supports, like the newly created ones in Pillar I (for cattle, for greening, and for young farmers). These are considered, namely, to bring higher returns in the form of common goods.

Most of the RDP's funds go to finance so-called agri-environmental measures. These entail compensation for farmers who carry out specified tasks or projects during a five-year period. Supports are available for grazing, for the restoration of grasslands, and for the upkeep of buildings or the maintenance of practices considered valuable from the standpoint of cultural heritage. Other supports within the RDP aim at stimulating rural entrepreneurship, or at extending broadband and other societal services and infrastructure. Supports are available, then, not just for farmers but also for rural entrepreneurs and for countryside dwellers in general. A large part of the budget for agri-environmental measures goes to grazing on semi-natural grasslands with high biodiversity, reflecting the government's decision to give equal support for grazing land and for cropland. Maintaining an open landscape through grazing has been an important objective of Swedish agricultural policy since the 1970s, when more intensive animal-farming techniques had prompted farmers to abandon lands previously used for grazing (Flygare 2004). The effects of reduced grazing pressure – with bush encroachment and lost biodiversity – had by then become evident.

The policy process

The EU and its member states have shared competence in agricultural policy, meaning that both the Union and its member states can enact laws regulating agriculture. Until the 1980s, however, the CAP had focused on subsidies and market regulations, the purpose being to facilitate free trade on the single market, while protecting European farmers from outside competition. The Single European Act of 1987 saw the introduction of the first regulations for food safety, animal welfare, and protection of the environment. These measures were regarded first and foremost as a means of reinforcing the single market. Common rules are thought to make for fairer competition (Oskam *et al.* 2011: 39). In Sweden, it bears noting, national legislation has generally been stricter in all these areas. For example, a number of pesticides which are forbidden in Sweden are allowed in the EU; pigs and chickens must have larger space per animal; and milk has to be pasteurised in Sweden. There is thus much discussion, in the agricultural sector in Sweden, of the need to harmonise legislation in order to ensure fair competition on the single market, especially since it is not permitted to allocate RDP expenditures to work or measures which just fulfil minimum demands stipulated by law. This means Swedish farmers cannot be compensated for complying with national laws, even when the effect of such laws is to raise their production costs above those of their counterparts in member states who face fewer exacting requirements. This issue has been taken up by a state commission, the members of which have argued that Swedish regulations for the protection of animal welfare and the environment should be adjusted (in effect lowered) to EU levels (SOU 2015:15).

Decisions on the CAP are made by the Council of Ministers, on the basis of proposals from the European Commission. The Commission then implements the decisions, issuing guidelines and regulations and monitoring their fulfilment. The SPS in Pillar I is financed wholly from the EU's budget, whereas Pillar II is funded both by the EU and by the member states. As a consequence, the influence of the member states is greater over Pillar II. Fewer national options are available within Pillar I. Most supports within Pillar I are mandatory, including the SPS and support for young farmers and for greening; but some are optional, such as support for farmland with lower productive capacity, or simplified rules for recipients of smaller payments. Sweden has chosen not to make use of the optional measures, on the grounds that it is better to use the RDP in Pillar II to channel support to specific farmers (Ds 2014: 6).

Pillar II is carried out through programmes drawn up by the member states on the basis of EU decrees. Ahead of each new RDP programme period, extensive discussions are conducted at both EU and national levels about what changes to introduce. The national RDP is drawn up by the Ministry of Enterprise and Innovation (as it has been since the Ministry of Rural Affairs was merged with the Ministry of Enterprise and Innovation in 2015); the Board of Agriculture is the administrative authority. In practice the Board of Agriculture exerts great influence over the design of the RDP, since its administrators produce documents for the Ministry which provide guidance on changes. Among the most important documents in this regard are the so-called technical reports *(tekniska underlagen)*, which present socioeconomic analyses of different support measures and suggestions for change based on these (see *e.g.* SJV 2012). Since the European Commission and the Swedish government have shared competence in this area, the national RDP proposed by the Swedish government must be approved by the EU. Then, once the Commission has granted its approval, it is the task of the Swedish Board of Agriculture to write up regulations on implementation and to stipulate requirements for different agri-environmental measures.

The implementation of the RDP is decentralised to a considerable extent. It is the County Administrative Boards that decide which agri-environmental measures will be available, as well as what share of the budget is to go to which payments within the county in question. These policies are set out in executive plans which must be approved by the Board of Agriculture (SFS 2007:481, §8). In effect, this means that different agri-environmental measures are applied in different member states, as well as in different counties in Sweden. Administrators at the county level have considerable leeway to decide – within the framework of the regional executive plan and the regulations laid down by the Board of Agriculture and the EU – which farmers are to receive what payments (Eriksson 2013).

The overall aim of the Swedish RDP is to achieve social, economic, and ecological sustainability (SJV 2010). The concept of sustainability, however, is not defined clearly in the programme – a point which has drawn criticism in evaluations of the RDP's efficiency (see, *e.g.*, SLU 2009). This points to a more general problem with assessing the efficiency of the RDP, in view of its replacement of previous quantitative targets like high production levels with qualitative targets, such as rich biodiversity, vibrant cultural heritage, and social sustainability. These targets are qualitative or difficult to assess, even as requirements relating to the assessment of efficiency and effectiveness are high in the EU. As a result, measurable criteria tend to be used for assessing progress towards complex and qualitative targets. This is a difficult task for administrators. As compared with previous policies, then, the new CAP demands administrative competence of a higher level and a partly different kind. (See Eriksson 2013 for a discussion of how this has manifested itself in the policy process in connection with agri-environmental measures for summer farming).

The political debate today centres on proposals to reform the CAP, by liquidating the SPS over the long run. On the one hand, the SPS provides support of a less distorting kind than previous policies did; on the other, it demands no more of farmers than that they follow existing regulations and keep the land in a usable condition. This has prompted criticism of the SPS from several quarters. The environmental movement want to see stricter demands placed on farmers to reduce negative environmental impacts. Neoliberal critics think the SPS subsidises European agricultural production in a way that distorts trade with countries outside the EU. Berkeley Hill, a professor of policy analysis, argues that due to these critiques, money currently paid out through the SPS will be successively channelled through the RDP instead – above all as agri-environmental measures to farms, since the most important argument that he identifies for continuing to subsidise agricultural production lies in the environmental value that the sector can yield (2012, 182). This argument matches what Swedish governments, on both the right and the left, have been urging since the turn of the millennium, as they have pushed for complete abandonment of the SPS in favour of the RDP (Ds 2004:9). The goals of the RDP may be diffuse, but the programme demonstrates that a new agenda for European farming has gained ground (even if, technically speaking, the goals laid down in the Treaty of Rome have not been altered). Agriculture today is expected to produce common goods in addition to just food, and it is being called upon to help solve environmental problems rather than causing them.

What has Happened in Swedish Farming Since EU Accession?

EU accession marked an end to the general feeling of apprehension and discomfort that had prevailed among Swedish farmers after the public criticism of agricultural subsidies during the 1980s, and the deregulation decision that followed in 1990. After the decision to deregulate the sector, many farmers chose to abandon cereals production in favour of for example energy crops, in order to receive support from the transition programme; and many left arable land fallow. Payments for leaving land fallow had been available even earlier (*träda-87*), the object being to reduce overproduction of cereals. This had clearly signalled to farmers that arable farming was not appreciated, and by extension that agriculture was thought to be causing problems for society rather than serving the common good. Then, after EU accession, subsidies for farming resumed – not only in an abstract sense through market interventions (of which the earlier Swedish policy had mainly consisted), but also in the form of direct support paid out to farmers. On the other hand, the direct payments involved have given rise to a stigma in public debate, with farmers being condescendingly described as recipients of social assistance. These direct supports have also entailed a control apparatus for assessing the effects of the subsidies – a control apparatus of which many farmers are critical.

Among members of the Federation of Swedish Farmers (LRF), there was a great degree of optimism as EU accession approached. They anticipated, namely, that entering the single market would open up export markets for Swedish farmers. Agricultural produce from Sweden, they believed, would be widely sought by European consumers, since it could be marketed as more environmentally friendly than food produced elsewhere in Europe. Marit Paulsen, for example – a politician who had an agreement with LRF to promote Swedish farming – campaigned on the slogan that only farms in Sweden could produce meat without the routine use of antibiotics (LRF undated-b).

Indeed, Swedish agriculture has undergone a rapid transformation since the 1990s. The number of farms fell by over 35 % between 1990 and 2016, from just under 97,000 to just under 63,000 (Statistics Sweden 2018, 38). Of these farms, only some 20 % generate full-time employment for one or more persons; and fewer than 5,000 of the latter are large enough to provide employment for two persons or more (Statistics Sweden 2014, 52). One of the most labour-intensive types of agricultural production is dairy production. The number of dairy farms has fallen even more dramatically over the same period – by 85 % (from just under 26,000 to just over 3,600). The number of dairy cows has fallen by almost 45 % – from around 576,000 to just over 322,000 in 2017 (Statistics Sweden 2018, 83). The number of persons receiving any part of their income from farming was just under 171,500 in 2016 (Statistics Sweden 2018, 106), which shows that a very large proportion of those with earnings from agriculture only work with it part-time. This is due to a combination of short-term seasonal work and a large number of small farms. Still, in 2013, farms of more than 100 ha made up less than 10 % of the total number of farms; however, they cultivated over half of the total amount of arable land in Sweden (Statistics Sweden 2014, 51). Farms are increasingly specialised, and it is becoming more and more common in Swedish agriculture to use high-tech machinery like tractors run with the help of GPS, and fully automatic robotic systems for milking.

LRF's expectation that EU accession would mean new export markets and better business opportunities for Swedish farmers proved wrong. On the contrary, domestic production has lost market shares to imports since 1995. Today Sweden imports food to a value double that of its food exports, making for a significant trade deficit (SJV 2013). It is impossible to say what the loss of market shares would have been if Sweden had not joined the EU and if the deregulation policy adopted in 1990 had been fully implemented, but it would likely have been larger still, for Swedish farmers in that case would have had to compete on the global market without benefit of any of the subsidies or regulations provided by the CAP. In any case, the low domestic production of beef and dairy products in relation to their consumption means that the goal of national self-sufficiency – which had been one of three main goals for Swedish agricultural policy up until 1990 – is not met today. Overall dependence on imports is furthermore difficult to estimate, since it is not only food that is imported but also inputs necessary for food production, such as fuel, fodder, fertilisers, and plant-protection products.

Another change seen in Swedish farming since the 1990s, in addition to structural rationalisation, is the widespread introduction of organic farming. Organic farming had risen in popularity since the 1970s due to the critique of the environmental impact of conventional farming, but it was still labelled 'alternative', and established agricultural organisations long viewed it with scepticism. Tracey Clunies-Ross and Graham Cox (1994, 66) describe how lobbyists for organic farming have worked to influence the CAP so that its support would be extended to organic farming. It has been important for such lobbyists that organic farming no longer be seen as 'alternative' to the norm. In Sweden during the 1990s, the Federation of Swedish Farmers underwent a notable change in this regard, gradually accepting organic farming as part of the Swedish agricultural scene. This became clear when the acting chair of the Federation at the time, Hans Jonsson, converted to organically certified production in 1999 (LRF undated-a).

A lot has happened since the 1990s to show that organic farming is now an established mode of agriculture, especially since many of the reforms made in the CAP have focused on the environmental impact of farming. Several of the supports offered by the RDP, for example, have been designed in such a way as to encourage organic farming. The way such measures are designed has a strong impact on the methods that future farmers will embrace. Organic cultivation has grown more profitable. In part this is thanks to specific measures of support from public agencies, but it is also due in part to the generally higher and less volatile prices which organic produce now fetches. The share of arable land on which organic production is carried on has increased, from 3.6% in 1995 to a bit below 20% in 2017 (Statistics Sweden 1996, 10; Statistics Sweden 2018, 148). However, almost half the land devoted to organic production is used as pastureland or for the production of fodder, and a large part of it is situated in areas of low fertility (Statistics Sweden 2018, 148). In other words, the largest change we have seen so far is that organic farming is now considered an established part of agriculture, rather than that a large share of food production is being conducted with organic methods.

The Role that Agriculture Plays in Society

Since the 1990s, according to the agrarian historian Janken Myrdal, agriculture has undergone a process of change as dramatic as that seen in the course of the great structural transformations that took place during the 'Green Revolution' in post-war Europe. Farmers have a 'new mission' now – as custodians of cultural, environmental, and recreational values, which are seen as an integrated part of agricultural production today. To some extent, in their use of the land, farmers create the rural environment – and not just for themselves, but for everyone who resides in the countryside or who visits it. This, Myrdal argues, entails a greater responsibility for farmers to care actively for future generations – which is a common definition of sustainability (Myrdal 2001, 2008).

The expansion of the CAP to encompass policies of rural development (as reflected in the change of name in 2011 from the Ministry of Agriculture to the Ministry of Rural Affairs) has consequences for how agriculture is conducted at farm level. Farmers are expected to move away from producing bulk products and to become an integrated part of service provision. They are encouraged to produce value-added products like cheese or charcuterie, and to sell these directly to consumers; or to offer farm stays and other recreational services on the farm (see Päiviö 2008). Some scholars refer to this new definition of what farming is and should be 'multifunctionality' (see Van Huylenbroeck & Durand; Wilson 2007). Others argue that this is really not so new. Britt Liljewall, an historian, contends that versatility has in fact characterised farming for centuries. The current 'rediscovery' of multifunctionality, she argues, reflects the earlier impact on public discourse of the postwar rationalisation programmes, which transformed the public image of what a farm should be more than they changed actual farm life. Swedish agriculture, she claims, is still characterised by family farms, physical labour, and multifunctionality, This has little to do, furthermore,with any new type of entrepreneurship; instead it illustrates continuity in the sector. Farming, she avers, remains first and foremost a lifestyle, rather than a capitalist endeavour (Liljewall 2000, 132).

In sum, what is new about the CAP today is what it signals regarding the role that agriculture should play in society. The versatile nature of farms – especially family farms – has been revalued and given new meaning, and terms such as 'multifunctionality' have become part of the public discourse of what farming ought to be. More than it had been during the postwar years, it is accepted today that there are many different ways to farm. The earlier focus on efficiency, specialisation, large-scale farming, and the rational use of land has come under challenge today. Whether this is an instance of Europeanisation or simply an effect of changing public discourse in late modernity is an open question. In any case it is clear that, when Sweden joined the EU in 1995, issues of cultural heritage and the environment were not integrated into Swedish agricultural policy. Since that time, however, such an integration has gradually taken place, especially as a consequence of the country's adoption of EU reforms that were introduced after Sweden joined.

Conclusion

In this chapter, we have seen how Swedish agricultural policy has changed since the 1980s, particularly since EU accession. During the post-war years, Swedish agriculture was regulated through fixed prices and market interventions. It was then deregulated in 1990, only to be re-regulated in 1995, when Sweden joined the EU and entered the CAP. Since that time, finally, the CAP has undergone substantial reform, so as to promote cultural and environmental values.

Decision-making competence in the area of agricultural policy is shared between Sweden and the EU, which means that all Swedish proposals must be made in accordance with regulations issued by the European Commission. Indeed, the Commission must approve them before they can be implemented. The overall aim of the CAP, and of EU-level laws and regulations generally, is to create equal opportunities for free and fair trade on the single market. Sweden has chosen, however, to continue imposing stricter regulations on matters of animal welfare and the environment. This has caused discontent among Swedish farmers, who have lost market shares to imports since the country entered the single market. Increasingly, therefore, the suggestion is made that Swedish legislation should be harmonised with EU legislation. This would entail, in practice, a softening of Swedish regulations. If this is done, it will no longer be possible to market Swedish produce as friendlier to animals and the environment. This in turn will undermine the market for Swedish produce, both in Sweden and abroad. Swedish policymakers thus find themselves in a difficult situation. Both options – maintaining stricter regulations and continuing to lose market shares or softening the regulations and losing marketing tools – seem like a dead end.

Over the last decade, the domestic production of beef and dairy products has fallen so low that the issue of food security has resurfaced in policy debates. Other consumer issues play a part here too. The position of Swedish meat production has been strengthened by reports about conditions elsewhere in the EU: *e.g.*, reports of poor practices in pig production; or the horsemeat scandal of 2013, when meat sold as beef was found to be horsemeat. It is too early to say what the long-term consequences of this new policy debate will be. In 2015, however, domestic meat production gained market shares relative to imports for the first time in decades (SJV 2015). Since then, moreover, it has increased somewhat every year.

The most radical change in public discourse on agricultural policy has taken place in the last few years, due to the new civil defence policy introduced by the Defence Act of 2015 (Swedish Government 2015). The aim of civil defence is to prepare society for war or prolonged crises. Naturally, a reliable production and distribution of food must be ensured under such conditions. The National Food Strategy of 2017 (Swedish Government 2017), the first of its kind, accordingly, required that measures be taken to increase Swedish agricultural production, with an eye to strengthening national self-sufficiency in food. A few months later, a report from the Swedish Defence Commission (2017) stated that policies for guaranteeing food provisions during war or prolonged crises should be reinstated. It further suggested an annual budget of 700 million SEK for this purpose, starting from the year 2021. It is too early to say what the exact implications of these rapid developments will be. It is clear, however, that the aim of ensuring free competition on the single market is likely to be an obstacle to measures for increasing domestic production. However, despite potential policy constraints from the CAP, the increasing salience of the issue of food security indicates that agriculture is once again embarking on a new policy path, where the question of national security serves once more as the main driver in debate over agriculture's main role in society.

References

Arvidsson, A. 1988. *Lantbruksnämnderna 40 år.* Jönköping: Lantbruksstyrelsen.

Clunies-Ross, T. & G. Cox 1994. 'Challenging the Productivist Paradigm: Organic Farming and the Politics of Agricultural Change' In: P. Lowe, T. Marsden & S. Whatmore (red.) *Regulating agriculture.* London: David Fulton Publishers.

Daugbjerg, C. & A. Swinbank 2007. 'The politics of CAP reform: trade negotiations, institutional settings and blame avoidance'. *JCMS: Journal of Common Market Studies* 45(1): 1–22.

Ds Jo 2004:9. *Genomförandet av EU:s jordbruksreform i Sverige.* Stockholm: Regeringskansliet.

Ds 2014:6. *Gårdsstödet 2015–2020: förslag till svenskt genomförande.* Stockholm: Regeringskansliet.

Eriksson, C. 2013. *Fäboden som politiskt rum. Att vara fäbodbrukare i den gemensamma jordbrukspolitiken.* Acta universitatis agriculturae Sueciae, no. 25. Uppsala: Sveriges lantbruksuniversitet.

European Commission 2015. 'CAP expenditure in the total EU expenditure.' CAP post-2013: Key graphs & figures. Available at: https://ec.europa.eu/agriculture/sites/agriculture/files/cap-post-2013/graphs/graph1_en.pdf, fetched July 20 2018–

— 2017. 'The European Union Explained: Agriculture.' Luxembourg: Publications Office of the European Union.

European Council 2005: 1698. 'Council Regulation (EC) No 1698/2005 of 20 September 2005 on support for rural development by the European Agricultural Fund for Rural Development (EAFRD).' *Official Journal of the European Union* 21.10.2005(L 277/1).

Flygare, I. 2004. 'Öppna landskap: det agrara landskapet i efterkrigstidens riksdagsdebatt'. [Open landscapes: the agrarian landscape in post-war parliament debates]. *Bebyggelsehistorisk tidskrift* 47(??): 30–48.

Garzon, I. 2006. *Reforming the Common Agricultural Policy: History of a Paradigm Change.* Houndmills: Palgrave MacMillan.

Grant, W. 1997. 'Butter Mountains, Wine Lakes and Beef Wars: The Commodity Regimes' In: *The Common Agricultural Policy.* London: Macmillan Education.

Hedlund, S. & M. Lundahl 1985. *Beredskap eller protektionism? En studie av beredskapsmålet i svensk jordbrukspolitik.* [Preparedness or protectionism? A study of the production goal in Swedish agricultural policy]. Malmö: Liber förlag.

Hill, B. 2012. *Understanding the Common Agricultural Policy.* London: Earthscan.

Ingemansson, J. & B. Olsson 1990. *Information om en ny livsmedelspolitik.* [Information regarding a new food policy]. Jönköping: Lantbruksnämnden.

Liljewall, B. 2000. 'Tradition som moderniserande kraft: alternativa mönster för historisk förändring'. [Tradition as a modernising power: alternative patterns for historic change]. *Kulturhistorisk tidskrift* 83(3): 129–149.

LRF undated-a. 'LRF och synen på miljön.' [LRF and our view on the environment] Abailable at: http://www.lrfhistoria.se/artikellista/synen-pa-miljon/. Fectched July 20, 2018.

LRF undated-b. Med LRF mot EU. [With LRF towards the EU] Available at: http://www.lrfhistoria.se/artikellista/med-lrf-mot-eu-/. Fectched July 20, 2018.

Myrdal, J. 2001. *Den nya produktionen – det nya uppdraget: jordbrukets framtid i ett historiskt perspektiv.* Stockholm: Regeringskansliet.

— 2008. *Framtiden – om femtio år: global utveckling och ruralt-urbant i Norden.* Stockholm: Institutet för framtidsstudier.

Oskam, A., G. Meester & H. Silvis 2011. *EU policy for agriculture, food and rural areas.* 2:a utg. Wagenigen: Wagenigen Academic Publishers.

Päiviö, E-L. 2008. *Det agrara landskapet på vinst eller förlust: biologiska och historiska värden inom lantbrukets nya uppdrag.* Acta universitatis agriculturae Sueciae, no. 95. Uppsala: Sveriges lantbruksuniversitet.

Regeringens proposition 2014/15:109. *Försvarspolitisk inriktning – Sveriges försvar 2016–2020.* Stockholm: Regeringskansliet.

Statistics Sweden 1996. *Jordbruksstatistisk årsbok 1996.* Örebro: Statistiska centralbyrån.

— 2014. *Jordbruksstatistisk årsbok 2013: med data om livsmedel.* Örebro: Statistiska centralbyrån.

— *Jordbruksstatistisk sammanställning 2017: med data om livsmedel – tabeller.* Örebro: Statistics Sweden

SFS 2007:481. *Förordning om stöd för landsbygdsutvecklingsåtgärder.* Stockholm: Regeringskansliet.

SJV 1993. *Uppföljning av livsmedelspolitiken.* Jönköping: Statens jordbruksverk.

— 2010. 'Vad är landsbygdsprogrammet?'. Hämtad 22 september 2010, från http://www.sjv.se/amnesomraden/mojligheterpalandsbygden/landsbygdsprogrammet/vadarlandsbygdspro grammet.4.7a446fa211f3c824a0e8000171998.html.

— 2011. *Sveriges första femton år som medlem i EU: Kontroll och revision av direktstöd till jordbrukare.* Jönköping: Statens jordbruksverk.

— 2012. *Tekniskt underlag: Landsbygdsprogrammet 2014–2020.* Jönköping.

— 2013. Sveriges produktion av nötkött och ägg ökar men importen tar ändå marknadsandelar. *På tal om jordbruk – fördjupning om aktuella frågor.* (red.). Jönköping: Statens jordbruksverk.

— 2015, 18/3 2015. 'Svenska marknadsandelar av kött, och några färska frukter och grönsaker.' Hämtad 2/1, 2016, från https://jordbruketisiffror.wordpress.com/2015/03/18/svenska-marknadsandelar-av-kott-och-nagra-farska-frukter-och-gronsaker/.

SLU 2009. *Slututvärdering av miljö- och landsbygdsprogrammet 2000–2006: Vad fick vi för pengarna?* Uppsala: Sveriges lantbruksuniversitet.

SOU 1946:42. *Riktlinjer för den framtida jordbrukspolitiken: betänkande. D. 1.* Regeringskansliet.

— 1966:30. *Den framtida jordbrukspolitiken: betänkande. A, Bakgrunden.* Stockholm: Fritzes offentliga publikationer.

— 2009:69. *En ny ransonerings- och prisregleringslag.* Stockholm: Fritzes offentliga publikationer.

SOU 2015:15. *Attraktiv, innovativ och hållbar, - strategi för en konkurrenskraftig jordbruks- och trädgårdsnäring.* Stockholm: Fritzes offentliga publikationer.

Swinnen, J. (red.) 2015. *The Political Economy of the 2014–2020 Common Agricultural Policy: An Imperfect Storm.* Centre for European Policy Studies (CEPS). London: Rowman & Littlefield International.

European Parliament 2004. The Treaty of Rome and the foundations of the CAP. Accessible at: http://www.europarl.europa.eu/facts_2004/4_1_1_en.htm. Fetched: July 20, 2018.

Van Huylenbroeck, G. & G. Durand 2003. *Multifunctional agriculture: a new paradigm for European agriculture and rural development.* Aldershot: Ashgate.

Wastenson, L., Å. Clason & B. Granström 1992. *Sveriges nationalatlas. Jordbruket.* Stockholm: Sveriges nationalatlas (SNA).

Wilson, G. A. 2007. *Multifunctional agriculture: a transition theory perspective.* Cambridge, MA: CABI.

Wästfelt, A. & Eriksson, C. 2017. *Det svenska lantbrukets omvandling 1990–2040: Exemplet Uppsala län.* Uppsala: Framtidens lantbruk, Sveriges lantbruksuniversitet.

5. Environmental Policy

The Challenge of Institutional Fit in a Complex Policy Area

Katarina Eckerberg & Therese Bjärstig

Environmental problems such as air and water pollution, carbon dioxide emissions and exhaustion of natural values and resources do not take account of national borders. The European Union (EU) member states have therefore decided to cooperate over environmental policy, with broad support among their citizens (Gerhards & Lengfeld 2008). The member states, however, also have certain discretionary power over the implementation of EU Directives and maintain decision-making power in some fields such as municipal planning. In other words, environmental policy is an area in which Sweden, in some cases, makes its own decisions, but also shares the decision-making power with the other countries within the EU, *i.e.* shared competence[1]. Furthermore, environmental policy is a truly difficult policy area to steer/govern, since these issues tend to permeate into many other policy areas. Consideration must be given to the environmental impact and consequences of various policy proposals and reforms. Neil Carter (2007) points to a number of features that make environmental issues difficult to handle. They are often:

- Collective goods: which means that all people have the right to the resources, such as air, water and what the earth provides us with;

1 Note, the conservation of marine biological resources are managed within the framework of the common fisheries policy, an area where the EU has the exclusive right to legislate, *i.e.* exclusive competence.

- Transnational: they do not follow political-administrative boundaries;
- Complex and uncertain: both in the connection inside and between ecological and physical processes and their effects on the environment and the conjunction and effects of different social phenomena on the environment;
- Irreversible: some changes in the environment may be impossible to restore;
- Varying over time and space: long-term effects are hard to predict and there is a wide variety of landscapes and physical/ecological conditions;
- Normative and cultural: how they are perceived depend on fundamental values regarding the relation of human-nature among different individuals in their social and cultural context (Carter 2007, pp. 174–179).

Consequently, environmental problems must be handled at all administrative levels (from local government to supranational level within the EU) and across policy areas, thus requiring an integrated approach (Jordan & Adelle 2012). In Swedish environmental policy, this is expressed in terms of both decentralization and centralization. Decentralization includes the important role played by municipalities in implementing environmental policy, while centralization is reflected both in the fact that much of the legislative power has moved to EU level, and that the national government wants greater control over local environmental work. In short, the responsibility for implementing environmental policy is largely decentralized to the local level, while steering comes from the top (Lundqvist 1998). It should also be noted that there are recurrent conflicts between environmental policy goals and other social goals, but also within environmental policy, something we will return to in our concluding discussion.

Sweden has often been regarded as an international forerunner in environmental policy, with high standards and ambitions (Eckerberg 2000; Hysing 2014; Kronsell 1997; 2002). But since Sweden's EU accession in 1995, environmental policy has advanced both internationally and nationally. The prevailing image might need to be reviewed and nuanced not least since environmental policy is not homogeneous.

For example, Sweden has been pictured as a climate policy pioneer (Zannakis 2015) but has been less successful in terms of reaching conservation targets for biodiversity (OECD 2015). The Commission has also raised criticism several times regarding Sweden's implementation of the Water Directive (*e.g.* EU 2014). Against this background, we ask 1) to what extent and how the EU membership has influenced Swedish environmental policy (both in terms of its form and content). And more specifically: 2) does EU environmental policy regulation comply with policy making at the national level, including existing rules, norms, and practices (thus making it 'easy' to implement)?

To answer these questions, we will briefly address the emergence of environmental policy within the EU and how environmental problems are generally managed within the Union, and then describe how Swedish environmental policy has evolved over time. In what way has the form and content of Swedish environmental policy changed since the EU accession? We will examine three different policy areas in more depth (climate, biodiversity, and water), which shows that the development is quite ambiguous. Based on this account, the concluding section discusses the complexity of the environmental policy area, including our findings on reciprocal impacts, and how these in turn affect environmental governance.

EU Environmental Policy

European environmental policy dates back to 1972 when the European state and government heads – in addition to the economic expansion – announced the need for Community-wide environmental policy and called for an action program. To date, seven subsequent environmental action programmes (EAPs) have guided environmental policy making in the EU. EAPs are drawn up by the Commission, span over several years, and describe legislative proposals and targets. In 2013, the Council and the European Parliament adopted its seventh EAP for 2014–2020 under the heading 'Living well, within the limits of our planet'. It sets nine priority objectives, including *e.g.* enhanced nature protection, improved ecological resilience, sustainable and resource-efficient growth in a competitive carbon economy, improved environmental integration and policy coherence, and minimized environment-related health risks.

European environmental policy has strengthened over time through a series of treaty changes. The 1987 Single European Act introduced a new environmental chapter that constituted the first legal basis for a common policy aimed at preserving the quality of the environment, protecting human health, and ensuring rational use of natural resources. Since then, hundreds of directives, regulations and decisions have entered into force in this area. More recent treaty changes have further strengthened Europe's commitment to environmental protection, as well as the role of the European Parliament in its elaboration. With the Maastricht Treaty in 1993, the environment became an official policy area, the co-decision procedure was introduced and qualified majority voting in the Council became a general rule. Another important point of departure is the Amsterdam Treaty of 1999 that introduced the obligation to integrate environmental protection into all EU policy sectors in pursuit of sustainable development. Furthermore, the 'fight against climate change' became a specific objective of the Lisbon Treaty in 2009, as well as the promotion of sustainable development in relations with non-EU countries. Its new status as a legal personality now allows the EU to conclude international agreements and act as a major player in global environmental issues (see Jordan & Adelle 2012 for a more detailed description of the development of the environmental policy in the EU).

Moreover, the content of EU environmental policy has gradually evolved. From the onset, 'traditional' environmental issues dominated, such as protecting nature and wildlife, and reducing pollution and emissions to air and water. Today, EU environmental policy aims for sustainable development, that is, more systematic strategizing that links economic, ecological, and socio-cultural developments (see also the chapter on agricultural policy). It has moved from focusing on 'repairing' damages towards preventing and minimizing negative environmental impacts – hence a turn from mainly reactive to more proactive environmental policy. Today, EU's environmental policy is based on the precautionary principle (*i.e.* a product may be forbidden if it might be considered hazardous even when scientific proof is insufficient), the polluter pays principle, and the principle of prevention of environmental harm at the source.

The EU has the power to act in all areas of environmental policy, but its scope of action is limited by the subsidiarity principle and the need for unanimity in the Council on certain issues such as tax issues, land use planning and land use. Environmental legislation includes noise, air quality, agricultural emissions, and protection of rare animal and plant species. However, the effectiveness of EU environmental policy depends on how it is implemented at national, regional, and local levels. Lack of application and enforcement is a problem in this respect, often referred to as an 'implementation deficit'. In this context, monitoring is crucial, both in terms of the environmental situation as such and the degree of implementation of EU environmental legislation.

Different private or public projects, plans and programmes (*e.g.* land use, transport, energy, waste, or agriculture) that are expected to significantly affect the environment must undergo an environmental impact assessment or a strategic environmental assessment procedure. At best, environmental aspects then become integrated at the planning stage and potential environmental impacts considered before a project is approved or authorized. In both procedures, consultation with the public is of central importance. This goes back to the Aarhus Convention, as implemented in the EU from 2003. According to this convention, public participation in decision-making is one of the public's three guaranteed environmental rights. The other two are: access to environmental information held by public authorities and the right to legal review if the two other rights have been violated. We will reconnect to the role of consultations and environmental organizations in our examination of various environmental policy areas.

Among the EU institutions, the European Parliament is the primary actor in the field of environmental policy (for more in-depth description of the EU institutions see Tallberg 2013 and see Blomgren & Bergman 2005 on how Swedish institutions are linked with EU equivalents). The European Parliament, as a co-legislator to the Council, has adopted a series of environmental regulations ranging from automobile and industrial emissions to electronic waste and plastic bags. The European Parliament has also repeatedly noted that improving implementation must be key priority. For example, the European Parliament criticized the unsatisfactory implementation level of environmental legislation in the Member States and put forward several recommendations for more efficient implementation such as dissemination of best practice between Member States and between regional and local authorities[2]. The EU mainly uses the Commission and the Council to press individual Member States in case of violations.

All Member States are required to inform the Commission how they transpose and implement EU directives at the national level. Failure by a Member State to comply with EU directives could lead to rectifying measures by the Commission. Christina Olsen-Lundh (2014) emphasizes three types[3] of infringements: firstly, that the Member State has not informed the Commission what national legislation incorporates the specific directive, which is considered most serious as it indicates that the Member State has made no effort to implement the directive. The second type of infringement concerns shortcomings in the adoption of national regulations according to the directive, while the third type implies that the Member State has failed in its implementation of national regulations that have sprung from the directive.

It is important to point out that one Member State may have more stringent and far-reaching rules than other Member States. The environmental guarantee provides an opportunity for EU countries to keep or introduce more stringent regulations than those required by EU environmental legislation. However, Member States are obliged to notify and justify their different national legislation to the Commission. Then it is up to the Commission to assess whether the rules are discriminatory, constitute a barrier to trade or otherwise violate the internal market, and decide on whether to allow the deviating legislation.

Swedish Environmental Policy

As already mentioned, Sweden has since long been viewed as a pioneer in environmental and sustainable development policy. From

2 The 2012 Resolution *Improving the delivery of benefits from EU environment measures: building confidence through better knowledge and responsiveness.*

3 These are non-communication infringements, non-conformity infringements and bad-application infringements.

its onset, environmental policy making was dominated by experts and developed as a reaction to increased environmental degradation resulting from industrialisation and urbanisation, but also from pressure by the growth of the environmental movement from the 1960s and onwards. The Swedish Environmental Protection Agency (SEPA), established already in 1967 and the Swedish Environmental Advisory Board from 1968 as an organ within the Government Offices, have since played important roles in the formulation of Swedish environmental policy. Initially, sectorial thinking dominated, and special organs were formed for nature and environmental protection, with regulation as the main policy instrument. It departed from the principle that environmental concerns should be balanced against competing interests within industrial and societal development (Lundqvist 1996). Physical planning flourished during the 1970s as a policy instrument both at national and local level of government, in which environmental interests were weighted against exploitation. The first UN environmental conference on *Human Development* held in Stockholm in 1972 spread the notion that environment and development issues should be mutually reinforcing, and that environmental issues should be integrated within all sectors and be seen as a prerequisite to development rather than a hindrance. This conference also inspired the development of EU environmental policy.

At the beginning, Swedish environmental policy was strongly centralised with SEPA as a node both for its formulation and implementation, but the County Administrations at regional level were gradually given increased responsibility for monitoring compliance and during the 1980s much of the implementation of environmental policy was delegated to the local authorities (Lundqvist 1996). The Ministry of Agriculture was initially responsible for environmental policy, with the Ministry of Environment formed only in 1988 to care for the environment overall even if environmental issues within the sectors of forest, agriculture and fisheries remained under the Ministry of Agriculture (since then, several ministerial reforms have occurred under different Governments). The principle of sector responsibility was introduced at the same time, which gave a number of economic sectors increased responsibility for environmental protection within their respective domains. The sector responsibility was further strengthened and became legally binding in 1996 (Persson *et al.* 2015). The entrance of the Green Party[4] in Parliament 1988 implied intensified political pressure on acting upon environmental issues. In 1991, a government reform reduced the role of SEPA to that of issuing permits and ensuring overall oversight in the decentralisation of environmental policy. In addition, SEPA should provide expert knowledge, function as advisor, and monitor the implementation on a general level. Environmental administration at the local level of government grew rapidly in terms of personnel, and new tasks for environmental permits and monitoring followed in rapid succession (Eckerberg 2000). The principle of producer responsibility was introduced in 1993, requiring industry and business to provide for recycling of their products. Hence, already before Sweden entered the EU, norms of the recycling society (more recently called circular economy) permeated environmental policy making.

This development was further triggered by several international commitments following from the Rio Conference in 1992 on *Environment and Development*, which emphasized the need for both all government and non-government actors to handle environmental issues. The notion of 'sustainable development' became the guiding principle for environmental policy at all levels, including the UN, EU, and national states, *i.e.* a development that meets the needs of the present without compromising the ability of future generations to meet their own needs. All sectors should practice the principles of long-term thinking, environmental justice, and precautionary action. At the time of Sweden's EU accession in 1995, environmental issues were high on the political agenda both in Sweden and the EU, and there were great expectations especially from the north European member states (Germany, Denmark and the Netherlands) that the environment would become further prioritized when Sweden, Austria and Finland would join (Andersen & Liefferinck 1997).

This change towards broadened environmental policy responsibility took place in parallel with increased reliance on new and 'softer' policy instruments both in Sweden and the EU. Higher priority given to environmental issues was also spurred by public opinion pressure,

4 The Green Party was established in 1981 in Sweden.

along with the so-called Cardiff Process that addressed article 6 in the Amsterdam treaty, namely, to fully integrate the environment into all Community policies. Economic instruments (mostly taxation and fees) and informative instruments (advice, education, campaigns, environmental labelling) were added to the already existing regulatory instruments. Furthermore, organisational instruments became increasingly important, *i.e.* allocation of responsibility and paths of decision-making that would steer towards taking environment into account in all activities. The introduction of the National Environmental Quality Objectives (NEQO) in Sweden in 1999 is a good example thereof, which implied that fifteen (later sixteen) overall environmental objectives were established by the Parliament, summarizing hundreds of previously adopted international and national policy goals (Eckerberg 2000). Through regular setting of sub-goals and follow-up mechanisms, the NEQO system has become an important tool among the implementing agencies and drawn public attention to the Swedish environmental policy achievements (Persson *et al.* 2015). In parallel, environmental legislation was also reformed in 1999 in the new Environmental Code, five regional environmental courts, and a Supreme environmental court, which replaced the previous Water Courts and the Concessionary Committee for Environmental Protection[5]. EU legislation was taken into account and incorporated into almost all areas in the Environmental Code, hence EU and Swedish environmental legislation became integrated in practice (Olsen-Lundh 2014).

National environmental policy today is formulated by the Parliamentary Committee on Environment and Agriculture, and by the Ministry of the Environment (MoE) together with the Ministry of Enterprise and Innovation (MoEI). The MoE is responsible for climate, hazardous chemicals and waste, recycling, energy use, and protection of nature and biodiversity, while the MoEI deals with transport, infrastructure, industrial and rural development, state en-

5 The Environmental Courts were later reformed in 2011 to become Land and Environmental Courts, with the task to also oversee the Planning and Building Act that had previously been under the Administrative Courts with the Government making final decisions.

terprises and land use (including forestry, agriculture, and tourism). A large number of agencies at the national and regional level carry out implementation tasks in line with the sector principle within environment and sustainable development. Hence, SEPA shares its responsibility for environmental policy with, for example, the Agricultural Agency, the Forest Agency, the Chemicals Inspectorate and the Agency for Marine and Water Environment, with the County Administrations at regional level assisting with planning, follow-up, and inspection tasks. As already mentioned, the 290 local authorities also play an important role by having responsibility for land and water use within their territory (Bjärstig *et al.* 2018). All these public bodies are required to implement EU environmental policy and directives, which we will describe further below.

The Effects of EU-Membership on Swedish Environmental Policy

As already stated, the environment is a very comprehensive and complex policy area that cannot be fully analysed in this chapter. EU environmental policy is commonly divided into three major areas: climate and energy, nature conservation and biodiversity, and water and waste. We have chosen to look into three particular examples of these areas. This will illustrate how EU membership has affected Sweden in different ways, including how Sweden has affected the EU in key environmental areas: climate, biodiversity, and water. We chose climate since it is prominent on the international agenda and highly prioritized both nationally and within the EU and global levels. We study biodiversity through the Nature and Habitats Directive with particular focus on the wolf issue[6], likewise attracting considerable attention internationally. Finally, we highlight the implementation of the Water Directive as this is one of The EU's oldest and most comprehensive directive within the environment area. As we will show, the environmental policy fits differently between these areas.

6 The wolf issue is deliberately chosen since it illustrates the tension between the national and supranational level when it comes to existing rules, norms and practices when implementing environmental legislation.

Climate

Through the establishment of the UN climate panel (Intergovernmental Panel on Climate Change, IPCC) in 1988, thousands of researchers around the world have continuously updated and synthesized the state of knowledge related to climate and drawn conclusions about the need for action together with policy makers. The work of IPCC has pressured governments, including Sweden and the EU, to find ways to mitigate as well as adapt to climate change. The Climate Convention was negotiated already at the UNCED conference in Rio, 1992, but several key countries did not sign. After several subsequent failures to bring the US and Russia on board, some 195 countries managed to agree on a global climate accord in Paris in 2015. It calls for zero net anthropogenic greenhouse gas emissions to be reached during the second half of the 21st century. The agreement included the goal to limit the temperature increase to 'well below 2°C' compared to pre-industrial levels, and 'pursue efforts' to limit the increase to 1.5°C. The parties also agreed to update and enhance their climate policy actions every five years starting 2023 and to increase the development aid to climate action.

Sweden has pursued an ambitious climate policy ever since the 1990s with its 'green tax reform' that introduced energy and carbon dioxide taxes. Indeed, Sweden was regarded at the forefront internationally, facilitated by its early development of hydropower and nuclear power, as well as extensive district heating based on bioenergy, which helped to decouple environmental degradation from economic growth. Sweden's emissions per GDP entity is therefore among the lowest worldwide (Samakovlis 2011). Sweden has already exceeded the EU goals to cut greenhouse gas emissions by at least 20 percent from 1990 to 2020 (Swedens' national goal is 40 percent), to lower energy use by 20 percent (where Sweden applies year 2008 instead of 1990 in the EU), to raise the share of renewable energy consumption to 20 percent (Sweden's goal is 50 percent), and to increase the share of bioenergy for transport to 10 percent (Ministry of Environment and Energy 2017a). Climate issues are high on the agenda both among Swedish citizens, enterprises, non-government organisations, and local authorities who are engaged in activities to promote reduced greenhouse gas emissions as well as to adapt to already ongoing climate change. The need for shared responsibility is particularly visible within climate work, with emissions generated locally while affecting globally. Sweden has therefore strongly pushed for more radical climate policy within the EU and the UN, taking initiatives to engage as many countries as possible in this work. Sweden's role as a pioneer and good example has helped to inspire other countries in this respect (Ministry of Environment 2007). For example, the EU Environmental Commissioner Margot Wallström (who is of Swedish origin) played an important role in securing that the Kyoto negotiations in 2005 would secure that the Climate Convention would not remain a paper tiger, and that it would allow emission trading. The EU Emission Trading Scheme (according to the Emissions Trading Directive 2003/87/EC (ETS)) was set in motion in 2005, building on the principle of cap-and-trade where companies can buy and sell emission rights within a set emission ceiling. A market price is given per ton of carbon dioxide, allowing trading among companies to reduce emissions at lowest cost, and promoting investment towards more eco-efficient technology. In Sweden, the ETS system covers 37 per cent of the total CO_2 emissions which were to be reduced by 21 per cent from 2205 to 2020 for EU as a whole (SEPA 2018). The Swedish emissions have, however, been lower than stipulated, and the Swedish Government has decided to cancel its allocated emission units at several occasions between 2013 and 2020. The ETS system has been criticised for not being sufficiently efficient since several sectors and countries are not included (Ministry of Environment 2007). Thus, Swedish climate policy has rather been driven by carbon dioxide taxes and by other policy measures within the NEQO system than by the ETS system.

In January 2018, Sweden's new Climate Policy Framework came into force through a cross-party decision. It includes achieving zero net emissions of greenhouse gases by 2045, and the setting up of an independent Climate Policy Council to annually review the Government's entire set of policies in light of the new national climate policy goals. The latter include reducing emissions from domestic transport (excluding domestic aviation that is not covered by the EU regulation) by at least 70 per cent by 2030 compared with 2010, and lowering emissions in Sweden in the sectors covered by the EU regulation by at least 63 per cent from 1990 to 2030, and at least 75 per cent by 2040 (Climate Policy Council 2018). These goals exceed those of the EU. Further, the Government is required to present a climate report every year in its Budget Bill, and to draw up a climate policy action plan every fourth year. So far, the government's policy has been assessed twice in annual reports by the Climate Policy Council, resulting in recommendations to increase the efforts substantially (Climate Policy Council 2019; 2020). Sweden's new Climate Policy Act represents a more holistic policy take than before, clearly acknowledging the need to consider the energy, transport, building and industry sectors as central to achieving climate policy goals, and lifting responsibility for climate policy to a new level. Still, it should be noted that Sweden's climate emissions remain on a relatively high level (about 10 tons per person) and that the share of emissions caused by consumption of imported goods produced in other countries, as well as from exports is growing. In fact, even if Sweden has indeed reduced its carbon dioxide emissions by 26 per cent since 1990, most of this happened in 2003–2014 and the traffic emissions are now increasing (SEPA 2018). Many local authorities have since long pursued climate policy in their societal planning and local investments, stimulated by a range of national subsidy programmes and networks towards environmental efficiency and by the legacy of Local Agenda 21 (Eckerberg 2010). An important network initiated by the Swedish Government ahead of the Paris climate meeting in 2015 called the Fossil Free Sweden initiative shows how enterprises, cities, municipalities, and organisations can lead force by contributing to climate efforts, along with several other environmental networks targeting different local actors. To date, eighteen roadmaps for fossil free energy use have been drawn up for different sectors, representing a large proportion of Sweden's CO_2 emissions, and more are underway (Climate Policy Council 2020, http://fossilfritt-sverige.se/in-english/). Fossil Free Sweden together with the municipalities' climate initiatives follow example of Sweden's tradition of soft implementation through societal mobilization. The local work with climate adaptation has more recently intensified as the societal effects of rising temperatures have become increasingly visible in the form of more frequent flooding and natural catastrophes but is still underdeveloped and suffering from problems of co-ordination and unclear allocation of responsibilities (Nilsson *et al.* 2012). Unlike climate mitigation policy, climate adaptation policy involves societal planning issues that are outside the EU policy domain. Also, in climate adaptation, the Swedish Government has recently adopted a national strategy requiring co-ordinated efforts among all relevant agencies and set up a National Expert Council for Climate Adaptation (SFS 2018:1428).

Biological Diversity

The EU has ratified the UN Convention on Biodiversity (CBD), which aims at the conservation and sustainable use of biodiversity, including land-based, marine, and other aquatic ecosystems and the ecological complexes in which these organisms are included as well as diversity within species (genetic), between species and of ecosystems. Sweden's work to comply with this convention fits within the framework of the 16 NEQOs, in particular the NEQO for a rich plant and animal life. Sweden's sixth report to CBD shows no major changes in status and trends of biodiversity, *i.e.* there is little evidence that the rate of loss of ecosystems, species and genetic diversity has halted. Actions such as specific species action programmes and EU LIFE projects have had a positive effect on a few species and habitats, but the overall trend is still negative, and many species are not viable in the long term in Sweden (CBD 2019). Based on the convention, the EU set the target to halt biodiversity loss by 2010, but this target has not been achieved. Plant and animal species both on land and in water continue to disappear and natural habitats and ecosystems are becoming depleted. A new strategy was therefore developed by the Commission in an effort to reduce the loss of biodiversity within the EU and globally. In its 2020 Biodiversity Strategy, the EU aims to restore 15 percent of damaged ecosystems in accordance with the UN Aichi biodiversity targets. The EU has established a network called Natura 2000 consisting of natural areas and habitats to protect threatened species in its member states. These protected areas should maintain or achieve viable populations (so-called favourable conservation status). Back in 1909, Sweden was a pioneer when establishing the first national parks in Europe, but today the proportion of protected land is second lowest in the European Union according to the European Environment Agency (EEA). The protection is certainly quite strong compared to many other member states' protected areas, but dominated by mountain areas with low productivity. Below the limit of mountainous forests, between 2.5 and 4.5 percent of all productive forestlands are protected, of which the least in Sweden (Swedish Forest Agency 2019). The protection of marine environments is also weak. Today, Sweden has more than 4,000 Natura 2000 areas, the majority of which are nature reserves or national parks. Nature protection is one of the largest items in the Government's environmental budget.

The EU Habitat Directive also calls for promoting biodiversity outside the protected areas. Even if Sweden has a good reputation for incorporating and complying with EU legislation nationally, the Habitat Directive is an example where Sweden has been criticized by the Commission (the Water Framework Directive, see next section, is another). In Sweden, wolves, stag beetles and aspen trees are protected in accordance with this legislation. The transposition of the directive into Swedish legislation also affected, in addition to the Environmental Code, among others, the Forestry Act, the Hunting Act and the Fisheries Act. There is a long-lasting and sometimes hot political discussion about how to define and interpret key concepts in the Habitat Directive, especially about the Swedish wolf population's management and conservation status (Olsen-Lundh 2014).

The management of the Swedish wolf population is thus an area that perhaps is not the most representative to display in relation to the Habitat Directive. However, since the wolf case has brought attention both nationally and internationally we think it is suitable to display and illustrate how Sweden, through its nationally-led policy, has been reviewed by the EU (see Darpö 2011 and Olsen-Lundh 2014 for a more detailed account of the legal implications). The wolf is protected under the Habitat Directive and a favourable conservation status must have been achieved before there can be any exceptions in terms of license hunting. From practically being extinct in 1966, when it became protected, the wolf population has recovered successfully and in 2008 the population counted 200 individuals, which was also the interim target. The year before, the Governments' carnivore investigation (SOU 2007: 89, 43) suggested that as soon as the target was reached, the population would be kept at that level. The report concluded that some limited hunting would likely increase public acceptance for carnivore management. The Government came to propose a license hunt for wolves, which was adopted by the Parliament after being debated intensively. In December 2009, the SEPA decided on license hunting of 27 wolves in the county of Dalarna, Gävleborg, Värmland, Västra Götaland and Örebro (SEPA 2009). SEPA perceived it as a conflict-mitigation measure that would eventually contribute to a favourable conservation status. This was considered to be in line with both the Hunting Act and the Habitat Directive. Also the following year, the SEPA decided on license hunting of 20 wolves, with a similar motivation. However, a procedure[7] had already been initiated against Sweden, since the Swedish Nature Conservation Association (Naturskyddsföreningen), the World Wildlife Fund (WWF), the Swedish Carnivore Association (Rovdjursföreningen) and Animal Protection Sweden (Djurskyddet Sverige) had reported the Swedish wolf hunt policy to the Commission. In January 2011, the Government received formal notification from the Commission with concerns about the wolves populations' unfavourable preservation status, namely that hunting of a protected species did not meet the strict conditions of the EU. In addition, it was pointed out that Sweden lacked an acceptable management plan for wolves. In June the same year, the Commission sent a reasoned opinion to Sweden, with the call to change the wolf policy. Against this background, the Government decided on a change in the hunting regulation, which implied a temporary halt of license hunt for wolves in 2012. Instead, the focus nationally was on how many wolves there should be for favourable conservation status should be considered to be reached. However, the Commission criticized the process of developing a management plan as well as its content. Among other things, it was considered not to be scientifically anchored and lacking measures to improve the genetic status of the wolf population. Sweden was

7 Actions for failure to fulfil treaty obligations are initiated by a procedure by the Commission, which provides a reasoned opinion to the Member State saying that it has failed to comply to Union law. If the State concerned does not comply with the opinion within the time specified, the Commission may refer the matter to the European Union Court.

asked to amend the hunting regulation to prohibit wolf hunting. Nevertheless, SEPA once again decided on license hunting for wolves in 2013. The two associations that previously had reported Sweden to the Commission now appealed against the decision to Stockholm's Administrative Court, with the aim of preventing the execution of the decision to save the wolves. The Administrative Court rejected the appeal, but the Court of Appeal decided on inhibition and the hunt was ceased. In autumn 2014, the Government presented the Bill *A Sustainable Carnivore Policy* (Government Bill. 2012/13: 191), which again proposed licensing hunting on wolves. Now it was the Parliament and not the SEPA that would decide on favourable conservation status. This again prompted the Commission to start a procedure against Sweden as the Commission saw a risk that environmental associations would appeal the license hunting to court (Additional reasoned opinion Art. 258 TFEU, 20104200 18/06/2015 Sweden Environment NATURE – Wolf hunting in Sweden). Here, however, the Aarhus Convention came into the picture (see p. 87). During the autumn of 2015, the Government rejected the criticisms that the Commission had directed against the Swedish wolf hunt, with the case is threatening to end up in the European Court of Justice. However, due to active action by the European Commission, it has been possible since 2016 to appeal hunting decisions taken by County Administrations and to bring them to trial (Infringement case 20142178, INFORMATION – Access to justice concerning hunting decisions taken by the County Administrative Boards, 26/05/2016). In 2018, licence hunting of 22 wolves was decided in the counties of Dalarna, Gävleborg, Värmland, Västra Götaland and Örebro. Also, this time, the decision was appealed, but the Supreme Court rejected the Swedish Carnivore Association's request for a temporary halt on hunting. However, motivated by a decreasing wolf population, and thus risking favourable conservation status, the SEPA recently decided on no license hunt of wolves in 2019. Regardless of one's view in this matter, Sweden cannot be regarded as an advocate of progressive environmental policy concerning the wolf issue. Instead, Sweden has made reference to the principle of subsidiarity, which means that the wolf issue will continue to be decided in Sweden, close to those concerned, rather than in Brussels.

Water

Clean water is a prerequisite for providing drinking water as well as for fisheries, aquaculture, agriculture, forestry, tourism, infrastructure, and regional development. At the same time, all those activities affect the water environment, both in terms of quality and quantity. Providing for good status of ground and surface waters therefore involves virtually all societal sectors. Since water runs freely through the landscape, collaboration over water resources is needed – across administrative borders – in line with the EU Water Framework Directive (WFD), stemming from 2000.

The WFD calls for sustainable management of all waters to achieve the two goals of 'good ecological status' and 'good chemical status'. It brings a holistic perspective on water management, with the water catchment area, or river basin, as the basis for the mandatory management plans. Control of the water status of all water bodies is required by the WFD, and preventative measures must be taken according to a list of priority substances for action, prioritised on the basis of risk; and the most cost-effective set of measures chosen to achieve load reduction of those substances, taking into account both product and process sources. Sweden implements the WFD through five regional Water Boards, guided by a National Water Board under the Swedish Agency for Marine and Water Management (see also its web page 2018). In practice, the Water Boards are located within the County Administrations. The 290 Local Authorities are still overall responsible for water management within their territory, which means that water management is carried out both at the local, regional, national, and EU levels. Administratively, this is a complex solution that brings about considerable lack of clarity in terms of who is responsible for what, where and when in achieving 'good water status'. In addition, the water regulation as such is complex and partly overlapping, with the WFD as the overall framework, complemented by the directives for Marine Water, Marine and Coastal Planning, Bathing Water, Drinking Water, Sewage Water and the Habitat Directive (SOU 2019).

These EU directives have been fully accommodated into the Swedish Environmental Code and accompanying regulations. The implementation of the WFD in Sweden was, however, highly debated at the time of the establishment of the five regional Water Boards, with the administrative responsibility placed on the County Administrations rather than the Local Authorities (Lundqvist 2004). Still, the administrative solution for water management is contested and has become subject to several government investigations with the aim to clarify responsibilities for effective decision making and financing of protection measures (SOU 2015; SOU 2019), the latter investigation to be presented in autumn 2019. Likewise, the Commission has criticized the implementation of the WFD in Sweden several times, including insufficient measures for monitoring, that Sweden has not developed detailed action plans, and that the principle of full economic compensation has not been fully implemented (EU 2014).

In the spirit of the Aarhus Convention, the WFD requires three levels of participation: *information* to citizens about the river basin management plans; *consultation* with affected societal actors about the water problems and their solutions; and *active engagement* in the development and implementation of the river basin management plans (2000/60/EG). Broad participation in the development of plans for action is needed to ensure implementation, and local engagement is realized both through established reference groups, tied to each of the five regional Water Boards, so called local water politicians from the local authorities, and Water Councils comprised by relevant stakeholders in each river basin. The Water Councils are expected to lead to a more holistic perspective on the water resources, and to applying the most appropriate measures in the right place, including improved legitimacy and possibility to affect decision-making (Eckerberg *et al.* 2012). The Water Councils in southern and middle Sweden were built upon already existing local water associations that were formed in the 1950s to prevent and manage water pollution in river basins, composed by both public and private actors. In north Sweden, however, the Water Councils were formed in 2008 by the regional Water Board as a direct result of the WFD.

It should be noted that Sweden has a long-standing tradition of water management since the time of industrialization and urbanisation in the beginning of the 1900s. At the time, water pollution was a prominent issue to handle, while the growing demand for energy involved massive development of hydropower. Still today, the apparent conflict between the demand for renewable energy and the protection of pristine rivers is highly vocalised, even if the political parties came to an agreement over Energy Policy in 2016 that limits the expansion of new hydropower and includes the creation of an environmental fund, sourced by the hydropower companies, to finance water improvement measures. The conflict between the goals for renewable energy and protection of biodiversity is also mirrored in EU programmes such as LIFE, which – among other things – includes subsidies towards restoration of river ecosystems affected by hydropower. Local water management plans were introduced during the 1960s, and sewage treatment expanded rapidly promoted by considerable state subsidies. Active stakeholder engagement within the water associations in south and middle Sweden could quite easily be transformed into the work of the new Water Councils. At the same time, however, there are remaining issues to be solved as to how norms and exceptions should be applied, how monitoring can be safeguarded in light of Sweden's very large number of water bodies compared to the rest of Europe, and how the financing of preventative measures can be secured (SOU 2019). The institutional fit of Sweden's water protection policy has thus struggled to adapt to the WFD requirements, and as Lennart Lundqvist (2004) emphasizes, the implementation of the WFD involves a triple dilemma of acquiring effectiveness, legitimacy and participation. It takes time and considerable effort to achieve the degree of participation as stipulated by the WFD, while the economic responsibility for action is not very clear in current regulation. Needless to say, these issues are commonplace in all literature about multiple level governance and collaborative natural resource management.

Conclusion

The EU membership has without doubt affected Swedish environmental policy making. Before the EU entry, there was a commonly voiced opinion that Swedish environmental regulation and protection was among the most ambitious, and that it built on appropriate and effective rule-making – ahead and beyond those of the EU. But the EU environmental policy has put pressure on Sweden to develop and adopt new policy instruments in pursuit of the EU targets for climate, biodiversity, and water, and to continuously monitor and report its progress. In some instances, the utilization of warnings and sanctions have also implied strong incitements for Sweden to remedy situations of non-compliance to EU requirements.

Even if the general picture of Sweden as an environmental policy forerunner is well founded in several respects, we have found that this picture is not consistent (see also Olsen-Lundh 2014). Due to the rather good state of environment in Sweden generally speaking (that in part is thanks to the small population dispersed over a large land area), there were, for example, not sufficient environmental monitoring in place (which became apparent with the implementation of the WFD). Also, Sweden has not always been successful in implementing effective policy instruments to reach its NEQOs. As for the wolf issue, the question of who should decide and at what level has become disputed, since national sovereignty has become promoted in light of the high level of (national/local) political conflict over wolf hunting. Here, the court system, and the right of environmental organisations to appeal Government decisions, has shown to be an important factor in respect to implementing the Habitat Directive.

As we have showed above in the examples of EU environmental policy implementation in Sweden, there is considerable variation in how well the EU regulation is fitting with the Swedish socio-political environment. Within climate policy making, Sweden remains a pioneer, and has advanced to be world leading with the recent introduction of its new Climate Policy Framework in 2018. There is a direct fit between Swedish and EU climate policy, not least explained by the fact that Sweden has been among the most active in international climate policy negotiations. Indeed, Sweden's high proportion of hydropower and nuclear power as well as bioenergy-based district heating that was largely in place even before the EU entry, along with its early green tax reform, has facilitated its role as a lead state in climate policy. As for the Habitat Directive and the WFD, the situation of fit is less clear and the pressure for national adaptation to EU regulation has therefore been higher.

Since Sweden was a pioneer in implementing waste and sewage treatment, and generally benefits from good water quality and quantity due to natural conditions, many of the requirements of the WFD came as a surprise when they were to be implemented. Initially, there was a view that Sweden had a favourable water situation but was shortly thereafter criticized by the Commission that data was lacking on a majority of its water bodies and that insufficient monitoring and action measures were in place. One could say that the Swedish authorities were a bit naïve in their way of interpreting the need for specification of preventative measures and their financing according to EU regulation. Sweden has regularly had to explain its particular situation to the Commission. There is a constant line of improvement in this respect, and in the latest Water Management Planning cycle much more detailed measures are listed. Still, however, the division of administrative and financial duties among the multiple level authorities as well as the private stakeholders is being debated and further investigated.

Both in terms of climate, biodiversity and water policy there is need to pay attention to the function of EU's rather rigid system for follow-up (which, in turn, is based on global commitments) that puts pressure on Sweden and other member states to document and provide continuity in environmental policy implementation. This is also a general means to try to reduce implementation deficit in the EU. One should keep in mind that environmental issues are neither 'neutral' nor solely 'technical' in character. Apart from cultural differences, previous environmental policy traditions between member states imply different interpretations of the various EU directives. From having been largely expert-driven issues, the environment is now high on the political agenda, displaying a range of different values and priorities. Environmental policy making continues to be one of the most contested policy areas, not least due to the inherent tension between economic growth and environmental protection, including the tensions between the urban and rural, north and south, and other issues of rights and justice. How one views environmental issues is therefore often dependent on place-making, as illustrated by the wolf issue. Hence, environmental issues and problems are perceived differently between different countries and administrative levels, and easily lead to goal conflicts, including between sector goals. It is therefore not surprising that Swedish environmental policy shows varying fit with the EU regulation, since common policy within the EU cannot fully take into account all the spatial, natural and cultural variation that is found among its members states.

As for the form and content of Swedish environmental policy, the accommodation of EU regulation – as well as with international conventions – is clearly visible in practice. Over time, Swedish environmental policy has become increasingly reliant on regulatory and mandatory policy instruments, with demands from the Commission to monitor and report. At the same time, both the private sector, citizens, and environmental organisations play an increasing role in managing the environment. Various forms of public participation and consultation with stakeholders have become commonplace, as a direct consequence of the EU's ratification of the Aarhus Convention. Furthermore, environmental policy is no longer treated as a separate policy area but has become increasingly integrated into sector policies at large – representing one of the most important prerequisites for future environmental work (Persson *et al.* 2015). This is clearly in line with EU environmental policy. Reaching the Swedish NEQOs and maintaining Sweden's role as a pioneering state is only possible by applying integrated ways of working across political levels, between different actors and sector areas. This way Sweden might be able to keep its role as a 'good practice entrepreneur' and norm-setter for progressive environmental policy both internationally and within the EU.

References

Andersen, M. S. & D. Liefferink. 1997. 'Introduction: the impact of the pioneers on EU environmental policy' In: M.S. Andersen & Liefferink D. (red.) *European Environmental Policy: The Pioneers.* Manchester: Manchester University.

Blomgren, M., & T. Bergman. 2005. *EU och Sverige: ett sammanlänkat statsskick.* [EU and Sweden: a linked government], Lund: Liber.

Bjärstig, T., C. Thellbro, O. Stjernström, J. Svensson, C. Sandström, P. Sandström & A. Zachrisson. 2018. 'Between protocol and reality – Swedish municipal comprehensive planning'. *European Planning Studies.* 26(1): 35–54.

Carter, N. 2007. *The politics of the environment: ideas, activism, policy.* 2 ed. Cambridge: Cambridge University Press.

CBD. 2019. *Sixth National Report to the Convention on Biological Diversity. Sweden.* (chm.cbd.int/pdf/documents/nationalreport6/242293/1, 2000-03-29).

Climate Policy Council. 2018. *Det klimatpolitiska ramverket* [The Climate Policy Framework*]*.Report #1 by the Swedish Climate Policy Council, Formas, Stockholm.

— 2019. Climate Policy Council Report 2019. Report # 2, Stockholm.

— 2020. Climate Policy Council Report 2020. Report #3, Stockholm.

Darpö, J. 2011. 'Brussels Advocates Swedish Grey Wolves: On the encounter between species protection according to Union law and the Swedish wolf policy.' SIEPS report.

Eckerberg, K. 2000. Sweden: progression despite recession In: W. M. Lafferty & J. Meadowcroft, (eds.). *Implementing Sustainable Development- Strategies and Initiatives in High Consumption Societies.* Oxford: Oxford University Press.

— 2010. 'Nationell och lokal klimatpolitik – låsning eller lösning? Sverige i nytt klimat – våtvarm utmaning' [National and local climate policy – Sweden facing the climate challenge]. Formas fokuserar, Forskningsrådet Formas.

Eckerberg, K., A. Zachrisson & G. Mårald. 2012. *Samverkan i Bottenvikens vattendistrikt: analys av vattenrådsarbetet* [Collaboration in Water Councils of the Bothnian Bay]. Länsstyrelsens rapportserie 6/2012, Norrbotten.

EU 2014. Skrivelse från Generalsekretariatet [Breaching note from the EU], överträdelse nr 2007/2239, 27.11.2014.

Gerhards, J. & H. Lengfeld. 2008. 'Support for European Union environmental policy by citizens of EU-member and accession states'. *Comparative Sociology*, 7(2).

Government Bill. 2013. *En hållbar rovdjurspolitik* [A sustainable carnivore policy] prop. 2012/13:191.

Hysing, E. 2014. 'A Green Star Fading? A Critical Assessment of Swedish Environmental Policy Change'. *Environmental Policy and Governance* 24(4).

Jordan, A. & C. Adelle. 2012. *Environmental Policy in the European Union. Context, Actors and Policy Dynamics.* 3 ed. London: Earthscan.

Jordan, A. & A. Lenschow. 2010. 'Environmental policy integration: a state of the art review'. *Environmental Policy and Governance* 20(3).

Jöborn, A., I. Danielsson & H. Oscarsson (eds.) 2006. *På tal om vatten. Om vägen mot en hållbar vattenförsörjning.* [Speaking of water: the road toward sustainable water use] Vastra report 6, Mistras wepage www.mistra.org

Kronsell, A. 1997. 'Sweden: setting a good example', In: M. S. Andersen & D. Liefferink (eds.). *European Environmental Policy: the Pioneers.* Manchester: Manchester University Press.

— 2002. 'Can Small States Influence EU Norms?: Insights from Sweden's participation in the field of environmental politics'. *Scandinavian Studies.*

Lundqvist, L. 1996. 'Sweden'. In: *Governing the Environment: Politics, Policy and Organization in the Nordic Countries.* Tema Nord, Nordiska Ministerrådets rapportserie no. 5, Copenhagen.

— 1998. 'Sweden: From environmental restoration to ecological modernization'. In: Hanf, K. & A-I. Jansen (eds.) *Governance and Environment in Western Europe: Politics, Policy and Administration*, pp. 230–252. Harlow: Addison Wesley Longman

— 2004. 'Integrating Swedish Resource Water Management: a multi-level governance trilemma'. *Local Environment*, 9(1): 75–90.

Ministry of Environment. 2007. Vetenskapligt underlag för klimatpolitiken. Rapport från Vetenskapliga rådet för klimatfrågor [Scientific basis for climate policy: Report from the Scientific Advisory Council on Climate]. Miljövårdsberedningens rapport 2007:03, Jo 1968:A, Stockholm.

Ministry of Environment and Energy. 2017. Sweden's Seventh National Communication on Climate Change. Government Offices of Sweden, Swedish Environmental Protection Agency.

Nilsson, A., Å. Gerger-Swartling & K. Eckerberg. 2012. 'Knowledge for local climate change adaptation in Sweden: challenges of multilevel governance'. *Local Environment*, 17(6–7): 751–767.

OECD. 2014. OECD:s granskning av Sveriges miljöpolitik: Sverige 2014 [Review of Sweden's environmental policy by OECD] available in Swedish at http://www.regeringen.se/contentassets/bdbff322aa1844948829ac268a13e6a2/oecds-granskning-av-sveriges-miljopolitik-2014 (2018-11-25).

Olsen-Lundh, C. 2014. 'En progressiv miljörätt? Hur 20 år i EU har påverkat den svenska miljörätten' [Progressive environmental law? How EU has impacted on Swedish environmental law over 20 years] In: Berg, L. & R. Lindahl (eds.), *Förhoppningar och farhågor-Sveriges första 20 år i EU.* Centrum för Europaforskning. Kompendiet: Göteborg. 97–126.

Persson, Å., K. Eckerberg & M. Nilsson, 2015. 'Institutionalization or wither away? Twenty-five years of environmental policy integration under shifting governance models in Sweden'. *Environment and Planning C: Government and Policy*, 0263774X15614726 pp. 1–18.

Samakovlis, E. 2011. *Klimatpolitikens utmaningar under mandatperioden*

[Challenges in climate policy over the government mandate period]. Special study no 5, Konjunkturinstitutet, Stockholm.

SEPA. 2009. Decision 2009-12-17, Dnr 411-7484—09 Nv.

— 2018. Fördjupad analys av svenska klimatstatistik 2018, Report 6848, December 2018, Swedish Environmental Protection Agency, Stockholm.

Swedish Agency for Marine and Water Management, 2018. Web page describing water governance https://www.havochvatten.se/hav/samordning--fakta/miljomal--direktiv.html (2018-08-08).

Swedish Forest Agency 2019. *Statistik om formellt skyddad skogsmark, frivilliga avsättningar, hänsynsytor samt improduktiv skogsmark* (Statistics on protected forests). SFA Report #18, 2019-06-27, Jönköping.

SFS 2018:1428 Förordning om myndigheters klimatanpassningsarbete. [Government decree on agencies' climate adapation work]. MoEE, Government offices, 2018-06-28.

SOU 2014:50. *Med miljömålen i fokus – hållbar användning av mark och vatten* [With the NEQOs in focus – sustainable land and water use]. Delbetänkande av Miljömålsberedningen, Miljödepartementet, Stockholm.

SOU 2015:43 *Vägar till ett effektivare miljöarbete* [Pathways towards more efficient environment work], Miljö- och energidepartementet, Stockholm.

SOU 2019:66. *En utvecklad vattenförvaltning* (A developed water administration). MoE, Government Offices, Stockholm.

Tallberg, J. 2013. *EU:s politiska system* [EU's political system]. 5 ed. Lund: Studentlitteratur.

Underdal, A. 2013. 'Meeting common environmental challenges: the co-evolution of policies and practices'. *International Environmental Agreements*, 13: 15–30.

Zannakis, M. 2015. 'The blending of discourses in Sweden's 'urge to go ahead' in climate politics'. *International Environmental Agreements: Politics, Law and Economics*, 15(2), 217–236.

6. Social Policy

Ingrid Grosse

Social policy is a central policy area for many Swedes (Svallfors & Taylor-Gooby 1999; Svallfors 2012). Social policy directly affects people's living conditions by protecting their rights, maintaining income, providing services, and by demanding taxes and contributions (Elmér *et al.* 2000). During their lifecycle, most Swedes will receive some kind of social benefit, whether in the form of education, healthcare or pensions. Most will also have contributed to social policy funding by paying taxes, contributions and fees.

Sweden's social policy is regarded as well-developed and as a special model internationally (Esping-Andersen 1990; Sainsbury 1999; van Kersbergen & Manow 2009; Tallberg *et al.* 2010). Swedish social policy is considered to be well-developed because the levels of compensation are generous; many different risks are covered; and there are relatively low thresholds to be eligible for support. In addition, a high proportion of gross domestic product (GDP), about 27 percent, goes to social benefits, while in the OECD the average share of GDP for social benefits lies at 21 percent, and in the USA and the United Kingdom at 19 percent (OECD 2018). Sweden's social policy is also considered to be a special model (Esping-Andersen 1990; Sainsbury 1999; Tallberg *et al.* 2010). Esping-Andersen depicts it as a social-democratic welfare regime, not as a conservative or liberal welfare regime. It is characterized by a high proportion of universal benefits, *i.e.* benefits based on citizenship and residence (*e.g.* child allowance and a guarantee pension), a large publicly funded welfare service sector (*e.g.* healthcare, education and elderly care), an emphasis on family services and insurance (*e.g.* parental allowance and preschool education), occupational income-related social insurance (*e.g.* unemployment benefits and occupational pensions), and a special legal and political position of union and employer organizations (*e.g.* who define wages via collective agreements and offer unemployment insurance). In contrast, conservative welfare regimes like Germany or the Netherlands are characterized by a predominance of generous employment-related social benefits, but less developed public services. Liberal welfare regimes like the USA or Australia have a stronger emphasis on means-tested social assistance and are overall less generous (Esping-Andersen 1990).

However, after Sweden's entry into the European Union (EU) in 1995, researchers have raised the question whether and to what extent social policy has been affected by membership. A complicating aspect of dealing with this issue is that Sweden implemented a number of social policy changes in the context of the economic crisis in the early 1990s. It is therefore important to distinguish as far as possible changes due to EU membership and those due to domestic initiatives. Major changes since the 1990s include, for example, the 1998 pension reform, reduced levels of compensation and increased social security contributions in several social security systems, as well as the introduction of private options. However, these changes to Swedish social policy are considered to be caused by domestic developments: partly because of the economic crisis and, partly because of ideological criticism of Swedish social policy (Vifell 2011; Dølvik *et al.* 2014; Kvist *et al.* 2012; Tallberg *et al.* 2010; Lindbom 2011; Hartman 2011).

The subject of this chapter is EU influence on Swedish social policy apart from these domestic changes. To what extent has Swedish social policy changed in its content (substance) and form (organization) as a result of EU membership? The chapter proceeds in the following way: Firstly, the historical development of Swedish social policy is presented. Then, a presentation follows of the EU social policy activities. EU activities are divided into whether they are directly or indirectly related to social policy purposes. In connection with this, examples of social policy changes and their implications for the member countries are highlighted. Then, a description of the consequences for Sweden's social policy follows, including both substantive and organisational changes. Finally, the EU's impact on Swedish social policy is summarized using the models of EU policy processes from Chapter 2.

The Historical Development of Sweden's Social Policy

The special position of Swedish social policy developed relatively late. Until the 1950s, Sweden had a less developed welfare state than several central European countries, such as Germany, France, the Netherlands and Austria (Cousins 2005). Despite its relatively higher prosperity in terms of GDP per capita around 1950, Swedish spending on social benefits has remained only on an average level (about 8 percent of GDP). It was only during the 1970s that the Swedish welfare state gained the special position it has today (since the 1980s, about 30 percent of GDP is used for welfare benefits; Cousins 2005; Blomqvist 2008).

The historical development went through several phases. Until the end of the 1950s, the main purpose of social welfare was to combat poverty. First introduced were the classical social insurances (accident, retirement, unemployment and health insurances). Then maternity allowance, child allowance, housing policy and local social welfare were introduced. The main purpose shifted after the 1950s. After the 1950s, the already established benefits were gradually expanded to cover, additionally, the needs of the rising middle classes: an income-related part of the pension system (ATP) was added and the maternity allowance was converted into an income-related parental insurance. Furthermore, social services were altered and expanded: healthcare became public, and childcare and elderly care were greatly expanded with the increased involvement of municipalities and the central state.

The financing of the increasingly generous social policy was made possible by increasing tax revenues in a growing economy. Ideologically, the emergence of the welfare state was supported by social-democratic ideas about a 'people's home', where citizens should receive the resources necessary to control their lives. Strong corporate organizations, such as trade unions, and strong public organizations, such as the central state, county councils and local authorities, were considered as the means of transforming these ideas into practice (Blomqvist 2008; Elmér *et al.* 2000).

The expansive phase ended with an economic crisis in the early 1990s. Sweden lost market shares in the export industry, and also incurred a high budget deficit and public debt. The economic crisis resulted in several cuts in the social security net: benefit levels were reduced (for example, unemployment insurance benefits, which is among the lowest in Europe until today); fees and private contributions for social services were increased; eligibility regulations were tightened; welfare personnel was reduced; subsidies for housing production were abolished; and, especially, a new, less generous pension system was introduced (Blomqvist 2008; Lindbom 2011; Hartman 2011).

Apart from these cuts, changes occurred which are not only related to the economic crisis. Choice was introduced in several welfare areas, which enabled clients to choose between public and private providers of schools, healthcare, childcare and elderly care. In addition, the proportion of private supplementary insurance schemes increased (for pensions, unemployment and healthcare). Several researchers believe that these changes were mainly due to an extended ideological criticism of an all-embracing social-democratic welfare state (Blomqvist 2008; Hartman 2011; Rothstein 2001). The criticism came (and still comes) from two main directions: a neoliberal-oriented right and a communitarian-oriented left.

The communitarian-oriented left has criticized the bureaucratic way of treating clients and organising services within the established social sector. It was argued that there was no opportunity for citizens and clients to exert an influence from below on the implementation of social policies. Furthermore, it was criticized that the established social systems did not take sufficient account of Sweden's increasingly heterogeneous society – including rainbow families and immigrants from several continents and nations. Therefore, critics from the left demanded that existing social systems should be increasingly opened to allow for more flexibility, choice and voluntary organizations.

The neoliberal right has criticized other aspects of the established social system. The comprehensive social policy was considered to be detrimental to economic growth due to the high costs of taxes and social security contributions. Social policy was also considered to lead to a decay in individual responsibility for one's own life and for others.

According to these critics, individual initiatives, labour morale and charity were undermined. Furthermore, it was criticized that the state forced citizens to consume in a certain way based on collective political decisions for welfare consumption and taxation instead of free individual decisions over individual resources. These critics therefore demanded that public social policy should be limited, taxes should be reduced, and choice and private options should be expanded.

In summary, researchers relate several major changes in Swedish welfare policy since the 1990s to domestic developments in the economy and ideological debates. Sweden's entry into the EU in 1995 came during these ongoing changes. To some extent, Sweden's entry is also a consequence of these economic and ideological changes. Nevertheless, the question for the forthcoming sections of the chapter is to what extent EU membership has had consequences for Sweden's social policy.

EU Activities in the Field of Social Policy

Within the EU competency catalogue, shared competencies of member states and the EU, the so-called second pillar, apply to only few social policy areas. Shared competencies apply to, for example, occupational safety and social security systems as far as they concern the free movement of workers within the common market. Predominantly, however, social policy belongs to the third pillar within the EU competency catalogue, meaning that the EU has only supporting powers in social policy (EU 2010). This implies, for example, that Sweden has a sole right to legislate about the major parts of social policy, such as taxes, healthcare, pension policy, housing policy, education policy and family policy. Likewise, member states can limit access to social benefits for other EU citizens (Kommerskollegium 2013). EU citizens must be residents in a country to access social benefits. Residence is only possible for those who work, those who are family members, or those who have sufficient funds to support themselves and who have health insurance. Social benefits are not given to EU citizens who only stay temporarily up to three months in a country. In addition, a country can deny EU citizens residence due to issues of public order, safety and public health (Kommerskollegium 2014).

Despite these formal rights of member states, several researchers argue that the EU has become an important player in social policy (Falkner 2012; Leibfried 2017; Scharpf 2002; Minas 2012). In order to better understand how the EU can affect member states' social policies, it is helpful to distinguish between direct and indirect EU social policy activity (Tallberg *et al.* 2010; Falkner 2012; Leibfried 2017). The EU's direct social policy largely follows the EU's official allocation of powers, while indirect social policy mostly has unintended consequences. Such consequences can flow from the EU's long-term goal of creating a common market for goods, capital, services and citizens since the Rome Treaty in 1957. In this regard, the European Court of Justice has played a key role. The EU's indirect role is described later, but first an overview of direct social policy.

EU's Direct Social Policy

EU institutions are active in social policy in a number of ways. Usually, three sets of policies are differentiated:

- Regulation (for example, regarding the working environment, labour law, gender issues and anti-discrimination)
- Reallocation of resources (such as the EU Social Fund and Regional Fund)
- Open Method of Coordination (implying reporting, review and development of state policies in several social policy areas, such as employment policy, family policy, health policy and pension policy)

Regulation of social policy in areas of direct EU competence is an old part of EU social policy. Regulation implies formal requirements, such as treaty regulations and directives, which are binding for member states. Various EU institutions (the European Parliament, the European Council, and the Council of Ministers) are involved in formulating these formal requirements, but the EU Commission, with its proposal right, and the European Court of Justice as interpreter are considered to be key players in social policy (Tallberg *et al.* 2010; Falkner 2012; Leibfried 2017).

At the time of the Treaty of Rome in 1957, the number of regulations was extremely limited, but regulatory competence has since developed, only slowly in the 1970s and 1980s, then faster since the 1990s. Today there are more than 90 binding rules (Falkner 2012). There are regulations governing the areas of gender equality (wages, labour market participation, parental insurance, etc.), anti-discrimination for several disadvantaged groups (immigrants, persons with disabilities, gender, etc.), working conditions and health and safety regulations. Multiple regulations also exist for the coordination of migrant employees' rights concerning the different national social security systems. Coordination of social systems takes place, for example, regarding the rights of employees to transfer social security entitlements when moving to or working in another EU country (Falkner 2012; Statskontoret 2005; Kommerskollegium 2013).

Working conditions and the working environment are regulated in terms of employee rights regarding the termination of contracts, information, part-time work and parental leave. The EU Working Time Directive regulates daily rest periods, weekly leave, holidays, breaks and weekly working hours (2003/88/EC). The Directive on Fixed-Term Work stipulates that member states should have an upper limit for the allowed number of fixed-term employment contracts (1999/70/EC).

Since the Treaty of Rome, EU regulations have clearly evolved to include ever more individuals and circumstances. Furthermore, a new level was reached with the Amsterdam Treaty in 1999, which opened for qualified majority voting instead of unanimity. However, it has been argued that not all EU rules have been de facto implemented in the national laws of all member states. It is often the case that implementation occurs only after the intervention of the European Court of Justice (Falkner 2012; Leibfried 2017; Obermaier 2009). Researchers assess the evolution of EU regulation in social policy differently: partly, it is considered to be an important part of social policy (Falkner 2012; Leibfried 2017), and partly, it is considered to be extremely limited (Minas 2012; Tallberg *et al.* 2010). Differences between the assessments depend mostly on whether the focus is on national sovereignty, which has been restricted by the EU, or if the focus is based on a comparative state perspective which still shows major differences between member states' social policies. Examples of existing state differences are that Sweden has a state-funded basic pension for all citizens without the need for labour market participation, while Germany's pensions are divided over dozens of private and public pension schemes granted only to employees and their relatives. A further difference is that Sweden has a well-developed childcare system, which makes parents' labour market participation possible, while most continental EU countries have only limited family services (Tallberg *et al.* 2010; Lindbom 2011; van Kersbergen & Manow 2009).

Redistribution of resources through the EU budget is perhaps best known in the form of EU agricultural policy. However, there is also the European Social Fund instituted by the Rome Treaty in 1957. Until the 1970s, the Social Fund mainly co-financed national projects related to the relocation, schooling and retraining of employees and the restructuring of the economy. Since the 1970s, the Social Fund has become more active and has begun specifying different target groups. Today, the Social Fund co-finances projects concerning target groups such as young jobseekers, the long-term unemployed, the disadvantaged and female employees. The overarching goal of the Social Fund is to improve employability and to promote self-employment (Falkner 2012; Statskontoret 2005).

In a broader sense, other EU funds also have social goals. For example, the European Regional Development Fund aims to help disadvantaged regions; the Cohesion Fund aims to help disadvantaged economies; and the European Adjustment Fund for Globalization aims to support workers who have lost their employment due to changed global trade patterns. In total, approximately 30 percent of the EU budget is used to co-finance projects related to market restructuring (Falkner 2012). Co-financing means that all these projects and programs are simultaneously funded by individual states and the EU. However, in comparison with the state budgets for social policy, EU spending is negligible (Leibfried 2017; Tallberg *et al.* 2010).

The Open Method of Coordination was promoted by the Swedish government in conjunction with its EU presidency. The Coordination Method became formalized with the Amsterdam Treaty in 1999. The Coordination Method is intended to open for dialogue and discussion between countries regarding socially relevant areas. Initially, the Coordination Method was used in employment policy, but then expanded to further areas, such as health, pensions and social inclusion (Falkner 2012; de la Porte & Pochet 2012).

The Coordination Method implies that the European Commission issues non-binding annual guidelines. Member states respond by submitting reports about their policies and policy plans on the basis of these guidelines. Meetings take place and the performance of the countries is discussed in order to facilitate mutual learning and mutual influence (Falkner 2012; de la Porte & Pochet 2012).

Researchers discussed the benefits and impact of the Coordination Method on national social policies. The majority considers that the Coordination Method has hardly resulted in significant changes of national social policy. Researchers could not identify convergent tendencies between the countries' social policies, which could be clearly linked to the process of the Coordination Method (Scharpf 2002; Leibfried 2017; de la Porte & Pochet 2012).

EU's Indirect Social Policy

Besides direct activities, the EU has been indirectly active in social policy. This has mainly occurred due to an ongoing process of creating a common market. This 'indirect' activity has had a strong impact on national social policy.

The creation of a common market with the free movement of goods, capital, services and employment in the EU is, according to most researchers, the dominant and most comprehensive policy objective from the Treaty of Rome in 1957 and beyond. The objective has been based on a political conviction that welfare and prosperity could best develop through free trade, competition and economic growth (Leibfried 2017; Falkner 2012). Social policy was judged to be politically subordinate to this general objective in the EU (Scharpf 2002, 2010; Leibfried 2017; Rhodes 2017).

However, free trade and competition have been considered to favour certain factors more than others in the economy. Easy movable parts, such as capital, can benefit more from an integrated market than less movable parts, such as, for example, employees without internationally requested abilities. An internal common market is therefore considered to generate a weaker negotiating position for employees (Falkner 2012; Leibfried 2017; Scharpf 2002). As employees and their organizations are regarded as playing an important role in shaping socially relevant conditions by some researchers, the weakening of employees' negotiating power is regarded to also have led to a weakened role concerning their ability to shape social policy (Korpi 1983; Esping-Andersen 1990; Scharpf 2010).

Furthermore, it has been stressed that increased mobility between countries has resulted in a weakening of countries' ability to determine and control key areas of social policy. This applies primarily to the design of tax revenues. It is easier for countries to tax non-movable incomes and assets, such as work income and real estate, than movable income and assets, such as capital and capital income (Scharpf 2010). As there is no uniform tax rate for all EU countries, the consequence can be tax competition with a tendency for a race-to-the-bottom process between the countries (Rieger & Leibfried 2003). A weakened ability to mobilize tax revenues would in turn limit the member states' ability to be socially active.

The European Court of Justice and the European Commission have most pronouncedly pursued the development of the common market. The member states, the European Council and the European Parliament were more hesitant about implementing various steps, but often agreed to accept changes afterwards. A number of court decisions in the 1990s became particularly known, because they were considered to infringe on the rights of the member states and, in part, exceed the powers of the European Court of Justice. Court decisions are regarded as having limited member states' rights in determining who has access to social benefits and shaping labour law issues. Furthermore, the Court is regarded as having limited business organizations' and trade unions' control over collective agreements (Leibfried 2017; Obermaier 2009; Statskontoret 2005).

There are several interesting examples of Court decisions. The famous *Kohll-Deckert* case concern the ability of national insurance to control costs. Kohll received dental care in Germany without applying for it in advance from his home country's social insurance in Luxembourg. Decker bought glasses in Germany without having applied in Luxembourg. In both cases, the European Court of Justice judged in favour of the citizens, implying that citizens should be compensated from their home health insurance. In subsequent court decisions, the European Court of Justice specified and expanded this interpretation of medical care rights. In the cases of *Gaerets-Smits* and *Peerboom*, the European Court of Justice ruled that citizens could also receive open care, *i.e.* care that does not require a hospital stay, in another EU country. On the other hand, in the cases of *Muller-Fauré* and *Van Riet*, the European Court of Justice ruled that hospitalization requires prior authorization from the home insurance system. The decisions of the European Court of Justice were later accepted by the member states through the adoption of the Patient Directive of 2011 (Martinsen 2013). As a result of these court decisions, it became possible for citizens to move freely as consumers of healthcare in the EU. Citizens do not need to migrate but can access healthcare even during temporary stays in another EU country. These court decisions also led to the development of a European Health Insurance Card (EU Card) 2004, which was intended to facilitate the administration of cross-border healthcare in 2004. It also can be interpreted as a first step towards a social EU citizenship (Martinsen 2013; Obermaier 2009; Leibfried 2017).

However, national constraints remain to some extent. According to the 2011 Patient Directive, member states may still require prior authorization from their citizens in the following cases: 1) for scheduled care, such as operations; 2) in the case of special risks for patients or the population; and 3) in the case of quality and safety doubts (Martinsen 2013).

A controversial consequence of the mentioned court decisions is that the court ruled that healthcare is a service like other services. Previous interpretations were that healthcare is a community service of general interest, which falls under national regulations according to the EU Competence Catalogue (TFEU, Protocol 26). By contrast, the Court's decisions imply that healthcare is to be regarded and legally treated according to the same market rules as other private services, such as banking, telecommunication, etc. As a result, the public sector cannot longer enter into particularly favoured agreements with, for example, 1) non-profit organizations, 2) semi-public organizations, and 3) publicly owned companies (as the European Court of Justice clarified in several rulings during the 2000s; Statskontoret 2005; Obermaier 2009; Martinsen 2013; Hancher & Sauter 2010).

Besides healthcare, the Court and the Commission have also pursued the development of a common market for the free movement of workers and service companies. A first expanded interpretation of EU law occurred already in the 1970s with the cases *Dassonville* and *Cassis de Dijon*. The European Court of Justice shifted the interpretation of the principle of non-restriction, applying to the four freedoms of the common market, towards a principle of non-discrimination (Höpner & Schäfer 2012). Thus, all national laws, which constitute barriers to the four freedoms, became non-legal within the EU. Furthermore, in the so-called *Säger* case in 1991, the European Court of Justice ruled that only serious reasons of national interest could lead to proportionate restrictions on service companies from other countries (Höpner & Schäfer 2012; Rhodes 2017).

In 2006, the Commission developed the Posted Workers Directive and the Service Directive, later adopted by other EU institutions. The directives aimed to facilitate free trade in services. While the Posted Worker Directive stipulated that rules and agreements applied according to the country where the service was performed, the draft version of the Service Directive contained the possibility that the company's homeland's labour laws and collective agreements should apply. In other words, it would be possible for an Eastern European service company, usually having lower wages, to provide services in a Western European country, usually having higher wages, to pay wages according to Eastern European wage levels. Trade unions were worried that this would lead to wage competition between different companies active in one country. Later, the Service Directive was amended following protests by unions and governments. It was clarified that the country's labour laws, social laws and fundamental rights (such as strike and contract law) would apply where the service was performed (Höpner & Schäfer 2012; Rhodes 2017).

Despite this regulation, the European Court of Justice ruled differently in the cases of *Laval, Viking* and *Ruffert* during the 2000s. The Latvian company Laval used Latvian workers to build a school in Vaxholm in Sweden. The Swedish Construction Workers Union found that Laval did not comply with Swedish labour law and took industrial action. However, the European Court of Justice ruled that the trade union's measures were disproportionate. According the Court, unions are only allowed to take industrial action concerning minimum standards. Thus, it became apparent that unions will find it difficult to enforce their full collective agreements in conflict situations with foreign companies. The judgement raised general questions regarding collective agreements and industrial action rights. The decision of the European Court of Justice may mean that unions and social partners cannot create binding collective agreements in the future without the legislative support of national governments. Several politicians and researchers have argued that the European Court of Justice exceeded its powers, but the EU countries could not agree on a new, clarifying legislation (Arvidsson 2009; Rhodes 2017; Höpner & Schäfer 2012).

Europeanization of Sweden's Social Policy?

In general, research shows that EU membership has not fundamentally changed national social policies (Falkner 1998; Scharpf 2010; Leibfried 2017). The same assessment has also been made for Sweden: changes to Swedish social policy have had predominantly domestic political reasons. Overall, it has been emphasized that Sweden is still different from other countries and that the 'Swedish model' is still an accurate description for Swedish social policy (Vifell 2011; Dølvik *et al.* 2014; Kvist *et al.* 2012; Tallberg *et al.* 2010).

Beyond this overall assessment, however, there are several researchers who highlight the importance of minor changes. These researchers take the view that the EU restricts national social policy sovereignty (Falkner 1998; Leibfried 2017; Obermaier 2009).

In the following, several examples will be presented showing how Swedish social policy activity has changed and is still changing through EU membership. What will be presented are illustrative examples since a comprehensive description would require too much space. In a first step, examples of Swedish adaptations are given which were caused by the EU's direct social policy activity – through regulation, redistribution of resources and the Coordination Method. In a second step, examples of Swedish adaptations are given which were caused by indirect EU social policy, that is, by adaptation to the principles of the common market.

Examples of Direct Europeanization of Swedish Social Policy

Swedish social policy has most obviously been influenced where the EU has been directly active. Sweden has had to adapt its *laws and regulations* at the national level regarding gender equality, anti-discrimination, working conditions for employees, health and safety aspects in the work environment, and the coordination of national social systems for migrant employees. The Swedish central administrative State Office (Statskontoret) assesses that 'the EU is affecting more and more, but not everything' (Statskontoret 2005: 93, translation by the author).

In a comprehensive report, the State Office described how Swedish local authorities and county councils have been affected in their role as welfare actors. County councils and local authorities are central actors in the Swedish welfare system. They have needed to adapt to several EU directives, *e.g.* directives on part-time work, fixed-term work and working time. The Part-time Work Directive (97/81/EC) stipulates that part-time workers may not be treated less favourably than full-time workers concerning their holiday, pension and health insurance rights. The Fixed-term Work Directive (1999/70 / EC) limited the number of fixed-term jobs that could follow each other. Both directives led to a comprehensive review of the employment conditions of local authorities and county councils. The estimated additional costs were 420 million Swedish crowns in 1996 (Statskontoret 2005). The Working Time Directive (2003/88/EC) – in combination with the European Court of Justice's decisions in the *Simap* and *Jaeger* cases – states that standby time and on-call duty hours are to be regarded as working time under certain conditions. This has led to new legislation by the national parliament: it was decided that working time regulations should not exceed an average of a maximum of 48 hours weekly working hours, eleven hours of continuous daily rest, and a regulation of working hours for night workers (SFS 2005: 16, prop. 2003/04: 180). In the white paper (proposition), it was stressed that these changes would require changes: 'Scheduling in accordance with the ECJ involves changes for the work organization of the county council and local authorities, especially regarding working hours for doctors but also for other healthcare professionals and for employees within local social care activities. The changes may result in a need for further personnel recruitment' (Prop. 2003/04: 180, translation by the author). Another example is EU anti-discrimination legislation. The Amsterdam Treaty issued the anti-discrimination principle to combat discrimination based on gender, race, ethnic origin, religion, disability, age and sexual orientation. This principle was then clarified in two EU directives on combating discrimination in working life. Swedish legislation was aligned to this EU legislation with the Swedish Anti-Discrimination Act (SFS 2003: 307: Statskontoret 2005).

Reallocation of resources, the second form of direct EU social policy, is of minor importance in comparison with Sweden's own social commitments. For example, Sweden received 604 million Euros for the period 2007–2013 from the Social Fund (ESF) for co-financed projects. Sweden's own public spending for social purposes amounts to over 124,173 million in one single year (*e.g.* year 2016; SCB 2018; Minas 2012).

Renate Minas has carried out one of the few evaluations regarding ESF resources in Sweden (Minas 2012). She evaluated the city of Stockholm's EU activity. Minas described that ESF projects involved the following work for the City of Stockholm: First, applications were submitted to project funds. Applications often required the participation of several local authorities or other organizations from different EU countries, which in turn required coordination. Then, if the funds were granted, the project's target group received some form of support: for example, unemployed young people received training or help to find work. Furthermore, project work involved mutual study visits and local meetings between participating project organizations. In the end, reports had to be written about the project.

Minas' analysis concluded that the projects did not lead to major changes in Stockholm City's general long-term work. When the project funds ran out, the social efforts financed by the ESF were usually terminated. Furthermore, policy learning between the different participating countries usually did not take place: new methods were rarely adopted or implemented (Minas 2012). From a Swedish point of view, it can be said that the importance of EU resources lies to a lesser extent in solving social problems – because the funds are comparatively limited in scope and time – but involving participants in exchanges and meetings beyond national borders within the EU.

Likewise, the third form of EU activity, the *Coordination Method*, has had a limited impact on Sweden according to researchers (de la Porte & Pochet 2012; Graziano 2012; Statskontoret 2005). Caroline de la Porte and Phillipe Pochet have investigated labour market policies and stressed that Sweden only in a 'reflective way' was affected by the social policy of other EU countries through the Coordination Method: Sweden only received confirmation of its own relatively well-developed standards (de la Porte & Pochet 2012). Paolo Graziano confirms this picture by considering that Sweden was a driving force for its peers in the EU but developed its labour market policy independently of the EU (Graziano 2012). In the same spirit, the State Office assessed that in the area of healthcare, the Coordination Method implied many meetings and exchanges of information between countries – concerning patient safety, evaluation of treatments and e-health care – but that there has so far not been a direct impact on Swedish healthcare (Statskontoret 2005).

Examples of Indirect Europeanization of Swedish Social Policy

Considering indirect social policy effects of the EU on Sweden, it is obvious that the EU had an effect. Sweden had to adapt its regulatory framework to the principles of the common internal market in general, including adaptations in the area of social policy (Statskontoret 2005; Kommerskollegium 2011, 2014).

The field of healthcare provides a good example of adaptations to EU regulation (Statskontoret 2005). The European Court of Justice's decision to increase patient rights beyond national borders, followed by the introduction of the European Health Insurance Card in 2004 in Sweden, implied that Swedish citizens could receive emergency care in other European countries. In the same spirit as the European Court of Justice, the Swedish Supreme Administrative Court ruled in favour of a Swedish patient (Jelinek) to receive compensation for rheumatism treatment abroad. Free patient mobility likewise applies inversely to non-Swedish EU citizens: visiting EU citizens have the right to seek emergency care in Sweden. An implication is that healthcare has become more difficult to plan and to control for county councils and the Swedish Social Insurance Agency. A further implication of EU integration is that funding for health has partly shifted. Remuneration for foreign care is payed for by the Swedish Social Insurance Agency and not the county councils, which normally fund healthcare in Sweden (Statskontoret 2005).

Other notable examples of Europeanization come from the areas of student loans and parental insurance. Study loan legislation only allowed persons residing in Sweden to reduce their repayments if their annual income was too low. By contrast, the Swedish Supreme Administrative Court ruled that persons residing in another EU country could also make reductions in order to insure free movement within the EU. In another case, the Swedish Supreme Administrative Court ruled that a Swedish citizen previously employed in Switzerland had a right to income-based parental insurance. The Social Insurance Agency had to change its decision to grant only the lowest, non-income-based level. The Swedish Supreme Administrative Court argued that the Social Insurance Agency had contravened rules on the coordination of social insurances in the EU (Kommerskollegium 2014). These examples show how the principles of the common market can have consequences for Swedish social policy.

A further implication of the EU is that public authorities and administrations have applied new work processes in order to implement EU legislation and in order to ensure that Swedish regulations do not violate EU legislation (Statskontoret 2005; Kommerskollegium 2011, 2014). The National Board of Trade (Kommerskollegium) is the authority in Sweden that organizes coordination between Swedish public authorities and administration and the EU (Kommerskollegium 2011, 2014). An example of this work is an assessment scheme developed by the National Board of Trade, which helps public authorities to systematically test whether their activities are compatible with the EU common market. Due to recurrent shortcomings in the application of EU rules by member states, the so-called Internal Market Information System (IMI) provides information and notifications. The name of the information system, 'Internal Market', is telling for how important the principles for the common market of the EU have become in a general way for EU activity.

As a final example, there are implications that derive from the EU directives on Public Procurement 2004 and 2014 (Directive 2014/24 EU on Public Procurement, earlier Directive 2004/18/EC; SOU 2014: 51). The directives intended to prevent distortions of the principles of the common market, but have effects on social policy, too. The EU Public Procurement Directive influenced the Swedish Public Procurement Act (LOU 2007: 1091; Swedish LOU became more stringent by including even contracts of low value and social services) and the Act on Freedom of Choice (LOV 2008: 962). Local authorities and county councils may no longer give special support, contracts or concessions to semi-public regional companies, local companies and start-ups of publicly employed personnel. The EU directives instead require a formal public procurement procedure (Kommerskollegium 2011). This implies that a promotion of municipal housing companies, non-profit service providers or sports associations has become more difficult (Statskontoret 2005). The State Office considers that the EU directives restrict the scope of local authorities and county councils to create special relationships with companies and organizations (Statskontoret 2005).

Furthermore, the EU directives and consequently Swedish legislation (LOU, LOV) demand high standards concerning the formal legality of procurement decisions. Decisions on awarding contracts must be able to hold in ex-post legal examination of the announced information to the tenderers. The detailed requirements have implied additional costs for public authorities in the form of technical, administrative and legal knowledge about procurement (Statskontoret 2005; Kommerskollegium 2011). The State Office believes that membership in the EU entails costly work for public authorities on all levels (Statskontoret 2005).

In summary, the EU can be considered to be influential for Swedish social policy via direct social policy *regulations* and via indirect effects from the EU common market regulation. Various directives regulating, among other things, working hours and employment forms have had an impact on Swedish social policy. Indirect effects of the EU also had great influence via changing administration and work processes, and via altering EU citizens' access to social benefits. The EU's direct social policies in the form of the *Coordination Method* and *redistribution of resources* has so far had much less influence on Swedish social policy. One can join with the assessment of researchers who consider that there has been a restriction of the national sovereignty of social policy content and organization since EU membership.

Conclusion

Sweden has needed to adjust its national social policy to EU requirements in several ways. Swedish national regulation has needed to be changed in the areas of healthcare, working environment, working hours, employment conditions, gender equality, discrimination and public procurement. Furthermore, local authorities, county councils and other public authorities have needed to adapt their working processes in a comprehensive way. In addition, Sweden has needed in a general way to adjust its eligibility criteria: firstly, to include European citizens living in Sweden, and secondly to include Swedish citizens living in other EU countries. Finally, public authorities needed to adapt routines in order to assure that Swedish legislation does not violate EU legislation, especially concerning the free movement of capital, labour, services and goods. Following most researchers, the development of Swedish social policy in the EU can be characterized as being situated between two different poles: on the one hand, the 'Swedish model', *i.e.* the special features of Swedish social policy, has not been changed due to EU membership, but on the other hand, Swedish national sovereignty for formulating its social policy has been limited by EU common market regulations. The State Office expresses the situation nicely with its assessment that 'the EU is affecting more and more, but not everything'.

Beyond an assessment of the degree of Europeanization so far, it will be interesting to see how future developments will shape Swedish society and social policy. Researchers have raised the question of whether the process of EU common market integration in the future will lead to an ever-stronger restriction of national sovereignty. What are the consequences, for example, of judicial decisions of the European Court of Justice for the model of the Swedish labour market, which rests on non-legal collective agreements? Is there a risk of wage dumping in the future? Several European unions are pressuring for the inclusion of a social protocol with the same legal standing as the four freedoms for capital, labour, services and goods. Another question concerns possible consequences for healthcare if access and volume can no longer be controlled in the same way? These are open empirical questions, which will be interesting to follow.

A question is how to theoretically classify EU social policy (see chapter 2 and Wallace *et al.*, 2017). Can it best be characterized as following the Regulatory Mode, Distributional Mode, Policy-Coordination Mode or Community Method Mode?

It is clear that the process of creating a common EU market has repercussions for national social policy. The creation of a common market has been most clearly driven by two EU institutions: the European Court of Justice and the Commission. The European Court of Justice has played a key role in pushing integration forward through several decisions (for example, for social insurance enabling the free movement of workers and against national wage agreements enabling free movement of service companies). The Commission has issued directives that were directly related to social policy issues (such as the Working Time Directive) and wages (such as the Service Directive). Due to the central importance of these two EU institutions, the social policy area in the EU policy can be classified as part of the Regulatory mode.

The Distributional Mode and Policy Co-ordination Mode are less able to capture the way EU influences Swedish social policy: Resources are limited which are allocated by the European Social Fund. The Coordination Method in social policy has had no further on-going effects on Swedish social policy. The Community Method is not relevant either, because member states are not eager to centralize the politically sensitive area of social policy.

References

Arvidsson, M. 2009. 'EU Labour Migration: Government and Social Partner Policies in Sweden' In: B. Galgóczi, J. Leschke & A. Watt (eds.) *EU Labour Migration since Enlargement: Trends, Impacts and Policies*. Abingdon: Ashgate.

Blomqvist, P. 2008. 'Den svenska välfärdspolitiken' In: L. Bennich-Björkman & P. Blomqvist (ed.) *Mellan folkhem och Europa – svensk politik i brytningstid*. Malmö: Liber.

Cousins, M. 2005. *European Welfare States: Comparative Perspectives*. London: Sage.

De la Porte, C. & P. Pochet. 2012. 'Why and How (Still) Study the Open Method of Co-Ordination (OMC)?' *Journal of European Social Policy*, 22(3).

Dølvik, S. J. E., T. Fløtten, J. M. Hippe & B. Jordfald (eds.) 2014. *Den nordiska modellen mot 2030. Et nytt kapittel?* FAFO rapport 2014: 46. Oslo: FAFO.

Elmér, Å., S. Blomberg, L. Harrysson & J. Petersson. 2000. *Svensk socialpolitik*. Lund: Studentlitteratur.

Esping-Andersen, G. 1990. *The Three Worlds of Welfare Capitalism*. Cambridge: Policy Press.

EU 2010. 'Konsoliderade versioner av fördraget om europeiska unionen och fördraget om Europeiska Unionens funktionssätt.' *Europeiska unionens officiella tidning*, 53(C83).

Falkner, G. 1998. *EU Social Policy in the 1990's: Towards a Corporatist Policy Community*. London: Routledge.

— 2012. 'European Union' In: F. G. Castles, S. Leibfried, J. Lewis, H. Obinger & C. Pierson (eds.) *The Oxford Handbook of the Welfare State*. Oxford: Oxford University Press.

Graziano, P. R. 2012. 'Converging Worlds of Activation? Activation Policies and Governance in Europe and the Role of the EU.' *International Journal of Sociology and Social Policy*, 32(5).

Hancher, L. & W. Sauter 2010. 'One Step Beyond? From Sodemare to Docmorris: The EU's Freedom of Establishment Case Law Concerning Health Care'. *Common Market Law Review*, 47(1).

Hartman, L. (ed.) 2011. *Konkurrensens konsekvenser: Vad händer med svensk välfärd*. Stockholm: SNS Förlag.

Höpner, M. & A. Schäfer 2012. *Integration Among Unequals: How the Heterogeneity of European Varieties of Capitalism Shapes the Social and Democratic Potential of the EU*, Working Paper. Cologne: Max Planck Institute for the Study of Societies.

Kommerskollegium 2011. *Inremarknadsguide för kommuner*. Stockholm: Kommerskollegium.

— 2013. *Att flytta till Sverige – hinder för den fria rörligheten för EU-medborgare*. Stockholm: Kommerskollegium.

— 2014. *Inremarknadsguide för myndigheter*. Stockholm: Kommerskollegium.

Korpi, W. 1983. *The Democratic Class Struggle*. London: Routledge.

Kvist, J. 2004. 'Does EU Enlargement Start a Race to the Bottom? Strategic Interaction among EU Member States in Social Policy.' *Journal of European Social Policy*, 14(3).

Kvist, J. & B. Greve. 2011. 'Has the Nordic Welfare Model Been Transformed?' *Social Policy & Administration*, 45(2).

Kvist, J., J. Fritzell, B. Hvinden & O. Kangas (eds.) 2012. *Changing Social Equality. The Nordic Welfare Model in the 21st Century*. Bristol: Policy Press.

Leibfried, S. 2017. 'Social Policy: Left to the Judges and the Markets?' In: H. Wallace, M. A. Pollack & A. R. Young (eds.) *Policy-Making in the European Union*. Oxford: Oxford University Press.

Lindbom, A. 2011. *Systemskifte: Den nya svenska välfärdspolitiken*. Lund: Studentlitteratur.

Martinsen, D. S. 2013. 'Welfare States and Social Europe.' In: U. Neergaard, E. Szyszczak, J. W. van de Gronden & M. Krajewski (eds.) *Social Services of General Interest in the EU – Legal Issues of Services of General Interest*. The Hague: T. M. C. Asser Press.

Minas, R. 2012. Europeisk socialpolitik möter den lokala arenan. EU:s inverkan på det sociala arbetet i Stockholms stad, arbetsrapport. Stockholm: Institutionen för socialt arbete.

Obermaier, A. 2009. *The End of Territoriality. The Impact of ECJ Rulings on British, German and French Social Policy*. Farnham: Ashgate.

OECD 2018. *OECD Data Social Spending*. Paris, November 2018. OECD. Accessed: https://data.oecd.org/socialexp/social-spending.htm.

Rhodes, M. 2017. 'Employment Policy: Between Efficacy and Experimentation' In: H. Wallace, M. A. Pollack & A. R. Young (eds.) *Policy-Making in the European Union*. Oxford: Oxford University Press.

Rieger, E. & S. Leibfried. 2003. *Limits to Globalization: Welfare States and the World Economy*. Cambridge: Polity.

Rothstein, B. (ed.) 2001. *Politik som organisation. Förvaltningspolitikens grundproblem*. Stockholm: SNS Förlag.

Sainsbury, D. (ed.) 1999. *Gender and Welfare State Regimes*. Oxford: Oxford University Press.

SCB 2018. *Nationalräkenskaper/Utgifter för det sociala skyddet i Sverige och Europa samt utgifternas finansiering*. Stockholm, November 2018. SCB. Accessed: https://www.scb.se/hitta-statistik/statistik-efter-amne/nationalrakenskaper/nationalrakenskaper/utgifter-for-det-sociala-skyddet-i-sverige-och-europa-samt-utgifternas-finansiering-esspros/pong/statistiknyhet/socialt-skydd-i-sverige-19932016/.

Scharpf, F. W. 2002. 'The European Social Model.' *Journal of Common Market Studies*, 40(4).

— 2010. *Community and Autonomy: Institutions, Policies and Legitimacy in Multilevel Europe*. Frankfurt am Main: Campus Verlag.

SOU 2014. 'Nya regler om upphandling'. 2014:51. *Statens Offentliga Utredningar*. Stockholm: Fritzes.

Statskontoret 2005. *EU:s påverkan på kommuner och landsting*. 2005:12. Stockholm: Statskontoret.

Svallfors, S. 2012. *Contested Welfare States: Welfare Attitudes in Europe and Beyond*. Stanford: Stanford University Press.

Svallfors, S. & P. Taylor-Gooby 1999. *The End of the Welfare State? Responses to State Retrenchment*. London: Routledge.

Tallberg, J., N. Aylott, C. F. Bergström, Å. C. Vifell & J. Palme (eds.) 2010. *Demokratirådets rapport 2010: Europeiseringen av Sverige*. Stockholm: SNS förlag.

Wallace, H., M. A. Pollack & A. R. Young 2017. *Policy-Making in the European Union*. Oxford: Oxford University Press.

Van Berkel, R., W. de Graaf, T. Sirovátka & P. R. Graziano 2012. 'Converging Worlds of Activation? Activation Policies and Governance in Europe and the Role of the EU.' *International Journal of Sociology and Social Policy*, 32(5/6).

Van Kersbergen, K. & P. Manow 2009. *Religion, Class Coalitions, and Welfare States*. Cambridge: Cambridge University Press.

Vifell, Å. C. 2011. 'Sweden: The Reluctant Follower' In: P. Graziano, S. Jacquot & B. Palier (eds.). *The EU and the Domestic Politics of Welfare State Reforms: Europa, Europae*. London: Palgrave Macmillan.

7. Education Policy

Charlotte Silander

Education is a sensitive political issue, especially within the European Union (EU). In all societies, education is viewed as a process in which adults convey opinions, culture and values to a younger generation. Hence, education relates both to national identity and solidarity. In the EU context, education has shifted from primarily being a device to create a European identity and strengthen unity amongst the people of Europe to increasingly becoming regarded as a means of competition for strengthening the European economic market and boosting democracy and citizenship in times of crisis and social division.

Prior to the turn of the millennium, there was no formal policy of education at the EU level, but there were a number of established educational programmes. This situation changed in the early 2000s, in part due to two processes: the Bologna Process and the Lisbon Strategy. The Bologna Process, built upon the Bologna Declaration, aimed to turn Europe into a cohesive sector for higher education. The Lisbon Strategy set out to establish Europe as the world's most competitive region and placed education at the centre by emphasising knowledge and education as the foundation of growth (European Council 2000). When the Lisbon Strategy was later replaced by Europe 2020, the relationship between knowledge and economic growth was highlighted once more as education was viewed as the foundation for growth. The Lisbon Strategy, followed by the Europe 2020 strategy and the implementation of the Bologna Process, along with frequent skills and knowledge assessments performed by the EU and the Organisation for Economic Co-operation and Development

(OECD), led to a new phase for how the EU coordinates the education policies of its member states.

This chapter will discuss how Sweden's EU membership has influenced the area of education. The chapter begins with an overview of the development of the EU's education policy from being a narrow area primarily involving exchange and a number of educational programmes to becoming increasingly significant due to the Lisbon Strategy and Europe 2020. The legal grounds for education policy in the EU treaties is described in more detail, as are the roles of the EU institutions in the policy process. A special focus will be placed on discussion of the Open Method of Coordination (OMC) and its significance. This chapter also addresses aspects formally outside the EU's framework, such as the Bologna Process.

Education Policy in Sweden

Education policy is an extensive field that cannot be easily grasped. Vygotsky described education as a process in which individuals are raised to understand their own knowledge of culture. Historically, Swedish school education has been supported by two ideas of community: Lutheranism and the nation. When schools were established as institutions in Sweden, education set out to transfer certain moral values to younger generations. This took place through religious schooling and education. In the late 1930s, this ethos became part of the creation of the Swedish *Folkhemmet* – middle way social democracy – as the nation was central and concepts such as 'folkhem' (lit. 'the home of the people') and 'one's country' became a uniting force in the structuring of Swedish society (Trägårdh 1993). Swedish education policy has been characterised by the long hold of the government power of the Swedish Social Democratic Party and their persistent ideology that education should be free and equal. Equality has been a central target, as education is perceived as a way to eliminate the class-based society (Rothstein 1986). Comprehensive reforms took place in the Swedish school system during the 1950s and 1960s. In 1962, the Riksdag ruled that schooling would be compulsory for children of a certain age, replacing the former educational system. By 1971, the creation of the new school system was complete; the previous parallel school system was replaced with a new, cohesive school system. The change was propelled by a growth in population and an increased demand for workers with an upper-secondary level of education, alongside an increased desire for education among the general population. One vital purpose of the reforms was to include all children and young people in a collective school system, regardless of class, gender and geographical location.

In the 1980s, criticism started to grow towards the uniform schooling, and there was an increased demand for reform of the Swedish school system coming from several political groups (Lindensjö & Lundgren 2002). In 1980, a new curriculum for the compulsory school was issued, where power was decentralised and transferred to the municipal school boards. The 1980s also saw an adaptation of the previous emphasis on democracy and equality, which now, due to a harsh economic situation, led to a more market-oriented perspective. All in all, the changes in the 1970s and '80s resulted in a more locally governed school system. The state governing of schools gradually declined, and by the start of the 1990s, the government only provided targets and guidelines for schools. In 1989, responsibility was transferred from the state to municipality with the purpose of giving municipalities greater freedom to organise activities (Swedish Government Bill 1990/91). The proposition on the freedom of choice and free schools (*Propositionen om valfrihet och fristående skolor)* (Swedish Government Bill 1991/92) set the path for private schools to be able to operate under the same conditions as municipal schools and receive the same government funding. The key concept of 'freedom to choose' was also followed by increased focus on evaluation, quality and efficiency (Arnman, Järneks & Lindskog 2004).

Higher education has also undergone significant changes in recent decades. The Swedish system of higher education is traditionally rooted in a long tradition of providing education for a limited elite, dating back to the founding of Uppsala University in the 15th century. Since then, the development of the 'mass university' (REF) has resulted in the establishment of a number of new higher education institutions, which has profoundly changed the expectations of the role of higher education. Today, 'higher education' is used as an umbrella term for universities and higher education institutions in Sweden, generally including all post-upper secondary education, which, since 2007, has been categorised into a first-, second- and third-cycle system.

Modern higher education began to take shape in the 1960s, with rapidly increasing student numbers placing new demands on the Swedish education system. By the end of the 1960s, a system consisting of fixed study paths was introduced in philosophical faculties, which expanded the access to higher education. Simultaneously, there was an increase in the geographical spread of education through the introduction of institutions in new areas: Umeå University in 1965, satellite campuses in Växjö, Örebro, Karlstad and Linköping in 1967 and Luleå University College in 1971. In 1968, a comprehensive government investigation into higher education (U68) was conducted and resulted in the 1977 Higher Education Reform, which has been described as the most comprehensive reform of the century for the sector (Fritzell 1998). The reform focused on how undergraduate education was governed and how accessibility could be increased, thus reducing socially uneven recruitment and providing the possibility for recurring education. Large parts of undergraduate studies were organised by cohesive study programmes, with most of their content determined by course syllabuses set by the University and Higher Education Office. Until this point, there had been a number of parallel higher education and post-upper secondary education institutions. The reform resulted in all post-upper secondary education being formally brought together in one system. This meant a widening of the concept of higher education, as parts of post-upper secondary education were transferred to higher education institutions, and courses such as nursing and teacher education now became classified as higher education courses. These were shorter and more vocational than the traditional academic courses.

The former independent teacher training institutes now became part of a university or higher education institution in their local area, and at the same time, new institutions were established. Over time, education related to healthcare was transferred to higher education institutions, followed eventually by engineering courses. The primary aim of the reform was not to expand existing university education but rather to meet the labour market's need for vocational training. The 1977 reform resulted in increased access to education as admission regulations opened up for new student groups, but what contributed most of all was the increased geographical spread. University colleges were restructured to become independent higher education institutions. New higher education institutions were established in Borås, Eskilstuna/Västerås, Jönköping, Kalmar, Kristianstad, Sundsvall/Härnösand and Östersund. Since 1977, additional higher education institutions have opened in Halmstad and Skövde (1983), in Karlskrona/Ronneby (1988), in Trollhättan/Uddevala (1990), in Södertörn outside of Stockholm (1997), on the island of Gotland and in Malmö in 1998 (Agency of Higher Education 1998). All of these smaller to medium-sized higher education institutions were given the primary task of offering undergraduate courses.

At the start of the 1990s, there were further calls for additional expansions of higher education. The organisation of undergraduate education into vocational programmes received criticism for significantly limiting the free choice of the students and for marginalising studies in humanities. Also criticised was the detailed regulation of the dimensioning of undergraduate studies with inaccurate prognoses which recurrently proved to be wrong, creating a system that failed to make local adaptations based on student requests (Fritzell 1998).

In the 1980s, decentralisation of higher education institutions had already begun with the abolishment of central syllabuses. In 1990, a process began that would later result in the 1993 higher education reform, in which the modern system for undergraduate education is rooted. The fixed system with centralised syllabuses was replaced by a system of qualifications, and the division into sectors was removed. Undergraduate studies would now instead take the form of courses that could be combined into a programme.

The reform represented a shift from regulation- and budget-based governance to target and results-based governance, which characterised the development in the public sector at the end of the 1980s. The purpose for higher education, as with other government sectors, was to divide responsibility and accountability in order to make organisations more efficient. With the 1993 reform, a new system for the allocation of resources was implemented, where higher education institutions received funding based on the number of students and their performance instead of the previously planned set of places.

Dimensioning education became a local matter that was to be managed within the framework of general funding agreement targets for the higher education institution. The 1993 reform therefore led to decentralisation and less central governance of higher education (Swedish Government Report 1996:21).

Between 1993 and 2010, the number of students in the sector increased considerably; however, towards the end of the 2000s, education policy changed from predominantly focusing on expansion to limiting the number of higher education places and recommending concentrations and profiling (Askling 2012).

The Historical Development of Education Policy in the EU

When the European Community (EC) was formed in the 1950s, the focus was economic cooperation; education was simply a matter for the member states to handle by themselves. Education first appeared in the European context at the start of the 1960s. In 1971, the European Commission established a unit for future cooperation within education. In 1973, this became a specialist unit in the newly established 'Directorate General for Research and Innovation' (DG XII) (European Commission 2006). In 1976, the first education action plan was passed in the form of a resolution for the period of 1976–1984 (*i.e.*, non-binding). This can be described as a statement of political ambition, where the countries declared an interest in cooperating within the education sphere, even though, at this time, there was no political intention to include education in the treaty (Wächter 2012). Education was formally introduced into the European cooperation through the Maastricht Treaty in 1993. Nevertheless, there was already scope for cooperation long before thanks to a legal judgment from the European Court of Justice (ECJ) in 1985, where in Françoise Gravier v City of Liège (C293/83), the court established grounds for the EU to react in matters of vocational training (Wächter 2012). The judgment, through Article 128 (on vocational training), created legal grounds that became a basis for the large EU education programmes *Commett* and *Erasmus*. When the Maastricht Treaty entered into force in 1993, and Article 149 gave the EU legal grounds to act on education, this only meant a codification of something that was already being practiced. The opportunity to act in the area of education through the Maastricht Treaty was, however, both then and now, limited to creating incentives for a European dimension to education, organising student and teacher exchanges, supporting cooperation between education providers, developing distance learning, working to recognise diplomas and periods of study and exchanging experiences about the education systems in member states (Treaty on the European Union, Article 126). The treaty excluded measures that led to the harmonisation of legislations and regulations and therefore limited the community's access to a number of practical measures.

Limited Provisions in Education and Training

Education has a weak legal basis in the EU. Prior to the Lisbon Strategy, the EU's role was limited and consisted mainly of implementing various forms of study programmes. The EU is only able to pass laws as part of the free movement framework, free right of establishment and recognition of diplomas. Articles 165 (education) and 166 (vocational training) in the treaty regulate the EU's targets for education, vocational training, youth and sport. The treaty stipulates that the EU shall: 1) develop the European dimension in education, particularly through the teaching and dissemination of the languages of the member states; 2) encourage mobility of students and teachers by encouraging the academic recognition of diplomas and periods of study; 3) promote cooperation between educational establishments; 4) develop exchanges of information and experience on issues common to the education systems of the member states; 5) encourage the development of youth exchanges and exchanges of socio-educational instructors, and encourage the participation of young people in democratic life in Europe and 6) encourage the development of distance education. Furthermore, the EU shall foster cooperation with third countries and international organisations.

To achieve the goals established in Article 165, the European Parliament and Council shall, in accordance with the Ordinary Legislative Procedure and after consultation with the Economic and Social Committee, reach decisions regarding incentives that, however, may not include any harmonisation of the laws or other ordinances of the member states. The Council can, upon proposal from the Commission, approve recommendations. Consequently, Articles 165 and 166 in the EU treaty exclude legally binding decisions and only allow for recommendations and incentives. The main principle behind these measures is for the EU to support and supplement actions taken by member states. The EU's actions are intended to increase quality by creating a European added value, but actions must not involve harmonisation of member states' laws and ordinances. The responsibility of each member state for the quality of teaching and organisation of the educational system is to be respected. The secondary right in the area primarily includes resolutions taken by the European Council, which are non-binding agreements, also referred to as 'soft law'. Additionally, several decisions exist on the establishment of various joint programmes to increase student movement and are based on the treaty (Articles 18, 20 and 21 of the Treaty on the Functioning of the European Union).

The restrictions in the treaty have resulted in a significant portion of EU education policy being based on programmes. The first European action programme (1976) in the field of education set the foundations for future exchange programmes. The most famous is the *Erasmusprogram,* which began in 1987. Erasmus is an exchange programme that enables several types of exchange for students and teachers. Further educational programmes were introduced based on proposals from the Commission. Examples include:

- *Commett* – to improve the exchange between higher education institutions,
- *Lingua* – to improve young people's language skills,
- *Force, Eurotecnet* and *Petra* – programmes for young people,
- *Tempus* – to support exchanges with the former Eastern European states,
- *Socrates* and *Leonardo* – for foundations and continued vocational training and
- *Commenius* – preschool, compulsory school and upper-secondary school.

In 2007, these programmes merged and became *the EU's Lifelong Learning Programme,* which was replaced in 2014 with the EU's new programme, *Erasmus+*, which is the EU's new education programme that replaces many previous programmes (Lifelong Learning Programme and its sub-programmes Erasmus, Commenius, Grundtvig and Leonardo da Vinci). Erasmus+ is aimed at preschools, schools, universities, vocational and adult education and youth organisations (European Commission 2014). All EU education programmes support similar activities (*i.e.*, student and teacher mobility, development of joint curriculums and course materials and summer schools). The programmes do not finance education systems but rather the cooperation between them, and therefore, they do not have a direct influence on structure and content. The majority of programmes require participation from several countries. The purpose of the programmes has always been to promote mobility and integration in the EU. In recent years, this has increasingly come to include contributions to solve the education and labour market problems facing the EU.

Even though the activities in the framework for EU education programmes are limited to practical operations such as exchanges, they have been indirectly significant for education systems in European countries. The Erasmus student exchange programme was built upon complete recognition of study periods abroad. In the early stages, a system was developed to overcome the difference in grading systems and the transfer of results across the grading scales of different countries – the European Credit Transfer and Accumulation Systems (ECTS). The third operative goal in the Bologna Declaration encouraged member states to introduce a common education credit system, and the ECTS was described as the system for the transfer and presentation of merits that would be used consistently throughout the European area for higher education (Proposition 2004/05:162). In 2007, the Swedish credit system changed to become compatible with the ECTS as part of the Bologna Process (Swedish Higher Education Ordinance 1993:100). Today, the ECTS is used as the grading system in many European countries, including Sweden. What had been designed to avoid harmonisation became – paradoxically – a tool for what the treaty expressively forbids: the harmonisation of education systems.

Towards a European Education Policy

The major change to the European cooperation in education policy took place in 2000, when the Lisbon Strategy for the first time gave the EU the role of being policymaker. At the European Council meeting in Lisbon, the EU member states agreed that in ten years' time, the region would be the world's most competitive. This was to be done via the Lisbon Strategy, where European member states compete with each other to improve national and European growth (European Council 2000). The goal established by the European Council that has a direct influenced on education was *'to become the most competitive and dynamic knowledge-based economy in the world, capable of sustainable economic growth with more and better jobs and greater social cohesion'* (European Council 2000). This goal formed a new link between education policy and employment policy, where improvements in the educational area became a precondition for a competitive EU. This link is central because the influence of the EU on education is justified by the creation of jobs, employment and growth. The Lisbon Strategy called for a European social model, in which economic growth would not exasperate existing problems of social exclusion, poverty and unemployment (*cf.* Chapter 3 on Economic Policy). In order to succeed, the European Council believed that a new plan for education of European citizens was needed: 'The European social system must adjust both to the needs of the knowledge-based society and to the need to raise the level of employment and improve quality' (European Council 2000). In their conclusions, they emphasised that they '... call on the council (education) to undertake a general reflection on concrete future objectives of education systems' (European Council 2000). This led the European Council to encourage member states to review their educational goals, which can be interpreted as support for the member states to move one step beyond what is stipulated in the legal grounds (that exclude binding policy) to achieve the EU's goals (Hingel 2001).

The Lisbon Strategy set comprehensive goals that were to be met by 2010, including how quality would be achieved in education. The European education systems would enable citizen mobility, and universities and higher education institutions would be given a special important role in the implementation of the goals (European

Commission 2003). In order to provide structure to the work in the area, additional reports on common goals were adopted (Education Council 2001), and a more detailed action plan was launched (Education Council and the Commission 2002). As a continuation of the Lisbon Strategy, in June 2010, a new ten-year strategy was approved for the EU, *Europe 2020*, with five principal targets: employment, research and development, climate change and energy, education and poverty and social exclusion. The fact that education is increasingly emphasised as the solution to Europe's problems is evident because one key target is to improve the quality and efficiency of education and increase creativity and innovation, as well as to include entrepreneurship at all levels of education (*cf.* Chapter 3, Economic Policy; Education Council 2009). Seven key initiatives have been linked to the targets to facilitate their attainment. The key initiative for education is 'Youth on the Move'[1]. This will strengthen results in the education system and facilitate a young person's entry into the labour market (Education Council 2009).

The main targets set out for education are *reducing the school dropout rate* to less than 10 % and increasing the share of the population aged 30–34 that have *completed tertiary education* to at least 40 % by 2020 (European Commission 2010). To support the achievement of the two main objectives, the Commission set another five benchmarks (Eurostat 2018:88): 1) at least 95 % of children between age four and the age at which education becomes compulsory should participate in early childhood education, 2) the rate of underachievement in basic skills for 15-year-olds should be below 15 %, 3) the employment rate of recent graduates should be at least 82 %, 4) at least 15 % of adults should participate in learning and 5) at least 20% of higher education graduates and at least 6 % of 18- to 34-year-olds with vocational education should have spent time studying abroad. How the member states progress in relation to these targets is monitored and reviewed annually by the Commission. As part of this monitoring,

1 *Other initiatives linked to education included* an Agenda for new Skills and Jobs and Innovation Europe. *Furthermore, there were principle initiatives,* A Digital Agenda for Europe, A Resource-Efficient Europe, Industrial Policy for the Globalisation Era *and* European Platform Against Poverty.

several methods are used, such as the Programme for International Student Assessment (PISA), which examines the reading, mathematics and science skills of 15-year-old pupils, and *Trends in International Mathematics and Science Study* (TIMSS), an international study that examines the mathematics and science knowledge of pupils in years 4 and 8. The Eurydice Network acts as a support and collects information about education systems and policy in Europe, as well as facilitating the exchange of information in these areas.

In the country-specific report for 2018, the Commission pointed out that Sweden scored high on many of the targets measured in the Europe 2020 process. The basic skills proficiency of the younger generation has improved, early childhood education has high participation rates (95.6% from age 4) (European Commission 2018: 282) and basic skills attainment has improved according to the PISA. Sweden's tertiary educational attainment rate is high. Of 30- to 34-year-olds, 51.3% have completed tertiary education, above both the EU average of 39.9% and the national Europe 2020 target of 45–50% (European Commission 2018:284), and the employment rate of recent tertiary graduates is among the highest in the EU. In 2017, 91.7% of graduates aged 20–34 were employed, above the EU average of 84.9%. Concerns expressed by the Commission are, for example, the growing inequalities in Sweden's school system, where a growing impact of socio-economic background on students' performance was shown in PISA 2015. The performance gap between foreign-born and native-born students is wide and increasing, reflecting changes in the composition of the foreign-born student population (European Commission 2018:283). Another concern is the growing teacher shortage, mostly in preschools and compulsory schools (European Commission 2018:283).

As national targets in the area of education, Sweden has set out that the proportion of 18- to 24-year-olds who have less than two years of secondary education and who do not participate in any kind of studies should be less than 7% in 2020. This figure has increased continuously since 2014 and reached 7.6% in 2017, which is better than the EU benchmark, but Sweden still has not reached the 7% national target (Swedish Government Offices 2018:24). The second national target was that the proportion of 30- to 34-year-olds with at least two years of secondary education should be 45–50% in 2020. In 2017, 51.1% was reached, which is above both the EU's benchmark and Sweden's national goals.

The Bologna Process and PISA

Two developments that have had a clear effect in Sweden are the implementation of the Bologna Process and the frequent assessments through PISA. The Bologna Process is formally outside of the EU cooperation, and the Bologna Declaration is not a legally binding document (Garben 2011). The declaration was given its name after a meeting in Bologna in 1999, when education ministers from 29 European countries signed a declaration that set a target to create a common European area for higher education before the end of 2010. This would increase competition and attraction to European higher education compared with countries outside of Europe. To meet this target, the participating countries were encouraged to introduce a system with clear and comparable diplomas, introduce a system that included two predominant levels (first- and second-cycle studies) and introduce a common model of credits. The overall purpose of the Bologna Declaration was to facilitate European cross-border movement for students and academics seeking employment. Today, over 45 countries are linked to this European cooperation. The comprehensive goal of the Bologna Process was for Europe to become a 'cohesive European area for higher education', in which mobility, employability and attraction as a continent of education was promoted (Eurydice 2007). Even though the Bologna Process has taken place outside of the EU system, it has been supported by the EU, and the EU has been involved in several ways (Garben 2011). In support of its implementation, the European Commission financed national groups of experts in the countries that worked with the Bologna Process. These experts supported the work at the higher education institutions and acted as advisors to those involved at Swedish universities and higher education institutions.

The Bologna-adaptation of the Swedish courses and programmes began at the start of the 2000s. This resulted mainly in higher education being divided into three levels (first-, second- and third-cycle), with specific learning outcomes being formulated for the first two cycles. For Sweden, which had followed a linear structure since 1977 and had programmes leading to vocational diplomas, the work with Bologna required considerable reviews of the content of the basic education (Askling 2012). In 2006, the Riksdag issued a decision on the structure of education and examination, and in 2007, the Bologna Process was formally introduced with the 2007 higher education reform, when a new Higher Education Ordinance came into force. Hence, the Bologna Process essentially changed the Swedish system of higher education. In the government bill that preceded the implementation of the Bologna Process, the government wrote that the 'purpose of this process is to create a common structure for higher education in cooperation with Europe's countries' (Swedish Government Bill 2004/162:26). In the period between 2001 and 2010, Sweden attained the six comprehensive targets of the Bologna Declaration. In addition the, the parliament ratified the Lisbon Convention that addresses mutual recognition of education in other countries. The Bologna Process now means that everyone that graduates from a programme receives a Diploma Supplement, which facilitates the use of the degree abroad.

In the same way as Bologna has left its mark on the Swedish higher education system, PISA and the results of its assessments have been subject to much attention, especially because Sweden has been ranked relatively low in the international rankings of skills compared to other countries. After several PISA studies with falling results, the result went up again in 2015, when the skills of Swedish 15-year olds improved. Reading comprehension and mathematics also improved, and within the field of science, there were signs of positive development. In the previous PISA survey, Swedish students performed below the average for OECD countries in all three areas of knowledge. The 2015 survey ranked Sweden as average or above average (Skolverket 2016). PISA is an instrument to assess the knowledge of the skills of pupils aged 15. The project is run by OECD, and the evaluations take place every three years, with examinations in mathematics, science, literacy and problem solving, but a number of non-OECD countries participate. In this regard, the EU and OECD have similar policy ambitions, and PISA has become an important part of the construction of a

European education area. It has also become the dominant comparative evaluation system in Europe (Greek 2009, Grek *et al.* 2009). The mathematics component tests pupils' ability to apply mathematical formulae to solve everyday problems. The literacy component tests pupils' ability to retrieve and reflect upon information and interpret and assess texts. The science component tests pupils' use and understanding of scientific theories, models and concepts. Hence, the PISA assessments aim to focus on problem solving related to real-life situations and measure skills such as literacy and numeracy, skills perceived as necessary to be successful in the European labour market. The critique has been that the emphasis on other educational targets such as democratic participation, artistic talent and understanding of political and historical events has been reduced and instead, a more instrumental approach to education in the form of its relevance to the labour market and lifelong learning has been emphasised (Greek 2009). Greek (2009) emphasised that the PISA highly affects national education systems and has an indirect, yet important, influence on the formulation of education policy. The PISA can be viewed as a component in a 'comparative turn' or 'scientific approach to political decision making' (Marten 2007:40), which has enabled the EU and OECD to influence areas where they formerly lacked the legal means to affect policy. Their production of statistics, reports and evaluations through the OMC are perceived as legitimate and neutral and are frequently used by politicians and decision makers, as well as researchers (Marten 2007).

Spread of Policies Through the OMC

As previously stated, education has a weak legal basis in the treaty. The EU's role is solely to promote cooperation between member states and, where necessary, support and supplement their efforts (Article 165 TEU). One way is enabling policy-creating measures in education as part of the framework for the OMC. The OMC is one of several methods for new forms of governance that build upon voluntary and informal ways to create policy through discussion and negotiation. This is not a new method for policy creation. It has been used successfully within the OECD for many years; it was, however, introduced to the EU as part of the package solution from the European Council meeting in Lisbon 2000. The method is generally used in areas where the EU only has the competence to support, coordinate or supplement the actions of member states and where no legally binding legislation is made. The OMC works in parallel with other more formal decision-making systems in the EU and forms a complex system of multilayered democracy consisting of informal lobbying mechanisms and agenda setting from the Commission in its attempts to influence policy.

The background to the introduction of the OMC can be traced back to the 1990s, when the EU reached a point where the economic integration process began to come closer to issues traditionally managed by the welfare state, for example, the labour market and social policy. Many believed that additional measures were needed from the EU to balance the economic integration, while at the same time, there was a reluctance amongst the member states to give up sovereignty in these areas. Hence, an alternative to the traditional community method was needed, through which the EU could continue to play a part without being viewed as a threat in sensitive issues on a national level (Borrás & Jacobsson 2004). Within the framework of the OMC, the Council invites member states and the Commission to jointly identify policy problems and establish common goals to solve them. Policy influence takes place through learning processes or policy learning (Alexiadou 2010), which, if successful, enables convergence of targets for education policy in the member states.

In this way, the OMC is a form of compromise, where member states retain responsibility for the policy area while the EU simultaneously is given a coordinating and policy-creating role that the member states are prepared to accept. It is a voluntary and informal model that contains policy proposals or solutions that do not constrain the member states but can still be included. 'Benchmarking' (*i.e.*, systematic comparisons of activities) and 'best practice' (*i.e.*, a practice that is believed to work) are central elements. The stages of the OMC are described in the European Council conclusions from 2000. In the first stage, the member states together agree on common goals and objectives that they will work towards in accordance with the agreed programme and schedule. The objectives are drafted in long and short terms, and a timeline is set for when they are to be reached.

In stage two, quantitative and qualitative measures in the form of indicators and benchmarks are developed. The third stage translates these targets into national and regional policies formulated with consideration of national conditions. Finally, periodic monitoring and evaluation take place based on peer-review methods, in which experts and participants assess and evaluate the development. This phase is organised as mutual learning processes, where representatives meet to discuss and exchange experiences from other countries and the Commission (Alexiadou 2010, European Council 2000). The method builds upon an idea of policy learning to influence and harmonise the policies of the member states (Alexiadou 2010). The work is organised into six workgroups for education. At its core, the OMC is a political process that builds upon that ideas of participatory democracy and with deliberative elements by the involvement of several actors. The Council and the Commission play important roles, while the Court and European Parliament – just like the national parliaments – are outside the process. The Council is responsible for coordinating the policies of member states and determining the targets, indicators and guidelines. It also has the final say regarding approving reports and Council conclusions. *The Education, Youth, Culture and Sport Council* comprises EU ministers responsible for the included areas. The role of the council is to approve frameworks and action plans for EU policy, while the priorities are established in cooperation between the member states and the Commission. Representatives from the Commission also participate in council meetings. The Council decisions mostly take the form of incentives and recommendations.

Within the Commission, the *Directorate-General for Education, Youth, Sports and Culture* (EAC) is the responsible directorate general for education. The Commission plays an important role as a driving force and can be considered the main agenda setter in the OMC process. The Commission coordinates representatives from the member states, the Commission and other stakeholders into a number of workgroups. The six working groups in the area of education address the themes of school policy, higher education, vocational education, adult learning, transversal skills and digital learning. Each group has a mandate lasting 1–2.5 years. In total, the groups involve 400 experts including decision makers, sector representatives and representatives from international organisations, all of whom participate in an array of meetings and seminars. The explicit purpose of the working groups is to benefit policy development in the member states through mutual learning and finding positive examples, all taking place within the framework of learning processes in which participants are to share experiences, examples and analyses (European Commission 2015a).

The stages of the policy can be separated analytically, but in practice, they flow together within the OMC process. This makes it difficult to distinguish the responsibilities between the agenda setting and implementation (see Chapter 2). The European Council, the Council of Ministers and the Commission all participate in agenda setting and formulation of policies; however, the Commission always stands behind the initiative. The entire process is political in its character, rather than administrative, mainly due to the role played by the Council of Ministers (Borrás & Jacobsson 2004). On one hand, the representatives of the member states take clear initiatives to create policies, which could risk limiting the role of the Commission as the initiator of policy processes. On the other hand, the Commission's role as 'broker' is clear, and it has the possibility to govern policy processes in the direction desired. Hence, the OMC procedure enables the Commission to take the initiative and expand the cooperation into areas formally outside the exclusive competence of the member states and provisions in the treaties. Even if the processes are intergovernmental, the OMC procedure still contributed to strengthening the influence of the Commission and made it possible for them to expand into new areas (Borrás & Jacobsson 2004:198).

Because the OMC procedure is not a legislative procedure, the working groups of the Commission are seldom involved in preparing proposals, nor are the working groups of the Council, which typically is the case when legislation is implemented in the EU. The standard procedure is also that COPREPER is not involved in the process. The Commission provides administrative support and is a member of the working groups which are to produce formal positions commissioned by the Council of Ministers and the Commission. This practice then differs from the Commission's expert groups and implementation committees, as well as from the working groups linked to the Council (Borrás & Jacobsson 2004:198).

The OMC process is characterised by the lack of a dividing line between decision-making and implementation (Radaelli 2003). A new policy might be implemented by a member state without any formal decision having been made, which creates uncertainty in terms of accountability. The method builds upon the cooperation between the Commission and the member states, which particularly takes place in the various thematic working groups. These groups have a unique position between the Council and the Commission. The working group meetings have the function of 'brainstorming', rather than engaging in regulatory negotiations with traces of deliberative democracy ideals, where the best argument should have an impact, rather than negotiation strength. No binding decisions are made; instead, networks and discussions take place. If the method works, the experiences of experts combined with creative discussions are expected to provide good solutions.

The OMC process is monitored through regular reports produced by the Commission. The Commission coordinates a comprehensive document for the entire EU, *The Annual Education and Training Monitor,* based on the national reports submitted by member states, and their representatives participate throughout the process. Additional country-specific reports are produced that are written by the Commission. This document has more of a 'naming and shaming' character, and often, the Commission will express criticism and present the extent to which member states have succeeded or failed in attaining the targets (Alexiadou 2010).

The weakness of the OMC can be found in the final phase. It is difficult to assign responsibility in the event of dissatisfaction, as well as to point out those responsible for lack of implementation. In line with this, the evaluation of the Lisbon Strategy showed that most of the targets set had not been reached, although nobody could be held responsible for the lack of progress. However, although the OMC is a relatively new phenomenon in education, and means a weaker policy-creating method, it has been a successful tool to promote integration because it has encouraged more participation from member states in the education sector (Warleigh-Lack & Drachenberg 2013).

Formal and Actual Influence on Swedish Education Policy

The EU's formal influence on individual member states' education policy is limited. However, there are signs that there is a measurable effect (Borrás & Jacobsson 2004, Alexiadou 2010, Sjöberg 2009, Whalström 2010, Lawn 2011), even if this cannot be precisely quantified (Cini & Borrogaran 2013, Alexiadou 2010). The OMC process can be seen as a way to circumnavigate the actual sovereignty in the area (Borrás & Jacobsson 2004). The method also means that joint action at the EU level is no longer synonymous with a formal transfer of power. This was summarised by previous Swedish Prime Minister Göran Persson, who said, 'The process is political, not legal. If any country fails it will not end up in front of the European court... The route chosen in Lisbon certainly means more cooperation, but it does not mean more supranationalism' (Riksdag Rapid Protocol 1999/2000:92). Helen Wallace (2001) described it as being a transfer of power through the distribution of tasks between the member states, and in formal terms, the EU is unchanging, but below the surface, there have been several changes in the member states (Wallace 2001:592). Common targets and guidelines are 'brought into' the European arena, even though this is formally a national matter. The method has also meant that the Commission has significantly increased its influence in an area where it was previously limited by the treaties, resulting in a large increase in policy output at the European level – a direct consequence of the use of soft power (European Commission 2008; Warleigh-Lack & Drachenberg 2011).

Sweden has been affected by EU targets set in the area of education. The clearest point made in the Commission's report for Sweden were the declining results in the PISA assessments (European Commission 2015b). Researchers in education state that the strongest influence on Swedish education policy from the EU is the emphasis on the link between education and economic growth. Quality education is perceived as a way for the EU to compete in a globalised world. The EU emphasises the connection between good results (measured in assessments such as the PISA) and EU competitiveness and growth. In this way, the education system is placed in an economic market-based discourse with a tight efficiency perspective (Sjöberg 2011). In order to reach economic growth and reduce social exclusion, the education systems need to be improved and adapt to the skills required by working life. The Lisbon Declaration emphasises the notion of education as a 'fresh product' and something that enables a flexible labour market (Sjöberg 2011). Sjöberg (2011) described how Swedish and European education policy has become characterised by an order of discourse where the responsibility for the acquisition of knowledge is placed on the individual. European citizens will need a number of basic skills that are believed to be essential for successful trade and economic growth. Teachers and pupils need to have an entrepreneurial approach in the sense that they can adapt to a changing society. Educational choices and methods of teaching must give the best possible returns, as education by the EU is predominantly viewed as a financial investment (Sjöberg 2011:75, Fanghanel 2011). However, it may still be difficult to distinguish the EU's role in a larger global context of policy changes. Many researchers have shown that recent decades have been dominated by a neoliberal development of education policy around the world (Sjöberg 2009, Lawn 2011). Ball (2008), for example, argued that education policy has come to be formed as a 'global ensemble' (Ball 2008:39), in which a flow of joined forces have contributed to reorient national education policy. Here, the EU has strongly contributed to the introduction of result indicators and performance goals. Steering through standardisation is at the core of EU education policy. The collection of information and data, evaluation of staff, organisations and systems corresponds to how the evaluating state is given a greater role (Power 1999, Lawn 2011:261). The governance that takes place through evaluations, ranking and standardisation do not require legislation and therefore it is easier and more flexible to implement because it is also in line with the subsidiarity principle (*i.e.*, that decisions are to be made at the lowest possible level).

By introducing overall guidelines and recurring benchmarks of member states, the EU has come to define what education should be. Lawn stated that in the EU, education has translated to 'learning' and 'lifelong learning', which should be supported by e-learning (where digital technology is used to support learning), where the focus is placed on the individual and on results and common standards (Lawn 2011:264). This understanding of what is 'quality' regarding education is seen as objective and self-evident and has been introduced as a basic presumption without any discussion. The problem is, consequently, that performance goals and result indicators are viewed as naturally given and have been introduced without any discussion of what they really represent (Ball 2008, Lawn 2011.) This system makes education policy in the member states more similar, and subsequently, education takes a more transnational characteristic. Comparative practices such as indicators, benchmarking systems and assessment (PISA, TIMSS) strengthen common EU discourse, and because similar policy content and policy descriptions appear in several contexts, the effect of these measures is viewed as neutral and taken for granted (Pontgratz 2006). The problem is that it becomes increasingly difficult to identify the source of power and government. Many actors participate, while accountability remains unclear in the OMC process.

The policy agenda of EU regarding education and the implementation of the OMC process can therefore be said to have had gradual impact on Swedish education policy. The OMC has brought change to the context in which education policy is shaped and has built in a link to competition rather than social values (Cini & Borrogaran Swedish). Despite the fact that participation through the OMC is voluntary, Swedish education policy is influenced through the creation of a common language and the introduction of a competitive culture as the international results are compared (Wahlström 2013). Researchers have criticised how the EU, through the practice of publications, recommendations and comparisons, prescribes what is 'good education' and constructs what is 'truth' for the policy area (Sjöberg 2009). Statements in the policy documents of what is the ideal future education policy will influence how institutions and individuals view education. Nordin (2012:202) argued that the EU has had an important influence on Swedish education policy through reinterpretations and shifts in meaning in policy documents on the journey between the EU and Sweden. This can be interpreted as a neoconservative subject orientation, in which detailed requirements of skill increase, which place more demands on quantitative knowledge in a culture of competition. The PISA is one example. The danger here is that education policy risks no longer addressing the content of what a person learns but how individuals should be (*i.e.*, flexible, able to learn and have an entrepreneurial spirit) (Simons 2006).

Conclusion

The formal influence of the EU on Swedish education policy has been limited. Education policy is an area in which the EU's role is only to support and recommend. The formal sovereignty that includes constitutionally regulated decision-making rights has not been affected by EU membership, and the EU can formally only support the education policy of member states. Nevertheless, the EU has had a direct influence on education in Sweden. Essential adaptations took place when in 2007, Sweden adapted its system to be a part of the Bologna Process, the implementation of which clearly changed the Swedish higher education system. The PISA skills and knowledge assessments play a central role in the debate of how the Swedish school system should be reformed. The Lisbon Strategy has also directly affected Sweden. The increased cooperation between the education ministers has resulted in an action plan that is the framework within which education policy development takes place. Several policy declarations and programmes have come out of the Lisbon Strategy, and consequently, Sweden now participates in common European discussions on the direction of education policy. Sweden has adhered to the Lisbon Convention for mutual recognition of foreign education, including education and training for access to study programmes and courses, crediting periods of study and admission to continued studies. The convention further means that the participating countries must recognise the different education and training in order to support access to employment in a country other than the one in which the original studies took place.

Education policy is interesting in terms of differences between formal and actual sovereignty because the EU activities in this area do not at all reflect the weak provisions in the treaties. Since the Lisbon Strategy was implemented, the EU has emphasised the connections between education and economic growth and welfare, which has given the area an important position in the EU cooperation. Through the OMC, the possibility for the EU to be a policy maker has become a reality. The developments in education have clear features of 'governance at a distance' (Castells 1997). Policy making is influenced by many participants, and there is an unclear central power. Instead, steering takes place through organised networks of public and private actors that lead the open policy towards common targets (Rhodes 1996). As for goals and guidelines, there are no real differences between Sweden and the EU. In terms of 'fit' and 'misfit' (*cf.* Radelli 2003) (*i.e.*, the existence of a distance between Swedish and EU policy that can be the basis of the Europeanisation of Swedish education policy), there is no such slack. Instead, there is an indirect Europeanisation process, in which the EU institutions and policy influence Swedish education policy.

References

Agency of Higher Education. 1998. *De första 20 åren: utvecklingen vid de mindre och medelstora högskolorna sedan 1997*. Stockholm: Högskoleverket

Alexiadou, N. 2010. 'Policy Learning and Governance of Educational Policy in EU'. *Journal of Education Policy*, 25(4).

Arnman, G., M. Järnek & E. Lindskog 2004. *Valfrihet – fiktion och verklighet.* Uppsala: Uppsala Univ.

Askling, B. 2012. *Expansion, självständighet, konkurrens. Vart är den högre utbildningen på väg?.* Göteborg: University of Gothenburg

Ball, S. 2008. *The Education Debate.* Bristol: Policy Press.

Borrás, S & Jacobsson K 2004. 'The open method of coordination and new governance patterns in the EU'. *Journal of European Public Policy,* 11(2).

Bråten, I. 1998. *Vygotskij och pedagogiken*. Lund: Studentlitteratur.

Castells, M. (1997). *Power of Identity: The Information Age: Economy, Society, and Culture*. Blackwell Publishers, Inc..

Cini, M, & N. Borragan 2013. *European Union Politics*. Oxford: Oxford University press.

Education Council 2001. *Report from the Education Council to the European Council: The concrete future objectives of education and training systems*, 14 February 2001, 5680/01 EDU 18.

— 2009, 'Education and Training 2020'. *Council conclusions of 12 May 2009 on a strategic framework for European cooperation in education and training* [Official journal of the European Union C119 from 28/05/2009].

Education Council and European Commission 2002. 'ET 2010.' *Detailed work programme on the follow-up of the objectives of Education and training systems in Europe*, Official Journal C 142, 14/06/2002.

European Commission 2010. 'Youth on the Move – An initiative to unleash the potential of young people to achieve smart, sustainable and inclusive growth in the European Union'. Luxembourg: Publications Office of the European Union.

— 2018. Education and Training monitor 2018. Luxembourg: Publications Office of the European Union.

— 1996. *Education, Training, Research: The obstacles to transnational mobility* COM (96) 462.

— 2003. *Communication from the Commission. The role of the universities in the Europe of knowledge.* COM (2003) 58 final.

— 2006. *The history of European cooperation in education and training: Europe in the making- An example.* Luxemburg: Publication Office of the European Union.

— 2008. *Education and training 2010: Main policy Initiatives and Outputs in Education and Training since the year 2000.*

— 2014. *Erasmus – Facts, Figures & Trends: The European Union support for student and staff exchanges and university cooperation in 2012–2013.* http://ec.europa.eu/education/library/statistics/ay-12-13/facts-figures_en.pdf

— 2015a. *ET working groups presentation 201.*http://ec.europa.eu/education/policy/strategic-framework/expert-groups/documents/et2020-presentation_en.pdf).

— 2015b. *Education and training Monitor 2015 – Sweden.* Publication Office of the European Union. Luxemburg:

European Council 2000. *European Council Meeting in Lisbon, 23 and 24 March 2000 – Conclusions.*

Eurostat (2018). 'Smarter, greener, more inclusive? Indicators to support the Europe 2020 strategy'. Luxembourg: Publications Office of the European Union.

Eurydice, 2007. *Focus on the Structure of Higher Education in Europe 2006/07 National Trends in the Bologna Process.* European Unit: Brussels.

Fanghanel, J. 2011. *Being an Academic.* New York & London: Routledge.

Fritzell, A 1998. *Hur styrs den svenska högskolan? Varför ser styrsystemet ut som det gör?* Stockholm: Högskoleverket.

Garben, S. 2011. *EU Higher education law – The Bologna Process and Harmonization by Stealth.* Alphen aan den Rijn: Kluwer Law International.

Grek, S. 2009. 'Governing by Numbers: The Pisa 'Effect' in Europe'. *Journal of Education Policy* 24(1).

Grek, S., M. Lawn, B. Lingard, J. Ozga, R. Rinne, C. Segerholm & H. Simola 2009. 'National policy brokering and the construction of the European Education Space in England, Sweden, Finland and Scotland'. *Comparative Education,* 45(1).

Hingel A. J. 2001.'Education Policies and European Governance: contribution to the interservice groups on European governance'. *European Journal for Education, Law and Policy*, 5(1–2)

Lawn, M. 2011. 'Standardizing the European Education Policy Space'. *European Educational Research Journal, 10(2).*

Lindensjö, B. & U. Lundgren 2002. *Politisk styrning och utbildningsreformer*. Stockholm: HLS förlag

Martens, K. 2007. 'How to become an influential actor – the 'comparative turn' in the OECD Education Policy' In: S. Leibfried, A. Rusconi K. Leuze, K. Martens, (eds.) *New Arenas of Education Governance – The Impact of International Organizations and Markets on Educational Policy Making*. London: Routledge

Nordin, A. 2012. *Kunskapens politik: En studie av kunskapsdiskurser i svensk och Europeisk utbildningspolicy*. Växjö: Linnaeus University Press.

OECD 2015. *Improving Schools in Sweden: An OECD Perspective*. Paris: OECD.

Pongratz, L. 2006. 'Voluntary self-control: Education reform as a governmental strategy'. *Education Philosophy and Theory*, 38(4): 471–82.

Power, M. 1999. *The Audit Society: Rituals of Verification*. Oxford: Oxford University Press.

Radelli, C. 2003. *The Open Method of Coordination – A New Governance Architecture for the European Union*. Research report, Swedish Institute for European Policy Studies 1.

Rhodes, M. 1996. 'Globalization and West European welfare states: a critical review of recent debates'. *Journal of European Social Policy*, 6(4), 305–327.

Riksdag Rapid Protocol 1999/2000:92

Rothstein, B. 1986. *Den socialdemokratiska staten. Reformer och förvaltning inom svensk arbetsmarknads- och skolpolitik*. Lund: Studentlitteratur.

Simons M. 2006. 'Learning as investment. Notes on governmentality and biopolitics'. *Educational Philosophy and Theory*, 20 (4).

Sjöberg, L. 2011. *Bäst i klassen? Lärare och elever i svenska och europeiska policytexter*. Department of Education, Communication and Learning; Institutionen för pedagogik, kommunikation och lärande.

Sjöberg, L. 2009. 'Skolan och den 'goda' utbildningen – för ett konkurrenskraftigt Europa'. *Utbildning & Demokrati*, 18(1).

Skolverket (2016). PISA 2015. 15-åringars kunskaper i naturvetenskap, läsförståelse och matematik. Rapport 450. Stockholm: Skolverket.

Swedish Government Bill 1990/91:18. *Ansvaret för skolan*.

— 1991/92:95. *Valfrihet och fristående skolor*.

— 2004:2. *Högre utbildning i utveckling – Bolognaprocessen i svensk belysning*.

— 2004/05:162. *Ny värld – ny högskola*.

Swedish Government report 1996:21. Reform och förändring – Organisation och verksamhet vid universitet och högskolor efter 1993 års universitets- och högskolereform. Stockholm: Statens Offentliga Utredningar.

Swedish Higher Education Ordinance (1993:100) Chapter 6 Section 2.

Treaty on the European Union (consolidated version 2012).

Treaty on the Functioning of the European Union (consolidated version 2012).

Trägårdh, L. 1993. *The concept of the people and the construction of popular political culture in Germany and Sweden 1848–1933*. Berkeley: University of California.

Wahlström, N. 2010. 'A European space for education looking for its public'. *European Educational Research Journal* (Online), 432.

Wallace, H. 2001. 'The changing politics of the European Union: an overview.' *Journal of Common Market Studies*, 39(4).

Warleigh-Lack, A. R. Drachenberg 2011. 'Spillover in a soft policy area? Evidence from the Open Method of Co-ordination in education and training'. *Journal of European Public Policy*, 18:7.

— 2013. 'Policy-making in the European Union' In: M. Cini & Borragan *European Union Politics*, 2013. Oxford: Oxford University press.

Wächter, B. 2012. 'An ever closer union? The role of 'Brussels' in shaping European higher education' In: D. Greenaway& C. Ennew (eds.) *The Globalization of Higher Education*, London: Palgrave.

8. Gender Equality Policy

From Equal Treatment to Intersectional Gender Equality

Sofia Strid

Gender equality is important to the Swedes. The country continuously rank high in European and global gender equality indices (EIGE, 2017; World Economic Forum, 2017), which is regularly reported in the national press and by the Swedish government's communication office. The current Prime Minister, social democrat Stefan Löfvén, claims to lead the world's first feminist government, meaning that 'gender equality is essential to the government's priorities' (the Swedish Government, 2016). Modern gender equality policy, from public child care provisions, paid parental leave and equal pay to safe abortions, brought onto the policy agenda in the 1960s with the challenging of sex/gender roles, have for a long time been mainstream and uncontroversial. Thus, many feared that Sweden's membership in the EU would dilute Swedish gender equality policy, stultify Swedish efforts to promote gender equality, and preserve Swedish welfare (Fridolfsson, 2006; see also the European Parliament (EP), 2015). In the Swedish debate, conceptions of Swedish gender equality were contrasted with what was framed as a regressive and unequal EU. That gender equality is one of the EU's basic values since the entrance into force of the Lisbon Treaty in 2009 is of little interest.

Simultaneously, the Swedish politicizing and prioritization of gender equality have recently sparked controversy and conflict. As in much of the rest of the EU, the last ten years has seen the rise of anti-feminist movements and anti-feminist politics. The third largest political party in the Swedish Parliament, anti-feminist, male dominated and with fascist roots (Lodenius, 2018), Sweden Democrats, argues for a limitation of abortion rights, the feminisation of parental leave, the primate of the heterosexual, biological, nuclear family, and the reinstatement of family/joint taxation, a serious disincentive for women's employment which was abolished in 1971 with the gender equality policy programs (SD, 2018). However, discourses framing Sweden as gender equal and the EU as unequal continue to permeate the Swedish debate.

This chapter provides a nuanced perspective on the EU's 'conservative' gender equality policy and 'feminist' Sweden. The focus is how the Swedish EU membership has affected the institutionalisation of Swedish gender equality policy in terms of *organisation* and *content*.

The first section below theorises gender equality and visions thereof. It exemplifies these theoretical perspectives by using Swedish and EU policy measures. The purpose is to conceptualise the actual and practical policies pursued and to highlight the issues involved in order to make visible the broad trends in gender equality policy developments shared by Sweden and the EU. The second section describes the emergence of Swedish gender equality policy and its content. It opens by addressing the question of what Swedish gender equality policy aims to achieve. The concrete gender equality policy developments are tied to a specific vision of gender equality. Differences and similarities to the development of the EU's gender equality policy are described. The third section describes the formal decision-making powers in the area of gender equality and the EU's gender equality policy base. Four policy fields, central to the development of and regulation of gender equality policy in Sweden and the EU, are examined: gender-based violence (GBV), equal treatment, employment and parenting. The fourth and final section discusses the Europeanisation of Swedish gender equality policy and the presentation of conclusions about how and to what extent Sweden's membership in the EU has influenced Swedish gender equality policy.

The Meaning of Gender Equality

The specific content and the implementation of gender equality in practice are highly debated and charged issues. In Swedish and European political contexts, the idea that gender equality should be pursued is relatively uncontentious (EP, 2015; the Swedish Government, 2015; the European Council, 2015). However, what is far from uncontentious is the question of *how* gender equality is to be achieved – by *which* means/strategies – and, more specifically, *what* is to be achieved, *i.e.*, the content of gender equality (Verloo *et al.*, 2011).

What, then, is gender equality? Gender equality can be seen as a means, as a strategy for achieving some other, higher-valued goal such as economic growth, social democracy, or reduced crime. In the EU, gender equality has historically tended to be seen as a means by which to achieve other more important goals, such as full employment and economic growth (the Amsterdam Treaty, 1997; the Council of Europe, 2011). Gender equality can also be an end in itself: a social and political vision to be achieved with the help of other political strategies, *e.g.*, paid parental leave, individual taxation, or fast track domestic violence courts (Armstrong *et al.*, 2009; Strid *et al.*, 2008; see also the QUING project 2006–2011).[1] This latter version, gender equality as a goal in itself, is a framing more suitable for Swedish gender equality policy (Kvist, 2008). There are at least four visions, or meanings, of gender equality:

- Gender equality as sameness: equal opportunities for women and men (the sameness or equal treatment perspective);
- Gender equality as difference: the equal valuation of women's and men's different contributions, functions, and positions (the women's perspective or difference-focused thinking);
- Gender equality as transformation: the restructuring of social structures and systems (the gender perspective; transformation) (Rees, 1998; Armstrong *et al.*, 2009);
- Gender equality as intersectionality: gender equality as inclusive of more than just sex/gender, women and men, and as explicitly based on the equality of social groups at the intersection of multiple, complex inequalities in addition to gender,

1 In Swedish research, another very common typology is gender equality as a rights argument, an interest argument, and a resource/benefit argument (see Jónasdóttir, 1991; Rönnblom, 1997; Wendt Höjer & Åse, 1999). However, as a vision or strategy, gender equality functions as a meta-typology.

such as ethnicity, class, religion, physical ability, and transsexuality (Strid, 2017, 2018; Walby *et al.*, 2012ab).

The first vision of gender equality, sameness, is to be achieved through equal treatment strategies and through the removal of formal barriers to equal participation (Booth & Bennet, 2002; Andersson 2017). The equal treatment perspective allows for the equal treatment of women and men in the public sphere. Women are to be given the opportunity to participate on the same terms as men. This perspective is tied to the first wave feminists, who fought for voting rights and education, equal pay for equal work, and equal rights for women and men. Legislation is the main medium used for the removal of formal barriers. This is therefore a form of negative freedom (Berlin, 1958) which guarantees equal opportunities for participation and the exploitation of women's resources. Two examples of how this vision is translated into concrete policy are the principle of equal pay for equal work outlined in the Treaty of Rome (1958) and the EU directive on equal pay for equal and equivalent work (European Council Directive 75/117/EG).

The second vision of gender equality, the equal valuation of difference, is to be achieved through specific measures directed solely towards women or (more rarely) men (Hearn *et al.*, 2016) and affirmative action. A women's perspective inspires initiatives aimed at promoting women as a disadvantaged social group, a group that can legitimately be treated differently than men. This form of policy aims to correct past injustices and prevent systematic, 'built-in' discrimination, *i.e.*, institutionalised discrimination. The women's perspective allows for different treatment of women and men and uses preferential treatment as a means by which to achieve equality (Phillips, 1998; Strid *et al.*, 2012). An example of such targeted measures and difference-focused thinking is the EU's introduction of two mandatory maternity weeks (Council Directive 96/34/EG), and, not least, affirmative action in the workplace, as outlined in the Amsterdam Treaty (1999).

The third vision, transformation, is achieved through the integration of a gender perspective in all policy areas. In European literature, this is referred to as 'gender mainstreaming' and in the Swedish context it is called 'jämställdhetsintegrering' (literally, 'gender equality integration') (Andersson & Hedlund, 2014). A gender perspective means that the focus moves from women to the relationship between women and men and a supportive policy foundation which aims to transform the organisation of society in a manner that leads to a fairer distribution of responsibilities. This involves the development of strategies that aim to not only change conditions for women, but also to alter the conditions for men and the relationship between the genders (Walby, 2005). The vision is realised by employing gender-aware and gender-sensitive tools in the creation of policy. Examples of such policy include the EU's gender equality mainstreaming of the European Commission's Action Plan 1991–1995 (the European Commission, 1990), gender budgeting (the European Commission, 1996) and the EU Parental Leave Directive (1996).

The emergence of a fourth vision – intersectionality – is further examined in this chapter. The theoretical starting point of such a vision is the debate of what intersectionality is and how it influences both gender equality and gender. In English, this has been theorised as the dynamic between 'intersectional gender' and 'gendered intersectionalities (Hearn *et al.*, 2016), and is here understood as a form of gendered intersectionality: gender equality as inclusive of more than just sex/gender, women and men, and is explicitly based on the equality of social groups at the intersection of multiple, complex inequalities in addition to gender, such as ethnicity, class, religion, physical ability, and transsexuality. (Strid, 2017, 2018).

The Emergence and Objectives of Swedish Gender Equality Policy

Swedish gender equality policy is based on a notion of equality as a matter of power between women and men, and the idea that measures to alter the current power relations must be aimed at transforming both formal and informal social structures (SOU 2005:66; SOU 2006:5; SOU 2015:78). The objective is that women and men are to have the same power and influence to shape society and their own lives. The goal was adopted in 2006 on the basis of the legislative bill *Makt att forma samhället och sitt eget liv – nya mål i jämställdhetspolitiken* ('The power to shape society and one's own life – new objectives in gender equality policy' (Prop. 2005/06:155; see also SOU 2005:66; the Power Inquiry (2006), and the objectives laid down in the 2015 Gender Equality Inquiry (SOU 2015:86)).[2]

In order to achieve the overall gender equality objective, the Swedish government is working towards six sub-goals:

- *Politics*: Gender equal division of power and influence. Women and men are to have the same rights and opportunities to be active citizens and to shape the conditions for decision-making.
- *Economy*: Economic gender equality. Women and men must have the same opportunities and conditions as regards paid work which give economic independence throughout life.
- *Education*: Gender equal education. Women and men, girls and boys must have the same opportunities and conditions with regard to education, study options and personal development.
- *Family*: Equal equal distribution of unpaid housework and provision of care. Women and men must have the same responsibility for housework and have the opportunity to give and receive care on equal terms.
- *Health*: Gender equal health. Women and men, girls and boys must have the same conditions for a good health and be offered care on equal terms.
- *Violence*: Men's violence against women must stop. Women and men, girls and boys, must have the same right and access to physical integrity.

Strictly speaking, the EU lacks formal decision-making powers in four of these six sub-goals of Swedish gender equality policy: political decision-making, family, education, and violence. The EU has no formal power to make binding decisions regarding Member States' internal decision-making processes, education policy, family policy, or efforts to prevent violence against women. However, the EU can

2 In the Swedish government's Gender Equality Inquiry, which was presented in 2015, two new target areas, education and health, were added to Swedish gender equality policy (SOU 2015:86).

use other instruments of change and control. As is described later in the chapter, this affects the development of EU gender equality policy and the Europeanisation of Swedish gender equality policy, especially with regard to the framework and the discursive construction of EU gender equality policy.

The institutionalised Swedish gender equality policy has its origins in the 1960s research report *Kvinnors liv och arbete* ('The Life and Work of Women') (1962), the introduction of the concept of gender roles, and the first motions to enact coherent legislation to prevent discrimination against women, drafted by the People's Party in 1970.[3] During the 1970s, gender equality gained legitimacy as a political area and was incorporated into the agendas of Sweden's political parties. The women's movement and feminist organisations played a very important role in this process (Bergqvist, 1999). In the 1970s, gender equality in Sweden became formally politicised. This shift was initiated by the government in power, which appointed the *Delegation for Equality* (1973). In research on the subject, the creation of the delegation is considered to have been a crucial step in the institutionalisation of Swedish gender equality policy.

In both the 1970s and 1980s, the central issue of gender equality policy was women's rights and the actual opportunity for full employment. The Swedish model of gender equality can be said to be based on the reduced gap in employment rates between women and men (Hedlund 2009; Hobson 2003). The increased participation of women in paid work was primarily made possible by three factors: women's increased participation in the education system, the development of public child and elder care and the transition from

3 Yet Swedish gender equality policy has a much longer history than that. In the 13th century, Birger Jarl enshrined the duty to protect women and the women's peace in law (Hearn *et al.*, 2016). In 1700s, certain women were granted the right to vote. The law ensuring equal inheritance rights for brothers and sisters was adopted in 1845. In the early 1900s, marriage legislation was modernised and a husband's formal power over his wife was abolished. The legislation gave married women and men equal responsibility for the family, and represented an early move away from the male single-provider model (Melby *et al.*, 2011). The 1930s saw an increase in paid work for women, and with the expansion of public child care, the gainful employment of women grew significantly in Sweden compared to the rest of Scandinavia and Europe. Paid work for women has been crucial to Swedish gender equality (Hernes, 1987; Esping Andersen, 2004).

joint taxation to individual taxation; the individual income tax was implemented in Sweden in 1970 (Florin & Nilsson, 1999; Lister, 2011). A fourth important gender reform was introduced in 1974, when Sweden became the first country in the world to introduce paid parental leave for fathers – a reform that has yet to be implemented in the EU – and transformed the maternity allowance into parental insurance (Klinth, 2002). Together, these reforms enabled the women's dual workload; the reforms freed up parts of the female labour force, and this 'womanpower' could be transferred from unpaid care work in the home in the private sphere to paid work in the public sphere. Along with improved incentives for paid work (both in terms of increased demand for labour and the transition from joint taxation to individual taxation), the fiscally and socially progressive policies of the Swedish (Nordic) two-provider model had a substantial effect on gender equality. Among Swedish women, the part-time employment rate is still one of the highest in Europe; 40 per cent of Swedish women work part-time, compared with 33 per cent of women in the EU.

In this case, gender equality as economic equality is made visible through the abandonment of the single-provider model and in the ideal of sameness and equal treatment: women should the same opportunities for paid work as men. At the same time, the introduction of a month of paid paternal leave led to a transformation of gender relations. There was a historical-institutional idea of a spill-over effect, namely that gender equality in the labour market could spill over into other areas of policy. In the Swedish context, this came to mean that the state became involved in what is traditionally and internationally considered the private sphere (in contrast to the public sphere). Not everyone favoured the imposition of legislation in this area; the Social Democrats, for example, were initially averse to the idea. The reason for this resistance was Sweden's strong tradition of negotiation between social partners, whose ability to negotiate and regulate the labour market was afforded a great amount of confidence. Despite the trade union protests, the 1970s came to be characterised by comprehensive gender equality legislation in both the economic policy area and the area of family policy: individual taxation, the right to free abortion, paid parental leave, expanded public childcare, equal pay and equality in education (Karlsson, 1996).

The Equal Treatment Act (Act 1979:1118) was adopted in 1979 under a government led by the Centre Party in coalition with the Moderate Party and the Liberals, who were the strongest driving force behind the law. It prohibits gender discrimination in the workplace and requires that all employers in both the public and private sectors actively promote equality (understood in this context as equal opportunities for women and men) in the workplace. It is worth noting that equal pay is not regulated in Swedish legislation. However, four years earlier the EU's Equal Pay Directive had enshrined that right in law (European Council Directive 1975/117/EG). Employers with 10 or more employees were ordered to adopt annual action plans addressing equal opportunities and equal pay. Gender equality was a liberal, emancipatory project based on a negative freedom ideal – that is to say, freedom from something (Berlin, 1958). In this case, women were guaranteed freedom from discrimination in the workplace. In tune with this policy, a special machinery (a gender equality machinery) evolved. The Gender Equality Delegation, the Gender Equality Commission, the Minister for Gender Equality, and eventually the Equality Ombudsman (1980) were all created, and together had a special mandate to monitor the implementation of the Gender Equality Act of 1980. In both Sweden and the European Union (albeit with a four-year gap), the form, content, machinery and legislation of the policy were developed. All are in line with the initial vision of gender equality based on equality between women and men, which is to be achieved through both equal treatment strategies and the removal of formal barriers. Both cases involve a principle of equal treatment that is intended to be applied in the public workplace.

A new Swedish Equal Opportunities Act (1991) extended the provisions of the earlier law to cover both direct and indirect gender discrimination and regulated more active measures to promote equality. The law allowed affirmative action on the part of under-represented genders and thus marked a departure from the previous equality and equal treatment principle of Swedish gender equality policy. In Swedish political governance, a concrete example of this thinking are the so-called Tham Professorships, named after Carl Tham, who served as the Minister for Education at the time of their creation. Established in 1995, the positions constituted a measure that was intended to increase the proportion of female professors in higher education. 30 professorships and 50 graduate assistantships were set aside for women (Bergqvist *et al.*, 2008). Because this approach implemented specific measures that only applied to women, it demonstrated the prevailing difference-focused thinking of Swedish gender equality policy. Affirmative action is not specific to Swedish gender equality policy. The European Commission's *Action Plan on Equal Opportunities for Women and Men 1982–1985* specified affirmative action as a means by which to combat discrimination against women in the workplace. The European Council recommendation, which was adopted in December 1984, advocates that the EU Member States to 'adopt a positive action policy designed to eliminate existing inequalities affecting women in working life and to promote a better balance between the sexes in employment' (the European Council, 1984; Article 1; *cf.* the European Commission, 1985).

In 1994, the Swedish Government made the decision to use gender mainstreaming as a strategy for achieving the objectives of the gender policy adopted in 1994 in the *Shared Power. Shared Responsibility* bill (1993/94:147). Gender mainstreaming means that a gender perspective should be incorporated into all decision-making processes, at all levels, and in all stages of the policy process, *i.e.*, in all planning and control of state and municipal activities. It can be a radical and transformative medium (Verloo, 2005; Walby, 2005), but has also been criticised because it often becomes a side strategy (Stratigaki, 2005). The EU introduced gender mainstreaming three years earlier, in 1991, through its *Third Action Programme for Equal Opportunities for Women and Men* (1991).[4]

An additional shift in the focus of Swedish gender equality policy came in 2006, when the parliamentary committee proposed 'coherent anti-discrimination legislation' (SOU 2006:22), thus calling into question the hitherto institutional, one-dimensional regulation of

4 Sweden is often regarded as the leading country in terms of gender mainstreaming. The government's 1994 bill is often cited as a reference. In fact, gender mainstreaming had been proposed nearly a decade earlier at the third United Nations World Conference on Women, held in Nairobi in 1985. The idea is thus a Swedish import rather than a national invention. Gender budgeting can also be traced to one of the UN women's conferences, namely the one held in Beijing in 1995 (UN, 1995).

anti-discrimination. In line with the national public inquiry, the government proposed a coherent anti-discrimination legislation (Bill 2005/06:155), a merger of the discrimination ombudsmen, an integrated Ministry of Gender Equality, and an integrated gender equality portfolio for the responsible minister. All of these proposals were in accordance with the UN's Paris Principles, which were adopted on December 20, 1993. In 2009, the Discrimination Act (2008:567) was adopted. It merged five anti-discrimination laws and seven grounds for discrimination: sex, gender identity, ethnicity, religion, disability, sexual orientation, and age. The Discrimination Act marks the institutionalisation of intersectionality in Swedish gender equality policy. Gender equality is no longer the sole focus. Rather, it favours an intersectional equality perspective that takes into account the way in which gender interacts with other axes of power/grounds for discrimination.

The development of Swedish gender equality policy encompasses all four of the initially presented visions of gender equality In the course of its evolution, policy has moved away from the initial equality and equal treatment perspective with a vision of gender equality based on the equality of women and men and equal rights in the workplace (1979). Affirmative action and quota strategies (1986) were the next step in the development. This was followed by the enactment of gender mainstreaming legislation (1994) which virtually institutionalised intersectional gender equality (2006). The last of these steps was made manifest through the creation of a coherent Discrimination Ombudsman and discrimination legislation (2009).

The development is by no means unique to Sweden; it is also evident in both EU Member States and at level of the EU itself (Lombardo & Verloo, 2009; see EU, 1993). The same four theoretical perspectives on gender equality dominate both Swedish and European discourse, and are an example of Europeanisation through the transfer of norms.

The Authoritative Powers of EU Gender Equality Policy

Seen from a European perspective, the Swedish model of gender equality has its foundations in an essentially Socialist welfare state model, with paid work as a basis (the Democracy Council, 2010).

Esping-Andersen (2000: 4) writes that what is striking about the Swedish and Nordic models are their 'emphasis on employment and the de-familiarisation of responsibility for providing welfare', which has maximized women's financial independence from men (see also Hernes, 1987). The EU, on the other hand, is often regarded as a market liberal deregulation project (Walby, 2005, 2015). The conditions which research has shown to strengthen gender equality – a high degree of female political representation, women's political mobilisation and social democratic politics (Bergqvist, *et al.*, 2008) – are weak throughout the EU.[5] The emergence of gender equality policy within the EU can thus be regarded as either contradictory (if gender equality is to be understood as an end in itself) or, in light of market economic objectives, as a rational political means and strategy for increased production and economic growth. The latter interpretation has often dominated.

EU gender equality policy is a coherent policy area with four priority areas: equal pay for work of equal value, equal decision-making opportunities for women and men, equal financial independence, and violence against women (the European Commission, 2016). These are the same four priority areas as in Swedish gender equality policy. Some researchers argue that because the EU does not have exclusive authoritative power in many of the issues which in Swedish politics are regarded as central to gender equality policy, Europe cannot be said to have a gender equality policy. Others argue that equality de facto falls within the EU's sphere of authoritative power: gender equality is one of the common objectives of the EU (The Treaty of Amsterdam, 1999), one of the Union's fundamental values (the Treaty of Lisbon

5 In the EU, the political mobilisation of women, as well as the mobilisation of other groups, has traditionally been regarded as weak. Among other things, conclusions about weak social movements have been based partly on the absence of a European civil society – a demos – and partly on the numerical lack of non-governmental organisations (NGOs). Based on access to decision-makers, networks, strength of organisation, and financing, the perception of the European women's movement as weak may be called into question. Since its formation in 1991, the European Women's Lobby (EWL) has brought together over 4000 European women's organisations in all the EU Member States. The lobby is funded by the European Commission and has official status in the European Parliament. In the early 2000s, there was talk of 'revolving doors' between the EWL and the Commission (Strid, 2009).

2009), and can be traced back to the principle of equal pay for equal work (The Treaty of Rome, 1958). Article I-2 of the Treaty on European Union (TEU) establishes that 'The Union is founded on the values of respect for human dignity, freedom, democracy, equality, the rule of law and respect for human rights, including the rights of persons belonging to minorities'. The values listed in Article I-2 are common to the Member States. Moreover, the treaty states that 'these values are common to the Member States in a society in which pluralism, non-discrimination, tolerance, justice, solidarity and equality between women and men prevail'. These values play an important role, especially in two specific cases. Firstly, respect for these values is a prerequisite for any new Member State joining the Union, pursuant to the procedure laid out in Article I-58. Secondly, a lack of respect for these values can cause the entitlement of a Member State to Union membership to be suspended (Article I-59).

Thus, the precise location of gender equality authoritative powers is not entirely clear. It can at least be established that certain powers within the gender equality policy area are located in part at the national level. Shared authoritative power applies in areas relating to the sociopolitical parts of the TEU, which are covered by treaties on economic, social and territorial cohesion, the area of freedom, security and justice, and common security concerns with regard to aspects of public health. The EU only has supportive authority in the area of protection and improvement of human health. Many issues related to gender equality thus fall within the scope of shared authoritative power. As previously mentioned, the Swedish gender equality objectives include power and influence, work, family, and violence. The EU has no power to make decisions in the area of violence against women (Kelly *et al.*, 2011),[6] but has shared authoritative power in the area of freedom, security and justice as well as the internal market, and also has exclusive authoritative rights in the area of customs union, *i.e.*,

6 This issue is debated. According to sociologist Sylvia Walby and her colleagues (2014), the treaty gives the EU the right to regulate violence against women: 1) violence against women involves combatting international crime (crossing borders), *e.g.*, trafficking and prostitution, and 2) violence is included in the gender equality policy, and gender equality is one of the fundamental values of the Union (the Treaty of Amsterdam).

the area relating to the crossing of borders. This means that the EU can make laws relating to specific forms of violence against women, provided they can be formulated in such a way that they fall within the scope of EU authority. Examples of this are the area of trafficking for sexual exploitation, which involves the crossing of borders, an EU area of authority. In connection with the 2010 football World Cup in Germany, the EU was able to invoke border policy as grounds for intervention in the German legislation on prostitution. The EU opined that Germany's construction of brothels adjacent to the stadiums would lead to the increased trafficking – crossing of borders – of women for sexual exploitation. There were no football brothels during the 2010 championship.

The EU has thus affected its Member States' legislation in the gender equality area of violence against women, despite the absence of specific authoritative power. However, some believe that the EU has the power to go even further. Because violence against women is defined as a form of discrimination against women by a number of major players in the field, including the EU and the Member States in connection with the ratification of CEDAW (UN, 1979) and the Council of Europe's Istanbul Convention (2011), the legislation from the EU's side is legitimised by Article 19 and Article 157 of the Treaty on European Union.

That said, there is no European gender equality law, gender equality commissioner, or directorate-general for gender equality. Instead, large parts of EU gender equality policy and action plans are implemented through the European Commission's communications, European Parliament resolutions and reports, or via the agreements of the Council of Ministers. There is no gender equality directive.

The Content of the Gender Equality Policy of the EU

In terms of its content, EU gender equality policy is based on the same four theoretical principles which are highlighted in the emergence of Swedish gender equality policy: equal treatment (the Treaty of Rome, 1957; Dir 75/117/EG), affirmative action (the Amsterdam Treaty, 1997), gender mainstreaming (the European Commission's Action Plan, 1991) and intersectional equality (the Anti-Discrimination

Directives, Directive 2000/43/EG; Directive 2000/78/EG; Booth & Bennet, 2002; Strid *et al.*, 2008). Three areas affected by these principles are equal treatment in the workplace, employment policy, and family policy. These are three areas in which either the EU shares authoritative power or the Member States have exclusive authority.

Equal Treatment and Pay Policy

The first EU gender equality measures, *i.e.*, the principles of the Treaty of Rome regarding equal treatment and equal pay, were intended to counter the imbalance in competitive advantages between the Member States. The principle of equal pay for equal work was introduced after France expressed concern that low women's wages and poorer social benefits for women in other Member States would give those countries competitive advantages in a single European market. The EU's earliest gender equality policy measures were not about equality in and of itself, but rather implemented equality as a means to an end: market principles, competition and economic growth justified equal pay. Thus, the EU's equal treatment policy is not founded on a women's rights perspective. Rather, its content is very narrow, even though the means – treaties and directives – which the EU has at its disposal can be characterised as very powerful. The EU-drafted policies in this area are legally binding for the Member States, and the European Court has the right to examine whether national legislation is in accordance with EU legislation.

There is comprehensive gender equality legislation which deals with *work*. The European Council Directive on Equal Pay for Equal and Equivalent Work (Dir 75/117/EG) and the Directive on Access to Employment, Vocational Training and Promotion, and Working Conditions (Dir 76/207/EEG), which were ratified by the Treaty of Amsterdam (1997), stated that women and men shall be treated equally, not just when it comes to wages, but also in terms of hiring, promotions and opportunities for further training.

The European Council Directive on Social Security (Dir. 79/7/EEG) ensures that women and men shall have equal rights to social security and public and private social insurance (sickness, pension, unemployment). The Swedish Gender Equality Act, which was added in 1981, was not sufficient for Swedish entry into the EU. Swedish membership necessitated the reinforcement and clarification of the Gender Equality Act. The law was thus both more diffuse and weaker than the EU directives. At least in part, this was due to the fact that the Swedish model is based on collective agreements and negotiations between social partners, rather than on legislation in the area (Bergkvist *et al.*, 2008). As mentioned earlier, the Swedish Gender Equality Act, met resistance from social partners, because legislation generally weakens these parties' influence on the labour market. The implementation of the EU directives called for clarification of how one should go about handling wage discrimination, a change that meant the law could apply to hiring instead of only to employment, and a definition of both indirect and direct discrimination. On these three points, Swedish gender equality policy has been Europeanised.

Employment Policy: Paid and Unpaid Work

EU employment policy constitutes the core of its gender equality policy. During the 1990s, European employment policy was designed to increase Europe's competitiveness and growth. In all EU Member States, more men were gainfully employed than women, and this remains the case. Increased employment for women was believed to contribute to increased growth, increased competitiveness, and (as a consequence or virtual side effect of this) increased equality. This meant that gender equality was once again used as a means by which to increase economic growth. As we have seen, the Swedish model of gender equality has its roots in the goal of reducing the gap in employment rates between women and men – which in itself is dependent on a redistribution of paid and unpaid work, as well as extensive public childcare – and in the individualisation of parental insurance. There are no EU directives in the field of employment, which instead is governed through the open co-ordination model. Because it relates to tax and welfare policies, Member States do not wish to assign formal decision-making powers to the EU in this area. Instead, the EU's Member States have formulated common objectives within the framework of the EU's employment policy, but have not established a binding directive. The objectives aim to increase the employment rate of women, in part through expanded public childcare. EU legislation in this area is referred to as 'soft law' and consists of common objectives, recommendations and action plans. Thus, it does not constitute Europeanisation in the sense of an assertion by the EU of overriding influence over national forms of governance (Olsen, 2003).

Family Policy: Children and Parenting

The EU's gender equality policy aims to facilitate women's employment by allowing the combination of paid work and parenthood. The low European birthrate has long been considered a challenge. One of the reasons is the difficulty of reconciling paid work with responsibility for unpaid work; that is, the difficulty of reconciling work with family life (work-life balance). Swedish gender equality policy in this area is transformative, meaning that the policy creates change through the regulation of parental leave and the power relationships between the sexes.

The EU regulates parental leave by means of a minimum directive (Dir. 96/34/EC) and childcare through norm-setting (the Barcelona Objectives). The Parental Leave Directive gives women and men an individual right to parental leave (without pay) for the care of children who are less than three months old. The fact that this right is individual means that the days cannot be transferred from one parent to the other. The reason why the directive does not stipulate parental leave with pay is that the EU does not have formal decision-making powers when it comes to compensation levels. The directive is a minimum directive; Member States can make laws providing longer leave, but not shorter.

The implementation of the directive forced many member countries, including the United Kingdom and Luxembourg, to introduce parental leave. In the Swedish debate, the conclusion was often drawn that the directive on parental leave and childcare had no consequences for Swedish legislation (Bergkvist & Junger 2008), but this assumption is incorrect. Sweden was forced to introduce two weeks of paid compulsory leave for new mothers, in connection with childbirth. The European Commission demanded that this be introduced, pointing out that the existing, gender-neutral Swedish legislation was not in harmony with the EU legislation. This adaptation to the EU parental leave regulations constitutes a step backward for the Swedish gender equality policy form, which was more progressive and gave men the possibility of paternity leave, whereas the European form instead forces women to take maternity leave.

Conclusion

This chapter has been based on the three visions of gender equality and EU policies by which to achieve them: equality, difference/equal valuation of different contributions, and social transformation. A fourth vision (which has come to resemble a strategy) has been described, and its development has been traced in contemporary European and Swedish gender equality policy. The chapter has set out the four objectives of Swedish gender equality policy, and the influence of the EU on the implementation of issues within the following areas been discussed: equality (politics), employment (economy), parental insurance (family) and violence against women. These four areas fall within the scope of both Swedish and European gender equality objectives, which are compared at the beginning of this chapter. In terms of form, the chapter has demonstrated how Swedish gender quality machinery has changed and become Europeanised. This has involved a form of 'streamlining' of interests and inequalities – partly through the EU's creation of privileges for certain types of organisations, and partly through the EU's demands and recommendations regarding certain types of institutionalisation.

Sweden's membership in the EU has led to a change in Swedish gender equality machinery, which has meant alterations in Swedish policy institutions (form) and policy (content), as well as discourses. In part, these changes are manifested in the creation of new institutions (the Discrimination Ombudsman), new political content (the clarification and extension of the Gender Equality Act, the establishment and abolition of affirmative action, mandatory maternity leave), and new political discourses (intersectional equality, anti-discrimination, and trafficking as border politics rather than as a form of violence). In terms of content, Europeanisation is evident in policies relating to equal treatment, employment, family policy and the violence policy.

From a feminist perspective, this Europeanisation has been both progressive and regressive.

In terms of norms, further Europeanisation has occurred in the course of the last decade. In this context, it has primarily had to do with a shift away from gender equality to what is referred to in this chapter as 'intersectional equality'. Theoretically, this means a shift away from studying a single ground for inequality (gender) in favour of studying multiple grounds for inequality (ethnicity, physical ability, sexual orientation, etc.) and the way in which a merger of these grounds has increased the focus on economic equality. The Europeanisation of gender equality policy discourse is clearly visible. In terms of form and organisation, Europeanisation is evident in the form of the merger of institutions, laws and government authorities through 1) the merger of the ombudsmen for different grounds of discrimination into a single Discrimination Ombudsman; and 2) the merger of the legal framework focusing on gender and gender equality into a single Discrimination Act that focuses on equality and multiple grounds for inequality (rather than gender alone).

The merger and institutionalisation of multiple grounds for inequality in both organisations and legislation reinforces the image of a Europeanised Swedish gender equality area. However, the conclusion that Swedish gender equality policy has undergone (and continues to undergo) a process of Europeanisation must be qualified and supplemented by two parallel phenomena. Firstly, during the same period in which its own policy has become Europeanised, Sweden has influenced both European and international gender equality policy. Certain politicians and scientists argue that Sweden has driven gender equality policy developments in the area of gender mainstreaming (Lindholm & Callerstig, 2015), the inclusion of violence against women in the agenda (*cf.* Strid, 2009), and the cultivation of the strong delineation between the personal and the political. It is difficult to distinguish between cause and effect in this area, because clear and measurable variables are often lacking. It is possible to say that gender discourses correlate with each other, but extending this to formulate conclusions about causality is difficult. Secondly, Europeanisation does not occur in a global vacuum; European and international organisations, such as the United Nations, the World Health Organisation (WHO) and the

Council of Europe, are strong influences on Swedish and European gender equality policy.

Herein lies part of the tension between the Swedish model and the European model. Swedish gender equality policy deals with gender equality as a goal in itself – a vision – whereas the EU's gender equality policy primarily focuses on equality as a means – as a strategy for achieving a different, more highly-valued objective.

References

Andersson, R. 2017. *Gender mainstreaming as feminist politics: A critical analysis of the pursuit of gender equality in Swedish local government*. Örebro: Örebro University Press.

Andersson, R. & G. Hedlund. 2014. 'Att göra kön i kommunal politik. Lokala variationer av gender mainstreaming och kvinnofrid'. *Tidskrift för genusvetenskap* 35(2-3).

Armstrong, J., S. Walby & S. Strid. 2009. 'What is quality?'. *Benefits* 17(3).

Bergqvist, C. 2004. 'Tillhör framtiden enbart männen? En analys av EU, framtidskonventet och jämställdheten' In: C. Florin & C. Bergqvist, (ed.) *'Framtiden i samtiden'- Könsrelationer i förändring i Sverige och omvärlden*. Stockholm: The Institute for Futures Studies.

Bergqvist, C., P. Adman & A-C. Junger. 2008. *Kön och politik*. Stockholm: SNS Förlag.

Bergqvist, C., A. Borchorst, A-D. Christensen, V. Ramstedt-Silén, N. C. Raaum, A. Styrkársdóttir (eds.) 1999. *Equal Democracies? Gender and Politics in the Nordic Countries*. Oslo: Scandinavian University Press.

Berlin, I. 2002/1958. 'Two concepts of liberty'. In: Berlin, I. 1969. *Four Essays on Liberty*. Oxford: Oxford University Press.

Booth, C. & C. Bennet. 2002. 'Gender mainstreaming in the European Union: Towards a new conception and practice of equal opportunities'. *European Journal of Women's Studies*, 9(4).

The Swedish Democracy Council's 2010 report. *Europeiseringen av Sverige*. Stockholm: SNS Förlag.

Eduards, M. 2002. *Förbjuden handling. Om kvinnors organisering och feministisk teori*. Malmö: Liber.

The Council of Europe. 2011. *The Istanbul Convention*. Strasbourg.

The European Parliament, 2015. *Report on the EU Strategy for equality between women and men post 2015. (2014/2152 (INI)). Proposal for a European Parliament Resolution*. The Committee on Women's Rights and Gender Equality. Available at: http://www.europarl.europa.eu/sides/getDoc.do?pubRef=-//EP//TEXT+REPORT+A8-2015-0163+0+DOC+XML+V0//SV [August 6, 2018].

The European Commission. 1985. *Equal opportunities for women. Medium term community programme; 1986–90*. Commission communication to the Council; transmitted

on December 20, 1984. Available at: http://aei.pitt.edu/3952/1/3952.pdf [August 6, 2018].
— 1990. *The European Commission's Third Action Programme for Equal Opportunities for Women and Men 1991-1995*. Luxembourg: Publications Office of the European Union.
— 1996. *Communication from the Commission: Incorporating Equal Opportunities for Women and Men in all Community Policies and Activities*. COM(96)67 final. Luxembourg: Publications Office of the European Union.
— 2006. *A roadmap for equality between women and men (2006-2010)*. COM(2006) 92 final. Luxembourg: Publications Office of the European Union.
— 2011. *Strategy for equality between women and men 2010-2015*. COM (2010) 491 final. Luxembourg: Publications Office of the European Union.
— 2016. *Strategic engagement for gender equality 2016-2019*. Available at: http://ec.europa.eu/justice/gender-equality/document/files/strategic_engagement_en.pdf [August 6, 2018].
— 1984. *Council Recommendation of December 13, 1984 on the promotion of positive action for women*. (84/635/EEC). Official Journal of the European Communities. Available at: http://eur-lex.europa.eu/legal-content/EN/TXT/PDF/?uri=CELEX:31984H0635&from=EN [August 6, 2018].
European Council Directive 75/117/EC.
— 96/34/EG.
— 2000/43/EC.
— 2000/78/EC.
The European Council. 2015. *Council Conclusions on the Gender Action Plan 2016-2020*. Brussels, October 26, 2015. Available at: http://www.consilium.europa.eu/en/press/press-releases/2015/10/26-fac-conclusions-gender-development/ [August 6, 2018].
EIGE (European Institute for Gender Equality) 2017. *Gender Equality Index 2017: Measuring gender equality in the European Union 2005–2015 – Report*. Available at: http://eige.europa.eu/rdc/eige-publications/gender-equality-index-2017-measuring-gender-equality-european-union-2005-2015-report [August 24, 2018].
Ferree, M. M. 2009. 'Inequality, intersectionality and the politics of discourse: Framing feminist alliances' In: E. Lombardo, P. Meier & M. Verloo (eds.) *The discursive politics of gender equality: Stretching, bending and policy-making*. London: Routledge.
Florin, C. & K. Nilsson 1999. *'Något som liknar en oblodig revolution…'. Jämställdhetens politisering under 1960- och 70-talet.* Umeå: The University Gender Equality Council.
UN 1993. *Principles relating to the Status of National Institutions (The Paris Principles)*. Adopted in the General Assembly Resolution 48/134 of December 20, 1993. New York: UN.
— 1995. *Fourth World Conference on Women: Platform for Action and the Beijing Declaration*. New York: UN Department of Public Information.
Fridolfsson, C. 2006. *Deconstructing political protest*. Örebro: Örebro University.
Hearn, J., S. Strid, L. Husu & M. Verloo 2016. 'Gendered intersectionalities in policy on violence

against women'. *Current Sociology*, 64(4).

Hernes, H. 1987. *Welfare State and Woman Power: Essays in State Feminism*. Oslo: Norwegian University Press.

Hobson, B. 2003. 'The individualised worker, the gender participatory and gender equity models in Sweden'. *Social Policy and Society*, 3(1).

Hoskyns, C. 1996. *Integrating gender. Women, law and politics in the EU*. London: Verso.

Karlsson, G. 1996. *Från broderskap till systerskap: det socialdemokratiska kvinnoförbundets kamp för inflytande och makt i SAP*. Lund: Arkiv.

Kelly, L., C. Hagemann-White, T. Meysen, & R. Römkens 2011. *Realising Rights: Case Studies on State Responses to Violence Against Women and Children in Europe*. London: CWASU.

Klinth, R. 2002. *Göra pappa med barn*. Umeå: Boréa.

Kronsell, A. 2005. 'Gender, power and European integration theory'. *Journal of European Public Policy*, 12(6).

Kvist, E. 2008. *Report Analysing Intersectionality in Gender Equality Policies for Sweden and the EU*, QUING Project, Vienna: Institute for Human Sciences (IWM). Available at http://www.quing.eu/files/results/ir_sweden.pdf [3 September 2018].

Liebert, U. 2003. *Gendering Europeanisation*. Brussels: Peter Lang.

Lindholm, K. & A.C. Callerstig 2015. 'Implementering av jämställdhets och mångfaldsmål' In: E. Deverell, D. Hansen & E. Olsson (ed.) *Perspektiv på krishantering*. Lund: Studentlitteratur.

Lister, R. 2011. 'Gender, citizenship and social justice in the Nordic welfare states: A view from the outside'. K. Melby, A-B. Ravn & C. Carlsson Wetterberg (eds.) *Gender equality and welfare politics in Scandinavia*. Bristol: Policy Press.

Lombardo, E. & M. Verloo 2009. 'Institutionalizing intersectionality in the European Union?'. *International Feminist Journal of Politics*, 11(4).

Lodenius, A-L. 2018. *Antifeministerna. Sverigedemokraterna och jämställdheten*. Stockholm: Arena förlag. Available at: http://arenaide.se/wp-content/uploads/sites/2/2018/08/rap-sd-antifeministerna.pdf [16 August 2018].

Magnusson, E. 1999. *Jämställdhet i många olika versioner. Mönster i den politiska retoriken för jämställdhet i svenskap 1990-tal*. Oslo: NiKK. Available at: http://www.nikk.no/wp-content/uploads/NIKKpub1999_ligestillingspolitik_Jamstalldhetimangaolikaversioner.pdf [August 6, 2018].

Mazey, S. 2000. 'Introduction: integrating gender – intellectual and 'real world' mainstreaming'. *Journal of European Policy*, 7(3).

Mazur, A. 2002. *Theorizing Feminist Policy*. Oxford: Oxford University Press.

McBride, D. & A. Mazur 2011. 'Gender machineries worldwide'. *World Development Report 2012*. Background Paper. The World Bank.

Nyheter24 2015. 'Feminismen har gått för långt nu'. Available at: http://nyheter24.se/debatt/788622-feminismen-har-gatt-for-langt-nu [August 6, 2018].

Phillips, A. 1998. 'Democracy and representation' In: A. Phillips (ed.) *Feminism and Politics*. Oxford: Oxford University Press.

Rees, T. 1998. *Mainstreaming Equality in the European Union*. London: Routledge.

Rönnblom, M. 1997. 'Halva makten? En feministisk granskning av politik' In: G. Nordborg (ed.) *Makt & kön: tretton bidrag till feministisk kunskap*. Stockholm/Stehag: Brutus Östling.

SOU 1995:60. *Kvinnofrid. Slutbetänkande av Utredningen som ska föreslå en nationell strategi mot mäns våld mot kvinnor*. Stockholm: Fritzes. Available at: http://www.riksdagen.se/sv/Dokument-Lagar/Utredningar/Statens-offentliga-utredningar/sou-1995-60-_GJB360/ [August 6, 2018].

SOU 2005:66. *Makt att forma samhället och sitt eget liv. Jämställdhetspolitiken mot nya mål*. Official Reports of the Swedish Government. Stockholm: Fritzes.

SOU 2006. *Maktutredningen 2006*. Available at: http://www.riksdagen.se/sv/Dokument-Lagar/Utskottens-dokument/Betankanden/Arenden/200506/AU11/ [August 6, 2018].

SOU 2007:108. *Slutbetänkande av Utredningen som ska föreslå en nationell strategi mot mäns våld mot kvinnor*. Report by the inquiry 'Kvinnor och män på maktpositioner i det svenska samhället'. Stockholm: Fritzes/The Government Offices of Sweden.

SOU 2015:55. *Nationell strategi mot mäns våld mot kvinnor och hedersrelaterat våld och förtryck*. Final report by the Gender Equality Inquiry, which shall suggest a national strategy to combat violence perpetrated by men against women. Stockholm: Fritzes. Available at: http://www.regeringen.se/contentassets/738becd6961e4a3d8d986c00b8c8bc9e/nationell-strategi-mot-mans-vald-mot-kvinnor-och-hedersrelaterat-vald-och-fortryck-sou_2015_55.pdf [August 6, 2018].

SOU 2015:86. *Mål och myndighet. En effektiv styrning av jämställdhetspolitiken*. Report by the Gender Equality Inquiry. Stockholm: Fritzes. Available at: http://www.regeringen.se/contentassets/fd7240295cab45df8130384abdb600fa/mal-och-myndighet---en-effektiv-styrning-av-jamstalldhetspolitiken-sou-2015_86.pdf [August 6, 2018].

Stratigaki, M. 2005. 'Gender mainstreaming vs. positive action. An ongoing conflict in EU gender equality policy'. *European Journal of Women's Studies*, 12(2).

Strid, S. 2009. *Gendered interests in the EU. The European women's lobby and the organisation and representation of women's interests*. Örebro: Örebro University.

— 2018. 'Patriarchy fights back. Violent opposition to gender equality in online contexts' In: M. Verloo (ed.) *Varieties of opposition to gender equality in Europe*. London: Routledge.

Strid, S. & M. Åberg. 2014. 'Våld som postdisciplinärt forskningsfält'. *Tidskrift för genusvetenskap*, 35(2-3).

Strid, S., J. Armstrong & S. Walby 2008. *Analysing intersectionality in gender equality policies for the United Kingdom and the EU*. Vienna: Institute for Human Sciences.

— 2014. 'Intersectionality and multiple inequalities: Visibility in British policy on violence against women'. *Social Politics*, 20(4).

Strid, S. & L. Husu 2014. 'The intersectional (re)structuring of equality architectures: comparing case Sweden and case Finland'. *Equal is Not Enough*. Antwerp, February 2-5 2015.

The Sweden Democrats. 2018. Party Program. Available at: http://partiprogram.se/sverigedemokraterna#sverigedemokraterna-familjen-och-jamstalldheten [16 August 2018].

The Swedish Government 2016. *Feministisk regering*. The Cabinet Office and the website of the Swedish Government. Available at: http://www.regeringen.se/regeringens-politik/feministisk-regering/ [August 6, 2018].

Van der Vleuten, A. 2007. *The price of gender equality: Member states and governance in the European Union*. Aldershot: Ashgate.

Verloo, M. 2006. 'Multiple inequalities, intersectionality and the European Union'. *European Journal of Women's Studies*, 13(3).

Verloo, M. *et al.* 2011. *Quality in gender+ equality policies. Final QUING Report*. Vienna: Institute for Human Sciences. Available at: http://www.quing.eu/files/QUING_Final_Report_Jan%2012.pdf [August 6, 2018].

Walby, S. 2005. 'Gender mainstreaming: Productive tensions in theory and practice'. *Social Politics*, 12(3).

— 2009. *Globalization and inequalities: Complexity and contested modernities*. London: Sage.

— 2015. *Crisis*. London & New York: Routledge.

Walby, S., J. Armstrong & S. Strid. 2012a. 'Intersectionality: multiple inequalities in social theory'. *Sociology*, 46(2).

— 2012b. 'Intersectionality and the quality of the gender architecture'. *Social Politics*, 19(4).

Wendt Höjer, M. 2002. *Rädslans politik. Våld och sexualitet i den svenska demokratin*. Stockholm: Liber.

World Economic Forum 2017. *The Global Gender Gap Report 2017*. Geneva: World Economic Forum. Available at: http://www3.weforum.org/docs/WEF_GGGR_2017.pdf [August 25, 2018.]

9. Asylum- and Migration policy

Guardian of the Swedish Model

Anna Parkhouse

During the autumn of 2015, the migration crisis in Europe[1] had developed into a political crisis for the Swedish government. In the European Union (EU), the political havoc was even more serious insofar that the free movement of people, the very foundation of EU cooperation, started to be questioned. If the large migratory movements were generated by efforts to escape war, hostility and poverty, but also of hopes for a better future in Europe, the breakdown of the Common European Asylum System (CEAS) was a clear example of a European migration governance crisis. Indeed, the failure to ensure solidarity between the EU Member States, as provided for by the Treaty of Lisbon (Art. 80 TFEU, Lisbon), became clear when several Member States, consecutively reintroduced national border controls. Sweden assumed a major responsibility in refugee reception, at least initially. However, from having had the most generous regulations in asylum policy, by January 2016, Sweden had developed into having one of the EU's most restrictive regulations in the policy area (Swedish migration agency). The temporary legislation, introduced as a means to reduce the number of asylum seekers coming to Sweden, is said to be conditional upon the implementation of the solidarity principle and burden-sharing in between EU Member States and has been prolonged until July 2021 (Swedish migration agency).

The nature of the policy area is politically sensitive to the extent

1 The number of asylum seekers in 2015 was unprecedented since World War II, having reached 1.65 million asylum seekers in the OECD area (OECD 2018).

that it is strongly associated with issues of national sovereignty and questions about citizenship and asylum, *i.e.* who is entitled to live, work and use the State's welfare system. The policy area is therefore closely linked to other policy areas, such as integration, foreign- and security- and development policy (Swedish government letter 2013/14: 73). With EU membership and the incorporation of the Schengen convention into the *acquis communautaire,* the boundary between internal and external security has become less distinct. This, in turn, has led to a situation where the control of territory and population no longer is the sole responsibility of the State, since this is shared with the EU (Nugent 2010). Although the policy area is not restricted to the supranational cooperation within the EU, since it is implemented in a wider international context, the aim of the chapter is limited to studying what impact the EU membership has had on the Swedish asylum- and migration policy area. By migration, we mean movements of people across state borders. These movements can take place in both directions, *i.e.* they can concern both emigration and immigration. This chapter is only concerned with immigration policies. In order to further clarify what we are talking about, we can divide immigration policy into different categories, such as asylum immigration, labour immigration and family reunification. After an overview of the development of the Swedish asylum- and immigration policy and its development within the EU, we analyse the impact of EU membership on the Swedish asylum- and immigration policies, both in terms of possible changes in policy development as well as in terms of its organisation.

Swedish Asylum- and Migration Policy Until 1995

It was during the Second World War that the Swedish State, with increased responsibility and financial resources, began to organise a system of refugee reception. Early on, there was an awareness that refugees did not constitute a threat but were positively seen insofar as their labour force could be 'utilised' in a post-war Sweden characterised by important shortages on the labour market. From the 1950s, the Swedish refugee reception also helped to strengthen both the self-image and the image of Sweden abroad as a moral superpower with a generous asylum- and immigration policy (Perlmutter 1996). In the aftermath of the Second World War until Swedish EU membership in 1995, the policy area can be divided into different time periods.

The first period extends from the beginning of the 1950s to the end of the 1960s and is characterised by extensive labour immigration. A labour immigrant can be defined as a foreigner who, for a shorter or longer period takes up legal employment in Sweden. This period of labour immigration coincided with a period of strong economic upswing and a high demand for labour. The immigrants originated mainly from the Nordic neighbouring countries but also from southern Europe (Bucken-Knapp 2009; Nilsson 2004). In the 1954 Aliens act, foreigners had in principle an unlimited right to take up legal employment in Sweden. The same year, Sweden, Denmark, Finland and Norway, entered into an agreement to create a common Nordic labour market (Spång 2008; Swedish government official report 1967: 18).[2] However, the slowdown in economic growth, followed by a sharp drop in labour demand, led to the introduction of a more restrictive immigration policy, initiated by the Social democratic government in 1967. The strongest advocates for a more restrictive policy were the trade unions, which considered the unregulated labour immigration as a threat to the Swedish labour market policy,[3] the Swedish workers, but also to the immigrants already residing in Sweden[4] (Hinnfors *et al.* 2012; Spång 2008). The regulations adopted by a unanimous Swedish parliament in 1968 meant that if Swedish employers wanted to recruit labour force from outside of the Nordic countries, they had to go through the Swedish public employment service.[5]

Since Swedish asylum- and immigration policy had primarily been unregulated up until the end of the 1960s, the main actors in the

2 In 1957, the Nordic passport union was established (Swedish government official report 1967: 18).

3 Trade union leaders feared that labour immigrants would be a threat to the process of industrial restructuring with a risk of lowering of wage levels (wage dumping), which would in turn create conflicts between Swedes and immigrants (Hinnfors *et al.* 2012).

4 The more restrictive immigration policy has also been tied to a more effective integration policy (Frank 2005, Öberg 1994).

5 This meant that all non-Nordic foreigners would have to provide proof of job offerings, work permits and certificate of residence to obtain entry permits (Hinnfors *et al.* 2012; Spång 2008; Swedish government bill 1968: 142).

decision-making process were the trade unions, such as the Swedish trade union confederation, and the Swedish employers' association. Since the laws of the Aliens acts, up until the late 1980s, had the character of framework legislation, this meant that the government had far-reaching powers to govern and to regulate the policy development (Spång 2008, Swedish government official report 1967:18). The role of the Swedish parliament, as legislator and as a forum for coordinated debate, was limited also in the domain of the asylum policy area and then in favour of the administration, which had an independent and prominent role. The administration was streamlined in 1969, when three units merged into one, forming the Swedish immigration board.[6] In 2000, the Board changed name to the Swedish migration agency (Swedish migration agency). The 1968 regulations entailed important changes insofar that Parliament became involved in the decision-making of asylum and migration policy (Spång 2008).

The period between 1970 and 1985 is predominantly a period characterised by asylum immigration and family reunification (Nilsson 2004). The right to seek asylum is anchored in international law, based on the human rights principle and the idea that 'all human beings are born free and equal in dignity and rights' (Art. 1 Universal Declaration of Human Rights, UN). Thus, everybody should enjoy the right to seek protection from political oppression and persecution in their home countries. In contrast to the legal protection provided by asylum law, rights protecting families and relatives are considerably weaker. However, the protection of families, and especially children's right to their parents, 'means that states have a duty to respond positively to applications of reunification of children' (author's translation, Spång 2008). The legal protection of asylum law was strengthened when Sweden ratified the Geneva convention in 1954.[7]

6 Up until the establishment of the Swedish immigration board, the Foreign affairs commission had had the responsibility for the permit issues. The cases pertaining to citizenship were transferred from the Ministry of Justice and adaptation issues from the Working party on immigration affairs were transferred from the Ministry of the Interior (Swedish migration agency).

7 The Geneva convention of 1951 and its 1967 protocol are the international legal documents regulating the rights of displaced people and the status of refugees. According to the Convention, a refugee is a person who a) is outside the country of citizenship or residence; b) has a well-founded fear of persecution there c) is perse-

A considerable part of the debate on asylum policy in the 1970s and 1980s was about the legal aspects of the asylum process, especially the long processing times but also the appeal process (Swedish government official report 1988: 2). Due to massive protests against a series of decisions of rejection, the government finally decided to delegate that responsibility to the Aliens appeals board, established in 1992 (Swedish government bill 1991/92:30).

Between 1985 and 1995, the number of asylum seekers in Sweden increased, primarily due to the large migratory influx, resulting from the wars in the Western Balkans between 1991 and 1995, but also due to increased efficiency in the asylum process and refugee reception. Asylum seekers, whose applications had been pending, were automatically granted residence permits. This situation led to a snowballing effect insofar that it entailed a large influx of asylum seekers. As a response to this, the government introduced more restrictive regulations, which in principle, meant the closing of national borders for a short period of time[8] (Nilsson 2004). The more restrictive view of asylum immigration that emerged in Sweden during the first half of the 1990s coincided with a period of deep economic crisis and political turbulence[9] (Abiri 2000; Appelqvist 2000). Even though Sweden was the country in Europe which received the majority of refugees (per capita) during the wars in the Western Balkans, this took place in parallel with the introduction of more restrictive regulations, *i.e.* introduction of visa requirements for certain groups of people.[10] In 1994, this was followed by the introduction of temporary permits. The system that emerged was based on two principles: on the one hand,

cuted because of race, nationality, belonging to a community or religion or political opinion, and d) cannot, or will not, avail himself of his or her home country's protection (Chapter 1, Geneva convention).

8 The restrictive regulations are known under the name of the *Lucia decision*, taken on December 13, 1989 by a Social democratic government. The decision was revoked in 1991 by the newly appointed Conservative government (Nilsson 2004; Spång 2008).

9 New democracy, a new political party with a populist and a clear xenophobic rhetoric in the party program, received 6.7% in the 1991 election to Parliament. Their sojourn in Parliament was brief and ended in 1994, after one mandate period (Rydgren 2005).

10 The visa requirement, introduced in 1993 especially for citizens from Bosnia and Herzegovina and the former Yugoslav Republic of Macedonia, meant that the number of asylum seekers decreased dramatically, from 7600 in June 1993 to 1200, a month later (Nilsson 2004).

the responsibility to protect major refugee groups in situations of mass influx of displaced persons; on the other hand, this protection should be based on temporary protection (Appelqvist 2000; Black & Koser 1999). This period also coincided with Sweden submitting an application for EU membership in 1991. In January 1995, Sweden joined the EU.

EU Common Asylum- and Migration Policy

Within the framework of Justice and Home Affairs (including 9 policy areas), asylum- and migration policy was established as a new policy area in the Treaty of Maastricht in 1993 (Ucarer 2013). The development of the policy area should be seen as a spill over from the completion of the single market and therefore as a logical consequence of the passport-free union (Nugent 2010). The policy area is therefore based on a paradox insofar that in order to guarantee the free movement of people, intra-EU, this requires more rigorous control and regulation of those who are outside, what in EU terminology is called third country nationals (Carmel & Paul 2013). Since the policy area, initially, was incorporated into the third pillar in the Treaty of Maastricht, it was limited to intergovernmental cooperation. However, the policy area developed rapidly in the successive Treaties. Already in the Treaty of Amsterdam, in 1999, and largely due to the impending Eastern enlargement, part of the policy area was 'communitarised', as issues pertaining to asylum, border control, visa and migration were transferred to the first supranational pillar (see chapter 1, Nugent 2010). Minimum levels of legislation and poor compliance with the regulations were however hampering to both implementation and policy development. Due to wars and conflicts in the European neighbourhood as well as people seeking a better future in Europe, increased irregular immigration has evolved into becoming one of the most difficult challenges for the EU to handle. At the same time and equally challenging, the *looming* demographic crisis and extensive labour shortages facing the EU, especially in certain sectors means that there is an increasing demand to attract third country nationals to the EU Member States (EC 2016).

In the negotiations leading up to the Treaty of Amsterdam, and as part of an agenda to combat irregular immigration, *i.e.* those who enter- and reside in the EU illegally, border management, especially towards the Mediterranean, was streamlined. The forthcoming Eastern enlargement in 2004 and the emergence of new borders to the East were also important incentives for incorporating the Schengen cooperation[11] into the EU *acquis communautaire*. However, the effectiveness of border protection has been weakened by the fact that membership in Schengen is neither complete nor is limited to the EU Member States.[12] These shortcomings were legally reinforced by the Treaty of Nice, which, in 2003, extended the principle of flexible integration to also apply to the area of asylum- and migration policy (Art. 40 TEU, Nice). This meant that both Ireland and the United Kingdom were granted the right to 'opt out' from the cooperation (Nugent 2010). In 2004, the Council of ministers decided on the setting up of a common authority for EU border protection, Frontex (EC 2007/2004). The effort to strengthen the Schengen cooperation,[13] with enhanced border protection, is morally controversial. Indeed, the development of a more locked-in and impenetrable EU, in EU-parlance known as 'fortress Europe' (Ucarer 2013), may paradoxically mean that not only the external but also the internal control is becoming increasingly rigid.

The five-year Tampere programme (2000–2005) was to be the first of a number of strategic action programmes aimed at strengthening the rights and the free movement of those legally residing in the EU. Another priority was to strengthen the fight against irregular immigration. The Tampere programme was also the starting point for the Common European Asylum System (CEAS), designed to harmonise national asylum systems. Minimum levels of legislation

11 The Schengen cooperation had been developed outside the EU Treaty since 1985 (Ucarer 2013).

12 The Schengen cooperation is composed of 22 EU Member States and States not having EU membership. Apart from Ireland, having an opt-out clause, Bulgaria, Cyprus, Croatia and Romania are not part of the cooperation. Non-EU Member States, such as Iceland, Liechtenstein, Norway and Switzerland are associate members of the Schengen cooperation. Although not *de jure* members of Schengen, Monaco, San Marino and the Holy Sea, are *de facto* members, keeping their borders to neighbouring States open (Ucarer 2013).

13 This was the second generation of the Schengen system, the Schengen Information System (SIS II) and the Visa Information System (VIS II) (Collett 2014).

combined with poor compliance with the regulations resulted in the Tampere programme's goals also becoming priority objectives in the subsequent policy programmes in The Hague (2005–2010) and in Stockholm (2010–2014) (Collett 2014). Up until the ratification of the Treaty of Lisbon in 2009, the division of competencies in the policy area had been divided according to the pillar structure introduced by the Treaty of Maastricht (see Chapter 1). Even though the whole policy area was 'communitarised' in the Treaty of Amsterdam, unanimity in the Council of ministers was guaranteed over a transitional period of five years (Ucarer 2013). This meant that the legislative powers of the European parliament remained severely limited.[14] From 2004, the decision-making powers of the European parliament were, however equalled to those of the Council of ministers. The European court of justice would also receive a mandate to interpret and judge in litigation. However, although a considerable part of decision-making was transferred to the supranational level, the rules and regulations of the Treaty of Amsterdam were examples of complex 'legal engineering'[15], for the purpose of political ends (Ucarer 2013:285). The Treaty of Lisbon involved significant reforms also in this policy area and in decision-making. With the disappearance of the pillar structure, shared authority was introduced as a legislative principle (Art. 4 TFEU, Lisbon). This means that the competence is divided between the EU and its Member States and that the EU can legislate and adopt binding acts in significant parts of the policy area (Art. 4 TFEU, Lisbon).

In May 2015, the Commission proposed the European agenda on migration. Based on four pillars, the aim of the Agenda is to create a more effective policy for legal migration at the same time as reducing the incentives for irregular immigration, primarily by streamlining the border protection management. The creation of a more robust CEAS, especially in terms of strengthening a more 'coherent implementation' of the system, was emphasised (EC 2015:12). The European migration

14 By using the consultation procedure, in which the European parliament only has an advisory role, in parallel to using the unanimity principle in decision-making in the Council of ministers, the legislative powers of the European parliament were limited (Ucarer 2013).

15 The maze of the rules and regulations in the area created a system that was difficult to comprehend even for legal experts (Ucarer 2013).

crisis that unfolded that same year was an example of the need to reform the system. The political turmoil that followed, leading some Member States to reintroduce national territorial border controls and more restrictive migration policies, contributed to further embed EU migration policy in the larger EU foreign policy and developmental policy areas. The Commission roadmap in 2017 was an initiative to build a collective engagement on a comprehensive deal on migration tackling the structural causes of migration. This would encompass the reinforcing of external border management, the more effective implementation on return and readmission arrangements and more generally to help public authorities in countries of origin and transit with both migration management but also assisting with socio-economic development. The strengthening of relations with international actors and neighbouring countries is a strategy that has been developed after the EU-Turkey deal in March 2016, which led to the drastic decrease[16] of migrants going from Turkey to Greece (Zimmermann 2017:97). Due to a lack of solidarity in between EU Member States, the Commission proposal for a reformed asylum policy package has to date been relegated to a political moratorium.

The Impact of EU Membership on the Swedish Asylum- and Migration Policy Since 1995

When Sweden joined the EU, it went from being a Nation state to becoming a Member State. Automatically this meant the transfer of parts of decision-making and sovereignty to a supranational level. This was also the case in asylum- and migration policy, a cooperation that started on EU level at the same time that Sweden became a member of the EU. In order to study how the EU-membership has impacted on the Swedish policy in the area, and vice versa, the chapter is limited to analysing labour immigration and asylum immigration. These categories are specifically analysed with regard to potential changes in policy development as well as in terms of organisation.

16 The EU-Turkey Statement has meant a drastic reduction in the number of migrants going from Turkey to Greece, from an average of 10 000 in 2015 to circa 80 on a daily basis in 2017 (Europe.eu).

Labour Immigration

When it comes to formulating a sustainable strategy for developing common rules for labour immigration and a more effective integration policy in the EU, progress has been rather slow. It was only in the Stockholm programme (2010–2014), with the aim of making the EU more competitive, that an action programme for a more demand-driven labour immigration, which would also include more effective integration policy measures, was formulated (Collett 2014). In the European agenda on migration this was further strengthened, specifically in regards to facilitating for highly skilled third country nationals to take legal employment in the EU. The fourth pillar of the Agenda zooms in on developing a more effective policy for legal immigration, thus strengthening the economic and social integration for the purposes of addressing labour market needs as well as to increasing the incentives for social cohesion (EC 2015).

When Sweden became an EU Member State, it immediately affected the Swedish labour immigration insofar that this automatically entailed a new category of immigrants; in the media referred to as 'EU migrants'. Since the freedom of movement[17] now also came to include the other non-Nordic EU citizens, labour immigrants in Sweden would henceforth be categorised as follows: 1) citizens from one of the Nordic countries;[18] 2) citizens from the EU/European Economic Area (EEA) and 3) third country nationals (Swedish migration agency). The issue of the non-Nordic labour immigration was therefore removed, at least initially, from the political agenda. In view of the Eastern enlargement in 2004, and because of concerns that the new (and poorer) citizens of the Union would become entitled to the extensive welfare system in Sweden, intense political debates ensued. The core issue was whether the EU 15 would introduce special rules for the 10 new

17 The 2004 directive on '*Freedom of movement and residence*', implemented in Swedish national law on 30 April 2006, states 'the right of citizens of the Union and their family members to move and reside freely within the territory of the Member States' (2004/38/EC). However, in order to work longer than 3 months, Union citizens, except citizens of the Nordic countries, must register this with the Swedish migration agency (Swedish migration agency).

18 Nordic citizens still have the most extensive rights since they have the legal right to reside and to work in Sweden without a permit, regardless of length of stay (Swedish migration agency).

Member States during a transitional period. In Sweden, the main advocates for this position came primarily from the Swedish Transport Workers' Union and from the Buildings Union. Concerns were also raised by the government where, then Social democratic Prime Minister Göran Persson, warned of 'social tourism' (Aftonbladet, November 21, 2003). However, in contrast to the majority of EU Member States,[19] Sweden finally decided not to introduce any transitional rules, neither prior to the enlargement of 2004, nor the following one in 2007 (Spång 2008). It was only in the late 1990s that discussions on a more organised labour immigration of third country nationals was brought onto the political agenda in Sweden (Swedish government official report 2000:7). The former restrictive policy was amended with the 2006 decision that opened up for regulated labour immigration from third country nationals.[20] In the labour reform, finally adopted in December 2008, the government-based labour market test[21] was removed and the hiring of third country nationals became the responsibility of the individual employer.[22] In parallel with the liberalisation of the 2008 regulatory framework in Sweden, the work towards a more demand-driven labour immigration in the EU began (Migrationsinfo.se).

The liberalisation of labour immigration in Sweden has resulted in the fact that the labour market parties no longer play an important role in decision-making. The politisation of labour immigration, especially since 1968, has also meant an increased role of the Swedish parliament, both as legislator and as a forum for a more coordinated discussion. The impact of EU-membership, in general, however, has

19 In the end, only Sweden, Ireland and the United Kingdom, decided not to introduce transitional rules (Nugent 2010; Ucarer 2013).

20 The new system included 'temporary residence permits for labour shortages, permanent residence permits due to labour market reasons, seasonal work and entrepreneurial activity' (author's direct translation from Spång 2008:83).

21 The government-based test was conducted by the National labour market board together with the trade unions. Until 2008, the test had been considered necessary with the argument that everyone living in Sweden have access to the Swedish welfare system (Swedish government official report 2006:87).

22 However, the basis for labour immigration from third countries is that there is both an offer for employment and that the forms of employment respect the Swedish collective agreements or the practice in the industry. The principle of preference for EU citizens is emphasised (Swedish government letter 2013/14:73).

meant a weakening of the legislative powers of parliament, in favour of the government. This is also the case in the asylum- and migration policy area. Subsequently, the role of parliament, both as legislator, but also as a forum for coordinated discussion, has diminished. The increased legislative powers of the Swedish government should however be relativised insofar that they are shared with the other Member States in the Council, since the decisions at EU-level are taken according to qualified majority voting (QMV), and also shared with the European parliament, co-legislator since 2004. Indeed, the shared authority in decision-making power, as institutionalised by the Treaty of Lisbon (Art. 4 TFEU, Lisbon), means that the EU can legislate and adopt binding acts in significant parts of the policy area. Decisions regulating 'who enters, on what basis, for how long and in what number', that is however still essentially Member State competence (Geddes 2015:78). In view of facilitating the rules and conditions for entry and residence of third country nationals to take up highly qualified employment, the EU launched the *Blue card directive*[23] (2009/50/EC), adopted in 2009. The directive was implemented in Swedish national law on 1 August 2013 (Swedish government letter 2013/14:73). In order to simplify entry and residence in more low-skilled professions, especially in sectors of services, care, industry and agriculture, the EU adopted the *Seasonal workers directive*[24] (2014/36/EU) in 2014. The directive was implemented in Swedish national law on 1 June 2018 (Swedish government bill 2017/18:108). Other directives to strengthen incentives for legal labour immigration are about facilitating for multinational companies to temporarily relocate their staff and also for third-country nationals to study, do research train or volunteer in the EU. The *Intra-corporate transfer (ICT) directive* (2014/66/EU) and the *Students and researchers recast directive* (2016/801/EU) were adopted in 2014 and 2016 respectively. Whereas the *ICT*

23 Apart from the higher education requirement, three years of working experience is also required in order to qualify to be a Blue card holder (2009/50/EC). Due to the inefficiency of the directive, the Commission has proposed its revision (EC 2016).

24 The *Seasonal workers directive*, governing both housing and working conditions, is temporarily limited and the seasonal worker may legally stay in the Member State between five and nine months. The time limit is determined by the Member State (2014/36/EU).

directive was implemented in Swedish law on 1 March 2018 (Swedish government bill 2017/18:34), the directive facilitating entry and residence for students[25] and researchers is proposed to be implemented on 1 January 2020 (Swedish government). Other directives, aimed at strengthening labour immigration, are the *Family reunification directive* (2003/86/EC), the *Long-term resident's directive* (2003/109/EC) as amended by directive (2011/51/EU) and the *Single permit directive* (2011/98/EU).

The consequences of the 2008 Swedish labour immigration reform primarily resulted in a significant increase in the number of work permits granted, especially in low-skilled sectors (Migrationsinfo). Although the increase was considerable, it started from very low numbers.[26] This means that, although Sweden has one of Europe's and the world's most liberal regulations, the rate of labour immigration has been below average for the OECD area (OECD 2011). In order to address some deficiencies regarding unfair employment conditions, especially for migrant blueberry pickers, having been the largest category of low-skilled immigrants, the Swedish government introduced stricter regulations from 2011. The control on the employers was also tightened since they were required to have collective agreement wages. The responsibility for overseeing the control was delegated to the municipality workers union. In 2012, stricter controls were introduced to check the employers' ability to pay salaries (Swedish migration agency). The *Seasonal workers directive* was integrated in the Swedish Aliens act on 1 June 2018. It is still too early to comment on the effect of the directive; presumably, however, it will mean the further tightening of the regulations, especially those regarding the rules on equal treatment (Swedish government bill 2017/18:108).

It is also the principle of equal treatment that is central to the discussions on the implementation of the directive on a '*Single application procedure for residence and work permit*' of 13 December 2011 (2011/98/EU). In order to fulfil the objective of the directive, the government

25 The 2011 decision to introduce tuition fees in Swedish universities for third country students meant an important decrease in the number of non EU/EEA students.

26 In 2005, 5376 third country nationals had been granted a work permit. In 2008, that number had risen to 14 513 third. Between 2013 and 2019, numbers have fluctuated between 15 357 (2013) and 19 415 (2019) (Swedish migration agency).

has announced that changes in the Swedish social insurance code will be required in order not to discriminate against third country nationals, who have been granted a work permit. This means that the current requirement for a minimum time period of residency in order to have access to the Swedish social security systems is removed (Swedish government directive 2014:109). The incorporation of the *Blue card directive* into national legislation was quite undramatic since Sweden already had introduced rules in this area. So far, the impact of the *blue card directive* has been minor. However, when comparing labour immigration in different sectors, the share of work permits granted to highly skilled third country nationals had, especially since 2017[27], increased relative to those of low-skilled sectors (Swedish Migration Agency). Furthermore, and especially in order to retain third country nationals, in December 2017, new rules, strengthening the legal rights of labour immigrants had been introduced.[28]

Asylum Immigration

A decade after the decision of the EU Heads of State or Government to establish a Common European Asylum System (CEAS), it was institutionalised in the Treaty of Lisbon (Art. 78 (1) TFEU, Lisbon). The right to asylum is anchored in the Geneva Convention[29] and is governed by the EU Charter of Human Rights (Art. 18 of the EU Charter). The Treaty of Lisbon also institutionalises the solidarity clause and the principle of fair division of responsibility between the Member States (Art. 222 TFEU, Lisbon). With the development of the migration crisis in 2015, the Commission's guidelines for a more effective asylum policy became more closely tied to the policies to

27 In 2017, the share of work permits granted to highly qualified third country nationals was 40% compared to 30% who had been granted work permits in low skilled sectors (Migrationsinfo.se).

28 Due to several cases of revoked work permits due to employers having made minor mistakes regarding employment conditions, especially in regards to IT-specialists, new rules, strengthening the rights of labour immigrants were introduced 1 December 2017 (Swedish government website).

29 The Geneva convention of 1951 and its 1967 Protocol are the international legal documents regulating the rights of displaced people and the obligations of the sovereign states having signed and ratified the documents (Zimmermann 2016:3).

combat irregular immigration.[30] This was also increasingly implemented through various protection programmes aimed at increasing the conditions for refugees either to return to their country of origin, to be integrated into the host country or to be resettled to a third country (Swedish government letter 2013/14:73).

In the light of the criticism that had been made against the Swedish asylum policy, the newly appointed Social democratic government had by November 1994 instigated a parliamentary inquiry to review asylum law.[31] Even though asylum policy in the EU was only at an early stage of cooperation, the government underlined that it was important to harmonise national legislation on asylum with the EU (Swedish government bill 1996/97:25). In 1995, the Swedish government had also applied for membership in the Schengen cooperation where Sweden became a member on 25 March 2001. The most controversial area with the Schengen membership came to be the issue of the extended carrier responsibility, decided by the Council of ministers in June 2001.[32] All political parties (in the Swedish parliament), except the Conservatives and the Social democrats, and in line with the United Nations High Commissioner for Refugees (UNHCR) as well as several non-governmental organisations, opposed the directive for fear that it risked undermining the right of asylum (Spång 2008). The directive was incorporated into Swedish national law on 1 July 2004 (Swedish parliament protocol 2003/04:114).[33] Between 2000 and 2005, the first legislative acts on asylum policy were adopted. Since the legislation initially only set minimum levels, they were later to be revised with a view to strengthening the CEAS.

30 In the European agenda on migration, published in May 2015, the Commission proposes more effective efforts to combat irregular immigration, for example by combating the trafficking in human beings within the framework of the Common security and defence policy (EC 2015).

31 The revisions focused primarily on broadening the grounds for asylum protection, with a particular focus on unaccompanied minors and children's asylum reasons, as well as lowering the need for proof (Swedish government bill 1996/97:25).

32 The extended carrier responsibility implied that the transport companies were responsible for checking passengers' identification and travel documents on public transports (2001/51/EC).

33 The Social Democrats, the Conservatives and one Christian Democrat voted for the amendment, adopted by 171 votes for and 126 votes against (Swedish parliament protocol 2003/04:114).

The Qualification directive, first adopted in 2004 (2004/83/EC) and amended in 2011 (2011/95/EU), sets out rules for what is considered to be the basis for international protection. As a consequence, two new grounds for protection were introduced in Swedish legislation, 'subsidiary protection' and 'other protection'.[34] The latter category, which has no international equivalent, was added to take into account those who would not be protected by the EU directive. Thus, the incorporation of the *Qualification directive* in Swedish law contributed to further extend the grounds for asylum protection in Sweden. In addition, the directive on *Temporary protection of refugees in situations of mass influx* (2001/55/EC) was implemented in the 2006 Aliens act. As a result, a large number of particularly Iraqi refugees and unaccompanied minors were granted residence permits in Sweden between 2006 and 2007 (Swedish migration agency). The incorporation of the *Temporary protection of refugees in situations of mass influx directive* into Swedish law was unproblematic since Sweden already before EU membership had implemented the policy on temporary protection, then in response to the reception of refugees from the Western Balkans in 1994. With the next massive refugee inflow, during 2013–2015 (mainly composed of refugees fleeing the war in Syria), and the collapse of the CEAS at the height of the European migration crisis in the autumn of 2015, the traditionally generous Swedish asylum policy had developed into becoming one of the EU's most restrictive[35] (Migrationsinfo.se).

Regarding the asylum process itself, the EU adopted the *Asylum procedures directive* in 2005 (2005/85/EC) and the *Reception conditions directive* in 2003 (2003/9/EC). Both directives, amended in 2013 (2013/32/EU; 2013/33/EU), set out the conditions for the application process and conditions regulating the reception of asylum seekers.

34 Up until November 2015, Sweden had five asylum protection bases: 'refugee according to the internationally regulated conventions'; 'person in need of subsidiary protection'; 'other protection' (no international equivalent); 'particularly embarrassing circumstances' such as severe illness (according to Swedish legislation) and 'UN quota refugee' (Swedish migration agency).

35 In view of reducing the number of asylum seekers, the government introduced temporary rules, which came into effect in July 2016 (working retroactively from 24 November 2015). This meant that the two bases of protection, 'other protection' and 'particularly embarrassing circumstances' were temporarily removed as asylum protection bases (Migrationsinfo).

The *Dublin regulation*, which was first adopted in 2003 (EC/343/2003), and forms the basis of the CEAS, is about establishing a Dublin State,[36] responsible for examining the asylum application. *The Eurodac regulation*, which was already adopted in 2000 (EC/2725/2000), was established as a support system for the more efficient application of the Dublin convention (Swedish government letter 2013/14:73). Since the *Dublin regulation* has been legally binding in Sweden, it has been controversial, especially with regard to the risk of undermining the right of asylum for unaccompanied minors (Spång 2008). The revised regulation, which came into effect 1 January 2014, strengthens the legal protection of unaccompanied minors and introduces a mechanism for early warning, should there be a crisis in the asylum system of a Member State.[37]

The Swedish migration agency has overall responsibility for the asylum process, from application to decision. Several other actors however, such as the County administrative boards,[38] the municipalities and the County councils, have special responsibility in their respective sectors to offer housing, education and care. Since 2013, the right to education and health care, including dental care, also include those who do not have a residence permit. Asylum policy in both Sweden and the EU, they are concomitantly, and increasingly, based on two pillars. On the one hand, focus is on strengthening the integration process for those who have been granted a residence permit, by 'shortening the path' to work and study.[39] This means that additional actors, such as the Swedish public employment service, has acquired a key role. On the other hand, and equally important, the focus is on streamlining the return process for those whose applica-

36 A Dublin State is an EU Member State or Norway, Switzerland, Iceland or Liechtenstein (Ucarer 2013).

37 On the basis of this mechanism, Sweden has decided not to send asylum seekers back to their country of origin, such as those coming from Greece, since the Greek asylum system is not considered legally safe (Swedish migration agency).

38 Since 2011, the County administrative boards have a special responsibility to negotiate with the municipalities on their readiness and capacity for the reception of unaccompanied minors (Swedish government letter 2013/14:73).

39 In the amended *Reception conditions directive*, there is also focus on the importance of increasing opportunities for asylum seekers to enter the labour market (2013/33/EU).

tions have been rejected.[40] Already in the mid-1990s, Sweden had concluded that possibilities to return is a human right and therefore 'should form an important part of refugee policy' (author's own translation, Swedish government official report 1995:75, 205). The *Return directive* was adopted in December 2008 (2008/115/EC) and incorporated into Swedish law on May 1, 2012 (Swedish government letter 2013/14:73).

Ever since the establishment of asylum policy in the EU, Swedish governments have pushed for more supranational decision-making, completely contrary to the traditionally intergovernmental Swedish stance. In particular, since the Treaty of Nice, Swedish governments have pursued an active policy aimed at increasing the EU responsibility, both in terms of more effective decision-making in legislation (removal of the unanimity principle in the Council of ministers) and a strengthened common asylum policy (second-generation asylum laws replacing the minimum standards) (Andersson 2008). In the context of the European migration crisis, the Swedish government initially continued to pursue a generous asylum policy, with the emphasis that the return policy was seen as a prerequisite for continuing to guarantee asylum law (Swedish government declaration, September 15, 2015). The failure to 'ensure greater solidarity between the EU Member States' (Swedish government letter 2013/14:73, 16) and in order to limit the influx of refugees to Sweden would, however, lead to a series of restrictions.[41] In December 2015, the Swedish government decided on the introduction of border controls and extended carrier responsibility[42] towards Denmark, set in place from the beginning

40 In case of rejection, the applicant has the right to apply for a review of decisions to two instances, the Migration courts and then to the Migration court of appeal (Swedish migration agency).

41 The government concluded in the cross-border agreement on migration in October 2015 that the urgent refugee situation required the introduction of temporary residence permits as a rule for asylum seekers, during a three- year period. In the agreement, it was also decided to temporarily remove one of the grounds for international protection in Sweden, namely 'particularly embarrassing circumstances'. However, among granted residence permits in 2014, only 5 percent had this ground for asylum as justification (Swedish migration agency).

42 The extended carrier responsibility means that all transport companies are responsible for controlling that everyone, without exception, who travels to Sweden from Denmark on ferries, buses, trains and flights, must be able to present a photo ID in

of January 2016. Paradoxically, this would mean that the policies and directives on stricter border controls, and the building of higher walls towards the exterior, that the Swedish government previously had reluctantly implemented, now were adopted with the distinction that these border controls were raised internally, within the EU. Indeed, from having been one of the Member States with the most generous asylum policies, the Swedish government had, by December 2015, downsized their policies to become aligned with the minimum standards as established at EU level (EC 2017). The temporary solution of more restrictive policies, conditional on solidarity and burden-sharing between EU Member States, was recently prolonged until July 2019 (Swedish migration agency).

Conclusion

The extensive Swedish welfare model was for long a decisive argument as to why a Swedish EU membership was considered impossible.[43] In the regulations of non-Nordic labour immigration in the 1960s, the protection of the Swedish labour market policy and the Swedish workers was central. The protection of the Swedish model and the Swedish social security systems has also consistently, and in particular in Social democratic governments, been central stumbling blocks in the discussions and the policy development that EU-membership and the liberalisation of labour immigration since 1995 would entail. The impact of EU membership on Swedish asylum policy is markedly different to the extent that Swedish governments have been pushing for more supranational decision-making and for the EU to take greater responsibility for a strengthened common asylum policy. Here, Swedish governments have rather had the role of a political entrepreneur and a proponent for policy development. The break with the traditionally Swedish intergovernmental stance, based on the nation

order to be admitted entry into Sweden. The ID controls were initially planned to be limited to six months (Swedish government website).

43 Tage Erlander, Prime Minister of the Social democratic government in 1961, gave a speech that became known as the 'Union speech', where he argued that the Swedish welfare model and the Swedish neutrality policy made it impossible for Swedish EU membership (*Svenska Dagbladet*, 22 August 2011).

state logic, is interesting insofar that the asylum policy area is strongly linked to issues of national sovereignty and security, touching upon core functions of statehood. Thus, the impact of EU membership on the two policy areas, under investigation, varies greatly, both in terms of the extent of the adaptation pressure but also in terms of who has had an impact on whom.

The impact of EU membership on labour immigration is difficult to distinguish from the more general liberalisation process that takes place concomitantly in Sweden in the early 2000s. Although the EU membership has meant an adaptation pressure on Swedish policy development in this area, it is limited. Limited to the extent that the policy developments in the EU have been slow and the few legal acts adopted, have been unproblematic to incorporate into Swedish national law, since Sweden already had legislated in this area (see the *Blue card directive*). The adaptation pressure has been more important in those areas that have a bearing on who should be considered to have access to the Swedish social security systems. This was blatant in the discussions on 'social tourism' that preceded the Eastern enlargements (2004 and 2007). It was also clear in the discussions about the implementation of the directives on work and residence permits for third country nationals. In this area, Sweden has to adapt its legislation in order not to discriminate against the principle of equal treatment and the right of third-country nationals to have quicker access to the Swedish social security systems. Although Sweden, since EU-membership, has opened its borders to non-Nordic labour force and since 2008 is one of Europe's and the world's most liberalised labour markets (OECD 2011, Swedish migration agency), labour immigration to Sweden has been slow. Even though there is a trend of increased labour immigration from third country nationals, especially since 2016, the low figures are worrying. Indeed, and given the *looming* demographic crisis in Sweden and the shortage of labour force, especially serious in certain sectors, like ICT, Health and Education, it is remarkable that the government has not been more active in attracting third country nationals in order to contribute to the needs and priorities of the Swedish labour market. Even though it is certain that the legal rights of labour immigrants have been strengthened by the law of 1 December 2017, making it more difficult to revoke work permits due to employers' mistakes, this is by no means sufficient. Furthermore, in the current political landscape of Sweden, with a considerable increase in nationalistic and xenophobic rhetoric, this has paved the way for a more restrictive labour immigration policy. This, in turn, is hampering both to the needs and priorities of the Swedish labour market but also to the survival of the Swedish welfare State.

The impact of EU membership in the field of asylum policy is considerably different. Here Sweden has pursued a policy that has been pushing the EU to develop a more effective common asylum system. Especially since the Treaty of Nice, Swedish governments, irrespective of party colour, have actively pursued a supranational policy with majority voting in legislation and the establishment of more uniform rules in the legislative acts. The agenda-setting role of Sweden was also evident during the autumn of 2015 when the crisis in refugee reception, led Sweden, together with Germany, to call for greater responsibility, solidarity and burden sharing between the EU Member States. Since EU migration management after 2015 increasingly has been tied to the policy of combating irregular immigration, this has also led to the establishment of a common policy for more efficient border controls. Here, the adjustment pressure has been greater insofar that Swedish governments clearly had been opposed to this development. The directive on *Extended carrier responsibilities* for instance met with large resistance in the early 2000s. Even though the directive later was incorporated into Swedish law, there was a fear that this would undermine asylum law, especially for the unaccompanied minors. Regarding the impact of EU membership on refugee reception, no real impact can be noted, at least not until 2015. In 1994, before EU membership, Sweden granted a large number of residence permits for asylum seekers from the Western Balkans. In 2006 and since 2013, Sweden has also granted a large number of residence permits mainly to Iraqi refugees (2006) and to Syrian refugees (2013-2015).

By the end of 2015, and as a result of the collapse of the CEAS, the traditionally generous Swedish asylum policy has evolved into becoming one of the EU's most restrictive. In addition to closing the border with Denmark, with the introduction of the rule of *extended carrier responsibility*, more restrictive legislation was also introduced in the domain of residence permits and family reunification. However, the reintroduction of national borders is not limited to Sweden, but the crisis in refugee reception led to a snowballing effect, insofar that several Member States closed their borders. This is not only contrary to the Schengen convention but also challenges the very foundation of the EU, based on the free movement. What can be noted is that the increasing irregular immigration, and how to manage it, has evolved into becoming one of the EU's most challenging priorities. Whether the new securitised EU policy with strengthened external border controls, where internal security is increasingly dependent on the external, is sustainable, is highly uncertain. Uncertainty also surrounds the outsourcing of EU migration management to third countries, as shown by the recent Turkish decision not to continue complying with the EU-Turkey Deal. What is certain, however, is that as long as lack of solidarity and burden-sharing in between EU Member States continue to hamper implementation of a reformed, more robust asylum policy, migration issues will continue to be one of the most decisive and divisive issues of both the EU as well as individual Member States, such as Sweden.

References

Abiri, E. 2000. 'The Changing Practice of 'Generosity': Swedish Refugee Policy during the 1990s'. *Journal of Refugee Studies*, 13 (1).

Aftonbladet, 21 November 2003.

Andersson, H. 2008. *Överstatlig flyktingpolitik*. Umeå: Boréa.

Appelqvist, M. 2000. 'Party Politics and the Bosnian question: the Swedish decision to grant permanent residence'. *Journal of Ethnic and Migration Studies*, 26 (1).

Black, R. & K. Koser. 1999. *The End of the Refugee Cycle. Refugee Repatriation and Reconstruction*. Oxford: Berghahn Books.

Bucken-Knapp, G. 2009. *Defending the Swedish Model: Social Democrats, Trade Unions and Labour Migration Policy Reform*. Lanham, MD: Lexington Books.

Carmel, E. & R. Paul. 2013. 'Complex stratification: Understanding European Union governance of migrant rights'. *Regions and Cohesion*, 3 (3).

Charter of Fundamental Rights of the European Union (2000/C 364/01), 18 December 2000.

Collett, E. 2014. 'Future policy development on immigration and asylum: Understanding the challenge'. *Migration Policy Institute Europe*, Policy Brief Series, No. 4.

Council directive 2001/51/EC, Extended carrier responsibilities directive, 28 June 2001.

— 2001/55/EC, Mass influx of dis-

placed persons directive, 20 July 2001.
– 2003/9/EC, Reception conditions directive, 27 January 2003.
– 2004/38/EC, Freedom of movement and residence, 29 April 2004.
– 2004/83/EC, Qualification directive, 29 April 2004.
– 2005/85/EC, Asylum procedures directive, 1 December 2005.
– 2009/50/EC, Blue card directive, 25 May 2009.
– 2008/115/EC, Return directive, 16 December 2008.
– 2011/95/EU, Qualification recast directive, 13 December 2011.
– 2011/98/EU, Single permit directive, 13 December 2011.
– 2013/32/EU, Asylum procedures recast directive, 26 June 2013.
– 2013/33/EU, Reception conditions recast directive, 26 June 2013.
– 2014/36/EU, Seasonal workers directive, 26 February 2014.

Council regulation (EC), 2725/2000, Eurodac regulation, 11 December 2000.
– (EC), 343/2003, Dublin Convention, 18 February 2003.
– (EC) 2007/2004, Frontex regulation, 26 October 2004.

Europe.eu

European Commission. 2015. A European Agenda on Migration. Brussels: COM(2015) 240 final.
– 2016. Press release on reforming the Blue card directive. Brussels, 7 June 2016.
– 2017. Annual Report on Migration and Asylum. European Migration Network. Brussels, 25 April 2017.

Frank, D. 2005. *Staten, företagen och arbetskraftsinvandringen: en studie av invandringspolitiken i Sverige och rekryteringen av utländska arbetare 1960–1972*. Växjö: Växjö University Press.

Geddes, A. 2015. 'Migration: Differential Institutionalization and its Effects' In: F. Trauner & A. Ripoll Servent (eds.) *Policy Change in the Area of Freedom, Security and Justice: How EU Institutions Matter*. London: Routledge.

Geneva Convention on the Status of Refugees, 28 July 1951.

Hinnfors, J., A. Spehar & G. Bucken-Knapp. 2012. 'The missing factor: why social democracy can lead to restrictive immigration policy'. *Journal of European Public Policy*, 19 (4).

Migrationsinfo.se

Nilsson, Å. 2004. 'Efterkrigstidens invandring och utvandring'. *Demografiska rapporter 2004:5*. Stockholm: Statistiska centralbyrån.

Nugent, N. 2010. *The Government and Politics of the European Union*. Basingstoke: Palgrave Macmillan.

OECD. 2011. *Recruiting Immigrant Workers: Sweden 2011*. Paris: OECD Publishing.
– 2018. 'International Migration Outlook'. Paris: OECD Publishing.

Perlmutter, T. 1996. 'Bringing Parties Back In: Comments on Modes of Immigration Politics in Liberal Democratic Societies'. *International Migration Review*, 30 (1).

Rydgren, J. 2005. Från skattemissnöje till etnisk nationalism: Högerpopulism och parlamentarisk högerextremism i Sverige. Lund: Studentlitteratur.

Spång, M. 2008. 'Svensk invandringspolitik i demokratiskt perspektiv'. *Current Themes in IMER Research 8*. Malmö: Malmö Institute

for Studies of Migration and Ethnic Relations (IMER), Malmö University.
Svenska Dagbladet, 22 August 2011.
Swedish government bill, 1968:142, 'Riktlinjer utlänningspolitiken, m.m.'.
— 1991/92:30, 'En särskild nämnd för utlänningsärenden'.
— 1996/97:25, 'Svensk migrationspolitik i globalt perspektiv'.
— 2017/18:108, 'Genomförande av säsongsanställningsdirektivet'.
Swedish government declaration, 15 September 2015.
Swedish government directive, 2014:109, 'Svensk social trygghet i en internationell värld', 17 July 2014.
Swedish government letter, 2013/14:73, 'Migration och asylpolitik'.
Swedish government official report 1967:18. *Invandringen. Problematik och handläggning. Utlänningsutredningens betänkande II*. Stockholm.
— 1988:2. *Kortare väntan.* Stockholm.
— 1995:75. *Svensk flyktingpolitik i globalt perspektiv.* Stockholm.
— 2000:7. *Långtidsutredningen 1999/2000.* Stockholm.
— 2006:87. *Arbetskraftsinvandring – förslag och konsekvenser.* Stockholm.
Swedish government.se (website of the Swedish Government)
Swedish migration agency.
Swedish parliament protocol, 2003/04:114, 12 May 2004.
Treaty of Lisbon
Treaty of Nice
Ucarer, E. M. 2013. 'The Area of Freedom, Security and Justice' In: M. Cini & N. Pérez-Solórzano Borragán (eds.) *European Union Politics*. Oxford: Oxford University Press.
United Nations, Universal Declaration of Human Rights
Zimmermann, K. F. 2016. 'Refugee and Migrant Labour Market Integration: Europe in Need of a New Policy Agenda'.
— 2017. 'Refugee and Migrant Labour Market Integration: Europe in Need of a New Policy Agenda' In: R. Bauböck & M. Tripkovic (eds.) *The Integration of Migrants and Refugees. An EUI Forum on Migration, Citizenship and Demography.* Robert Schuman Centre for Advanced Studies.
Öberg, N. 1994. *Gränslös rättvisa eller rättvisa inom gränser? Om moraliska dilemman i välfärdsstaters invandrings- och invandrarpolitik.* Stockholm: Almqvist & Wicksell.

10. Crime Prevention Policy

Between National Priorities and EU Commitments

Rebecka Villanueva Ulfgard

Can European Union (EU) Member States fully trust each other's criminal justice systems? (Block, 2017; Bureš 2016; Hufnagel and McCartney, 2017; Spapens, 2017) The 'EU Justice Agenda for 2020', launched by the European Commission in 2014, highlights the need for strengthening trust, mobility and growth, underlining that 'enhancing mutual trust' between relevant actors is key for the EU (Hufnagel and McCartney, 2017). Against the background of religiously motivated terrorist attacks, unprecedented migration flows and increasing cross-border crime in recent years, the EU is facing serious threats to the core spirit of its *raison d'être*; securing democratic and peaceful societies where fundamental freedoms and liberties are respected. The European integration process rests on four freedoms; free movement of capital, goods, services, and individuals (labour). The aim with these freedoms is to contribute to the dismantling of border controls between the Member States and increase EU competitiveness in the global arena. At the same time, this unique feature of the European community has produced unwanted consequences such as uncontrolled immigration and complex cross-border crime (Colvin 2002; Den Boer 2001; Den Boer and Doelle 2002). To compensate for the loss of control at the borders, the Member States have agreed on a number of so-called compensatory measures, for example, the Schengen cooperation framework and extended intelligence agreement within and between police and customs (the Europol agency) and the Prosecutor's Office (Eurojust). By mere involvement in these, the Swedish police organisation and law enforcement practices have become Europeanised, which this chapter seeks to problematise.

Initially, EU police and judicial cooperation in criminal matters was of intergovernmental nature (Colvin 2002); each country had the right to veto decisions and the EU could not control how its members actually implemented the rules in their national legislations. Cooperation has since developed and deepened, especially after the terrorist attacks that hit the United States and Europe from the early 2000s onwards (Casale 2012; Carrapico 2013; Cocq and Galli, 2017; Den Boer 2002a, 2002b, 2003, 2011, Felia and Den Boer 2013, Lodge 2002, 2004, 2009; Paoli, 2014; Scherrer, Jeandesboz and Guittet 2011; Smyrl 2007). The EU then decided on a set of rules to combat terrorism, for example the European Arrest Warrant (EAW) (2002) and the Directive on the retention of data generated or processed in connection with the provision of publicly available electronic communications services or public communications networks (Directive 2006/24/EC).

Since December 1, 2009 with the entry into force of the Treaty of Lisbon (amending the Treaty on European Union and the Treaty establishing the European Community), cooperation in criminal law and police matters is supranational in character (Bossong and Rhinard 2015; O'Neill, Swinton and Winter 2013). This means that EU and the Member States 'share power' to decide on rules and measures, though it is the countries themselves who are responsible for maintaining law, order, and security within their own borders. Put differently, in the name of the EU there are common rules to combat trafficking in human beings, but the EU does not have the power to, for example, prohibit prostitution (the Member States decide for themselves).

Two questions are central in this chapter: To what extent has Sweden adapted its policy in law enforcement to requirements resulting from its EU membership? What does the adaptation process look like? What are the different kinds of pressures regarding the content of this policy (substance) and form (organisation)? Additional questions are: To what extent is Sweden involved in the agenda-setting of the EU's law enforcement agenda, thereby making the compliance issue less likely to cause friction with national policies, and, hence 'easier' to implement directives nationally? What are some of the challenges surrounding the implementation process of EU law enforcement in the national arena? The last question deserves special attention given the intense debate in Sweden on the Data Retention Directive, where precisely the 'fit' between Swedish and EU legislation became a sticking point.

In order to answer the above questions, the chapter first traces the development of EU law enforcement. Next, it sheds light on how Sweden's law enforcement policy has evolved over time in the light of its EU membership, distinguishing between direct and indirect effects of Europeanisation. Subsequent sections address substantive changes and organisational changes, with special emphasis on deepened EU cooperation in two interconnected areas; fight against global terrorism and prevention of cross-border crime. The concluding section summarises the key findings and reflects on the degree to which Sweden's law enforcement has become Europeanised as consequence of EU membership, and whether there is a need for deeper Europeanisation in this particular area of cooperation.

Development of European Law Enforcement

The evolution of European law enforcement is marked by ideas of continuity and new institutional/organisational initiatives but also incidents and critical junctures, from the early days of the TREVI cooperation over the latest Lisbon Treaty, to the debates on preventing Islamist radicalisation of young men and women across Europe, all of which in various ways has contributed to qualitative changes in police cooperation at the EU level.

To account for police cooperation in today's EU, an international context is required taking its starting point in the creation of the International Criminal Police Commission (ICPC) in 1923, since 1956 better known as Interpol (International Criminal Police Organization). A dilemma for Interpol under the post-World War II era concerned how to handle the principle of neutrality when its mission collided with sensitive issues of political, ethnic or religious nature. Doubts that prevailed on this point partially paralysed Interpol's ability to act forcefully in the fight against political terrorism, which posed a serious threat to both individual and state security, undermining political stability in some European countries in the 1970s (The Red Army Faction (RAF) also known as the Baader-Meinhof Group in then West Germany; the Revolutionary People's Struggle, and the Revolutionary Organization 17 November in Greece; and, the Red Brigades in Italy). It was not until 1984 when Interpol decided to include the pursuit of terrorist-related crimes in its mandate. The ambivalence on the side of Interpol caused disappointment among political leaders in West Germany, France, the Netherlands, Belgium and Luxembourg, who decided to take matters in their own hands and created the so-called TREVI cooperation ('Terrorism, Radicalism, Extremism, Violence, Internationalism') in 1975. Its dynamic was intergovernmental under the leadership of the interior ministers assisted by representatives from the respective police authorities (Colvin 2002:87). By 1989, TREVI boasted four working groups: political terrorism, police cooperation, organised crime, and free movement of persons. These were supervised by a group of senior officials responsible for preparing the decisions adopted later by the Council of Ministers concerned. It is no exaggeration to that claim that discussions within the TREVI group served as source of inspiration for the continued intergovernmental cooperation where the Schengen Agreement from 1985 became a cornerstone for EU police cooperation.

What is the Schengen Agreement about? Again, the Franco-German axis was determinant in bringing about the idea of eliminating border controls in the European Community area, securing wider endorsement at the European Council in Fontainebleau in 1984. However, the agreement was not signed by all then European Community members; on June 14, 1985, only Belgium, France, Luxemburg, The Netherlands, and West Germany ratified it. In 1990, the Schengen Agreement was transformed into the Schengen Convention that aimed for the complete elimination of systematic internal border controls and a common visa policy (Colvin 2002:88), but it did not take force until 1995. Importantly, the Schengen Agreement was not anchored within the European community institutional or legal structure until the Amsterdam Treaty (1999) when certain provisions became replaced by new EU legislation (for example, concerning the Schengen Borders Code). Importantly, the incorporation of the Schengen acquis was only possibly after agreed opt-outs for Ireland and the United Kingdom, who did not wish to be included in the Schengen Area for political reasons. Moreover, in December 1996, Norway and Iceland signed an association agreement with the signatories of the Schengen Agreement to form part of the Schengen Area. Now, this agreement never materialised, but later on both countries joined the Schengen Area after ratifying similar agreements with the EU. In fact, the Schengen Convention itself was not supposed to be open for signature by non-EU member states, so, for example Switzerland could join the Schengen Area but not the Convention in 2009. Bulgaria, Croatia, and Rumania do not participate but are technically speaking obliged to join, and Cyprus has a temporary derogation; only future will tell whether they actually will one day. After the Nordic enlargement of the EU in 1995, it was not until 2001 that Denmark, Finland, Iceland, Norway, and Sweden joined the Schengen Convention. In response to the massive influx of migrants especially from the Middle East since autumn 2015, early September that year the German government decided to introduce temporary controls on its border with Austria to get better control of this situation. The following year, border controls were temporarily reintroduced in some other Schengen countries; Austria, Denmark, Norway, and Sweden. During the past years, the government has recurrently extended the period for the border controls. On October 31, 2019, the government decided to keep border controls until May 12, 2020. The decision is based on the government's assessment that there is still a serious threat to public order and domestic security in Sweden.[1]

The loss of internal border controls in the EU area has successively been replaced with enhanced border control at Schengen countries' external borders and the European Border and Coast Guard Agency (better known as Frontex) plays an important role in this regard. The external borders comprise land and sea borders of the signatory states as well as airports and ports as per the Schengen Convention not

1 "Fortsatt gränskontroll vid inre gräns." Press release from the Swedish Department of Justice. Published Oct. 31 2019. https://www.regeringen.se/pressmeddeland-en/2019/10/fortsatt-granskontroll-vid-inre-grans/

counted as internal border. Furthermore, the convention establishes conditions to be met by incoming people to the Schengen Area and facilitates black listing undesired third country nationals who seek to enter the territory of the signatory states. As the signatory states are obliged to impose rules on this in national legislation, for Sweden this has meant changes in the Aliens Act Sweden, Passport Act, and the Police Data Act. In fact, there is an ongoing revision of these acts during 2018-2020 by a one-man commission of inquiry (a common form for the government to make expert consultations ahead of new legislation).[2]

In order to compensate for the loss of direct border control, the EU countries who are signatories to the Schengen Convention have agreed on a range of compensatory measures, including data-based personal files/registers (Colvin 2002:93). The Schengen Information System (SIS) II-currently in its second phase since 2013, is a common inquiry system, established 1995, which is used, *inter alia*, in border controls and police investigations, and when issuing visas and residence permits.[3] In this system, the Schengen countries register data about wanted persons and objects, as well as information that will prevent expelled or qualified as security risk third-country nationals from entering the Schengen area. Member States exchange information about convicted and wanted persons and objects, supported by mutual access to various registers containing data about DNA, fingerprints, and vehicles. When an EU citizen is convicted of a crime in another EU country, home country will receive information about the verdict. A particular EU country may also request the criminal record from the home country of a suspect in order to get a fuller picture

2 Regeringskansliet. 'Regeringen ser över regelverk för att öka skyddet mot säkerhetshot', August 24, 2018, at https://www.regeringen.se/pressmeddelanden/2018/08/regeringen-ser-over-regelverk-for-att-oka-skyddet-mot-sakerhetshot/.

3 SIS is in operation in 30 European countries, including 26 EU Member States (only Ireland and Cyprus are not yet connected to SIS) and four Schengen Associated Countries (Switzerland, Norway, Liechtenstein and Iceland). While it operates the SIS, since the UK has chosen not to join the Schengen area, it cannot issue or access Schengen-wide alerts for refusing entry or stay into the Schengen area. European Commission. Migration and Home Affairs. 'Schengen Information System.' Last update: 28/08/2018. At https://ec.europa.eu/home-affairs/what-we-do/policies/borders-and-visas/schengen-information-system_en.

for an ongoing investigation. Article 93 in the Schengen Convention establishes that the aim of SIS is to preserve order and public security, including state security, by means of using data transferred via SIS. Hence, SIS has the task of compensating for the loss of internal border controls and is therefore used by police and customs authorities at external border controls. Every police station, not just located at the external borders of the Schengen area, as well as mobile police units, shall be connected to SIS. SIS is made up of national sections and a central office, based in Strasbourg. The ambition is that national sections should be similar in organisation and procedures for handling data, and contain all data from all the signatory countries, while SIS should be continuously updated via the central office. SIS contains information about age, gender, nationality, and in some cases, criminal record. The SIRENE register; Supplementary Information Requests at the National Entries, complements SIS. If a police, customs or Coast Guard officer when performing a search in the SIS in conjunction with a control of a particular person or object finds out that there is a statement regarding this person, then the reporting state should be notified about this. Situations like these are dealt with directly between SIRENE offices of the two countries concerned. Each signatory country has a SIRENE office serving as national contact point and is responsible for exchanging information in the event of a 'hit' in the SIS. The Swedish Police Authority has a special branch within the National Operations Department (NOA) functioning as a link between police, customs, and coast guard authorities, along with national migration offices and other Schengen SIRENE offices.

Another important measure to compensate for the assumed 'security deficit' resulting from the elimination of internal border controls in the Schengen area is the possibility for Schengen countries to conclude bilateral agreements to allow so-called 'cross-border hot pursuit'. This means that a supposedly criminal who crosses the border to another country may be persecuted (and even arrested) within a certain territorial range by the police force in that country where the actual criminal act was committed, provided that the bilateral agreement allows for this. How this looks in practice varies from Schengen to Schengen country, meaning that it is unilateral in nature. Yet another crime prevention measure allows the signatory states to conclude bilateral agreements to send out police officers from one Schengen country for work in another Schengen country. A recent example is from June 1, 2018, when the Nordic Justice and Home Affairs ministers presented a declaration of intent to facilitate for operational police work in each other's territory to a greater extent than what provisions allow for today. Among other measures, the nearest police patrol even from another Nordic country should be allowed to intervene in an ongoing crime scene. Another proposal is that police officers from a Nordic country should be allowed to patrol and secure law and order across the border of another Nordic (neighbouring) country.[4]

Justice and Home Affairs (JHA) became institutionalised through the Treaty on the European Union (also known as the Maastricht Treaty), Title VI, Articles 29–42, which entered into force on November 1, 1993. As mentioned elsewhere in this volume, the EU rested on three pillars; the first one of supranational character (the European Community dealing with agricultural policy, competition policy, external trade policy, among others), the second one intergovernmental since it concerned the Common Foreign and Security Policy (CFSP), and the third one intergovernmental since it covered Justice and Home Affairs. The Maastricht Treaty drew the guidelines for joint law enforcement envisioning a common Police Authority (later, Europol) and a union-wide information exchange system. The fact that JHA were given priority on the EU agenda was due to two interwoven factors; increased reporting in the media on illegal immigration and sex trafficking raised public attention and protests in several EU countries resulting in responsible politicians' growing awareness that cross-border crimes would be increasingly complex and rapidly expanding, hence requiring common efforts to be fought efficiently.

A few years later, the JHA Council adopted a special action plan against organised crime in April 1997, approved by the European Council at its meeting in Amsterdam in June that same year. The legal base for intensified police cooperation was procured by Article 30 in the Amsterdam Treaty, which entered into force on May 1,

4 Regeringskansliet. 'Nordiskt polissamarbete fördjupas', June 1, 2018, at https://www.regeringen.se/pressmeddelanden/2018/06/nordiskt-polissamarbete-fordjupas/.

1999. Among others, it emphasised Europol's mission to facilitate investigative work and promote cooperation between investigators and specialised prosecutors and judges. The novelty was that asylum and immigration issues, as well as civil law cooperation and the Schengen provisions were transferred from the third to the first pillar. Accordingly, the third pillar kept Police and Judicial Cooperation in Criminal Matters (PJCCM); drug trafficking and weapons smuggling, terrorism, trafficking in human beings, organised crime, bribery and fraud. Decisions were adopted by unanimity and the legal instruments previously applied were replaced *inter alia* with so-called Framework Decisions; determining what should be achieved, but leaving the Member States certain freedom to decide how to go about it.

At the European Council meeting in Tampere on October 15-16, 1999, the heads of state and government announced the creation of an 'Area of Freedom, Security and Justice' for the EU. To facilitate for this vision to come true, decisions were made to increase efforts in police cooperation, facilitate for the application of the principle of mutual recognition in both civil and criminal cooperation, and develop a common asylum and refugee policy (Colvin 2002:90). On this same occasion, it was also decided to set up Eurojust based in The Hague. This evolution can be summarized like this: 'Measures to combat terrorism and international organised crime have been adopted on a piecemeal basis, often in response to particular problems. [...] Each element seems to be discrete but each has become part of a wider package of instruments designed to enhance the EU's ability to combat international criminal activity with a view to realising a zone of freedom, security and justice in an enlarging EU. Member governments have ditched the security taboo and acknowledged the obvious inseparability of internal and external security matters.' (Lodge 2002:6)

The radical change to the EU's treaty structure came with the amending of the two treaties forming the constitutional basis of the EU, initially named the Reform Treaty, and finally entitled the Treaty on the Functioning of the European Union (TFEU), agreed in Lisbon (hence, the Lisbon Treaty), which entered into force on December 1, 2009. In conjunction with this shift, cooperation in criminal justice and police matters became supranational and the Member States thereby lost their veto power over new laws in this area, but they have 'shared power' with the EU institutions to decide about new rules.[5] In concrete terms, the European Commission shares the right of initiative with the Member States provided that they are represented by a quarter of the members of the Council (Article 76 TFEU). The dialogue with the European Parliament is comparatively limited. The European Council sets out the guidelines and the JHA Council sets the agenda, assisted by the General Secretariat of the Council. The CJEU is guiding the JHA Council and the Member States in their implementation of EU law enforcement directives. Supporting actors at the supranational level are Europol, Eurojust, Frontex, CEPOL, and the EUPCN. In addition, the Lisbon Treaty introduced the so-called solidarity clause (similar to NATO's Article 5 mutual defence clause), which originated after the terrorist attack in Madrid in March 2004. Expressed in Article 222, it states:[6]

> 1. The Union and its Member States shall act jointly in a spirit of solidarity if a Member State is the object of a terrorist attack or the victim of a natural or man-made disaster. The Union shall mobilise all the instruments at its disposal, including the military resources made available by the Member States, to:
>
> (a) – prevent the terrorist threat in the territory of the Member States;
> – protect democratic institutions and the civilian population from any terrorist attack;
> – assist a Member State in its territory, at the request of its political authorities, in the event of a terrorist attack;
>
> (b) – assist a Member State in its territory, at the request of its political authorities, in the event of a natural or man-made disaster.

5 It is important to mention that Denmark, in accordance with Protocol 22 on the position of Denmark, and the United Kingdom, Protocol 21 on the position of the United Kingdom and Ireland, were granted special derogations with respect to the EU's Area of Freedom, Security and Justice, (for example, in relation to Europol and CEPOL), annexed to the TEU and to the TFEU.

6 EUR-Lex. Treaty on the Functioning of the European Union, at https://eur-lex.europa.eu/legal-content/EN/TXT/PDF/?uri=CELEX:12012E/TXT&from=EN

However, given the politically sensitive nature of this issue, the European Council agreed that this commitment 'shall not prejudice the specific character of the security and defence policy of certain Member States'.[7] For Sweden (and neutral Ireland), this means that it can preserve the doctrine of 'military non-alignment in peace aiming at neutrality in war', that is, keeping one of the few remaining European Cold War legacies in foreign policy matters.

Supporting Institutions and Networks Coordinated at Supranational Level

Europol (https://www.europol.europa.eu/), the European Union Agency for Law Enforcement Cooperation, formerly the European Police Office, plays a supportive role for cooperation between the Member States' crime prevention and law enforcement authorities (Bruggeman and Den Boer 2007; Bureš, 2016; Cocq and Galli, 2017; Paoli, 2014; Schalken and Pronk 2002), in particular, in the area of criminal intelligence. One of its objectives is, precisely, to improve the effectiveness and cooperation between Member States' competent authorities in preventing and combating different forms of international organised crime. In others words, Europol functions as a service agency and information centre for the EU countries. As mentioned earlier, the TREVI-countries' JHA ministers held discussions on the need for European police cooperation, but it was not laid down until Maastricht and the first tangible step came in June 1993 in Copenhagen when these ministers decided to set up the Europol Drugs Unit (EDU), as a precursor to Europol. In October that same year it was decided that EDU would have its office in The Hague. Initially, EDU would only work with international illicit drug trafficking, but gradually its duties expanded into other areas (Den Boer 2001:264; Lodge 2002:46), like illicit trafficking in radioactive and

7 EUR-Lex. Consolidated version of the Treaty on European Union – TITLE V: GENERAL PROVISIONS ON THE UNION'S EXTERNAL ACTION AND SPECIFIC PROVISIONS ON THE COMMON FOREIGN AND SECURITY POLICY – Chapter 2: Specific provisions on the common foreign and security policy – Section 2: Provisions on the common security and defence policy – Article 42 (ex Article 17 TEU), at https://eur-lex.europa.eu/legal-content/EN/TXT/?uri=CELEX%3A12008M042.

nuclear substances, and stolen vehicles; crimes involving clandestine immigration and trafficking networks, and networks for spreading child pornography; crimes against life, health and freedom; illicit trade and environmental crimes; crime against private and public property; counterfeiting and counterfeiting of other means of payment; terrorism, and money laundering in relation to these aforementioned crimes.

The Europol Convention was ratified by all EU countries in 1995 and entered into force on October 1, 1998 following an extended ratification process in the Member States. After a number of acts had been adopted as a result of the convention, Europol became operational on July 1, 1999 (Colvin 2002:94), replacing the EDU. On January 1, 2010, Europol was 'upgraded' to EU authority, following the Council Decision 2009/371/JHA, hence the convention became obsolete and new administrative simplifications and budgetary procedures and controls entered the picture, involving the European Parliament. Another feature of this transformation process was the expanding of its mandate to include crime that is not strictly connected with organised crime. This means that Europol can support a Member State with intelligence and analysis resources in conjunction with major international events (for example, sports events and festivals). In addition, Europol will also support Member States to collect and analyse information from the Internet.

To sum up, Europol's mandate includes offering analysis to support operations in the EU countries, as well as to assist these with strategic reports and criminal investigations based on information and information provided by them. In terms of resources, Europol can act as coordinator and provider of expertise and technical support for investigations and activities to be carried out within the Member States under the auspices of corresponding authorities (Colvin 2002:95; Helmius 2000:52). It should be pointed out that Europol has no independent, executive power tools, but is entirely in the hands of the political wills of the Member States (Schalken and Pronk 2002:74). Europol thus assists by facilitating exchange of information in accordance with national laws. This exchange occurs, for example, between Europol's contact persons working at Europol's office in The Hague and their contact persons representing various national law enforcement agencies (Sweden has a designed liaison officer at the National Operations Department (NOA) within the Swedish Police Authority.

The JHA ministers are responsible for guidance and control of Europol, appointing the Executive Director and adopting the budget. Since May 2018, Catherine De Bolle (former commissioner general of the Belgian Federal Police) holds this function. It is relevant to mention the procedure for this designation: Just as with other EU agencies, the management board of Europol had drafted a list of potential candidates, passed on to the JHA ministers. With their approval, De Bolle attended a hearing at the Committee on Civil Liberties, Justice and Home Affairs (LIBE) of the European Parliament, who, in turn, issued a non-binding positive opinion. Following this, the JHA ministers could then ratify (by unanimous decision) the designation of De Bolle as Europol's new Executive Director for a four-year term period.[8]

The Management Board of Europol consists of one representative of each member state (and an alternate), entrusted with the general task of monitoring the organisation's activities. The Swedish government, through the Ministry of Justice, has appointed this representative from the NOA. It is worth noticing that Europol is under scrutiny by the Joint Parliamentary Scrutiny Group (JSPG), created at the EU Speakers Conference in Bratislava on 23–25 April 2017, enabling for both the European Parliament and national parliaments to gain deeper knowledge about its activities.[9]

Since 2005, Europol supervises the Europol Information System (EIS) that is equivalent to a 'criminal information and intelligence database' as it keeps track of 'all of Europol's mandated crime areas, including terrorism'. This 'reference system', which extends 'beyond national or organisational jurisdictions', operates in 22 languages.

8 Europol. 'THE COUNCIL OF THE EU APPOINTS CATHERINE DE BOLLE AS NEW EXECUTIVE DIRECTOR OF EUROPOL', n/a, Press release, March 08, 2018, at https://www.europol.europa.eu/newsroom/news/council-of-eu-appoints-catherine-de-bolle-new-executive-director-of-europol. n/a. Europol. 'GOVERNANCE & ACCOUNTABILITY', at https://www.europol.europa.eu/about-europol/governance-accountability.

9 Europol. 'Governance and Accountability', n/d, at https://www.europol.europa.eu/about-europol/governance-accountability.

Besides, it enables 'storage and automatic cross-checking of biometrics (DNA) and cybercrime-related data'. 'In 2015, 24 countries and organisations began using the EIS to share lists of foreign terrorist fighters (FTFS) [...], which had grown to over 7800 contributed by 24 countries, by December 2016.' No doubt, it is a key instrument to uphold Europol's mission and consulted by 'Europol officials, Member State liaison officers, and seconded national experts stationed at Europol headquarters, as well as staff in the Europol National Units and in competent authorities in the Member States. In addition, some of Europol's cooperation partners can store and query data via Europol's operational centre. '[10]In order to track down FTFS in the EU, Europol has a special group of experts gathering in the framework for the so-called Europol Analysis System, hence, the Analysis Project Travellers is a valid focal point for exchanging experiences regarding the return and possible reintegration of these individuals.[11]

It is also worth mentioning the possibility to set up so-called joint investigation teams (JITS), which involves police and judicial cooperation between at least two countries, saving time from administrative procedures regarding requests for mutual legal assistance.[12] This particular modus operandi helped the French and Belgian police/judicial systems to track down connections between the terrorist attacks in Paris, November 2015, and Brussels, March 2016.

To facilitate for Member States sharing information and data between themselves and with Europol and other relevant EU law enforcement actors, the European Counter-Terrorism Centre (ECTC) was launched on January 1, 2016, which also provides 'Direct and immediate on-the-spot support' for example through 'Emergency Response Team (EMRT)' and 'Live investigation support' and 'Incident response

10 Europol. 'EUROPOL INFORMATION SYSTEM (EIS)', n/d, https://www.europol.europa.eu/activities-services/services-support/information-exchange/europol-information-system.

11 Europol. 'EUROPOL ANALYSIS PROJECTS', n/d, at https://www.europol.europa.eu/crime-areas-trends/europol-analysis-projects.

12 ELSJ. Reséau universitaire européen. 'The Paris Terrorist Attacks: Failure of the EU's Area of Freedom, Security and Justice?', P. de Bruycker, D. Watt, H. Labayle, A. Weyembergh, C. Brière, January 8, 2016, at http://www.gdr-elsj.eu/2016/01/08/cooperation-judiciaire-penale/the-paris-terrorist-attacks-failure-of-the-eus-area-of-freedom-security-and-justice/.

and coordination'.[13] It is important to keep in mind that, '[w]hereas police information sharing is subject to EU legislation, adopted under the EU competencies in police cooperation in criminal matters, [...], intelligence sharing does not fall within the EU competencies, and the EU is prevented from taking any action in this regard'. Nonetheless, one could actually ask whether the EU countries are not moving into a grey zone, especially when some of the intelligence measures constitute a potential threat to fundamental rights and freedoms, besides, 'intelligence service might be reluctant to cooperate extensively with law enforcement, judicial or other authorities'.[14]

Eurojust (http://eurojust.europa.eu/Pages/home.aspx) comprises national prosecutors, judges and/or police officers assists national authorities in their fight against terrorism and organised crime involving more than one EU country by 'coordinating investigations and prosecutions, helping to resolve conflicts of jurisdiction [and] facilitating the drafting and implementation of EU legal instruments, such as European Arrest Warrants and confiscation and freezing orders'.[15] Eurojust was launched in 2002 following a decision by the European Council. Similar to Europol, Eurojust cannot conduct preliminary investigations or prosecute on its own. Practically, Eurojust arranges meetings and coordination centres with prosecutors, judges and law enforcement officers from the EU countries (and third countries on special occasions), providing facilities and translation services and reimbursing travel and accommodation expenses, and it also funds and offers expertise to assist Joint Investigation Teams (JITS), which has proven an efficient form of collaboration between EU countries in combating organised crime. Moreover, Eurojust auspices 'the Secretariats of the European Judicial Network, the Joint Investigation Teams Network and the Network for investigation and prosecution

13 Europol. 'EUROPEAN COUNTER TERRORISM CENTRE – ECTCN', n/d, at https://www.europol.europa.eu/about-europol/european-counter-terrorism-centre-ectc.

14 ELSJ. Réseau universitaire européen. 'The Paris Terrorist Attacks: Failure of the EU's Area of Freedom, Security and Justice?', P. de Bruycker, D. Watt, H. Labayle, A. Weyembergh, C. Brière, January 8, 2016, at http://www.gdr-elsj.eu/2016/01/08/cooperation-judiciaire-penale/the-paris-terrorist-attacks-failure-of-the-eus-area-of-freedom-security-and-justice/.

15 europa.eu. 'Eurojust', Overview, at https://europa.eu/european-union/about-eu/agencies/eurojust_en.

of genocide, crimes against humanity and war crimes (Genocide Network)'.[16] Eurojust is governed through the 'College', which is made up of one senior prosecutor or judge from each EU country under the leadership of an Administrative Director. The Data Protection Officer works independently of the Administrative Director. Collaboration partners are Europol, OLAF (the European Anti-Fraud Office), the European Agency for the Management of Operational Cooperation at the External Borders of the Member States of the European Union (Frontex), Interpol, and United Nations Office on Drugs and Crime (UNODC), among others.

In 2002, the Member States decided on a common definition for locating organised crime and that it is a crime to participate in criminal organisations. The underlying idea is to approximate sentencing of criminality across the EU. In fact, the whole purpose of judicial cooperation in criminal matters aims for the Member States' mutual recognition of judgements and punishments in this area, but also, to harmonise law enforcement measures and making them more comparable. Therefore, under certain conditions, the EU can decide on minimum rules, for example regarding handling evidence and rights of victims. Individual Member States can then apply stricter rules if they so wish. There are also certain areas where the JHA ministers can reach agreement on minimum rules regarding legal provisions and punitive measures; areas that largely coincide with Europol's mandate: terrorism, trafficking in human beings and sexual exploitation of children and women, drug trafficking, trafficking in arms, money laundering, corruption, counterfeiting, cybercrime, organised crime, and terrorism.

Supporting bodies to Europol and Eurojust are, for example, the European Crime Prevention Network (EUPCN) with office in Brussels (http://eucpn.org/), seeking to 'connect local, national and European level and to promote crime prevention knowledge and practices among the EU Member States', 'disseminate qualitative knowledge on crime prevention', and 'contribute to the EU policy and strategy of crime prevention and to take part in various aspects of crime prevention with respect to the strategic priorities of the EU'. Funding is dependent on the Member States' degree of interest in the EUCPN's

16 *Ibid.*

activities and the ability to seek support from various EU financial programmes managed by the European Commission.

CEPOL, the European Union Agency for Law Enforcement Training (https://www.cepol.europa.eu/) since the Regulation 2015/2219 of the European Parliament and of the Council of 25 November 2015 (taking force on July 1, 2016), situated in Budapest, is entrusted with new knowledge creation and sharing, and education of EU countries' law enforcement officials and by invitation from third countries, in tight relation with the multi-annual EU Policy Cycle to tackle serious and organised crime.

Frontex (https://frontex.europa.eu/) established in 2005, today the European Border and Coast Guard Agency, located in Warsaw, had its mandate transformed and expanded in 2016. The allocation of more resources to Frontex came as a consequence of increasing challenges at the EU's external (Schengen) borders; in particular, the migration flows since the war began in Syria in 2011 and ensuing escalating conflicts in the Middle East and Afghanistan, generating more violence and political and religious extremism forcing people to flee their homes in unprecedented numbers since World War II. Sweden's national contact point for Frontex is affiliated with the NOA. It is rather conspicuous that Frontex is conducting 'regular vulnerability tests' in the EU countries to detect flaws and obstacles in law enforcement measures, sharing this information with national authorities and EU institutions. Frontex is also involved in migration enforcement; not just with respect to securing the EU/Schengen borders but also return operations. Not surprisingly, its increasingly operational function has led to demands (especially from human rights groups) to safeguard fundamental rights of migrants. Indeed, today Frontex has both technical and theoretical capacity for this, but its image remains abstruse with quite many Europeans. Being 'more operational than ever', Frontex boasts 'some 1,700 officers deployed at the EU's sea, land and air borders, assisting EU Member States in surveillance, registration, finger printing and security checks'. Moreover, the 'rapid reaction pool' can assist national law enforcement authorities in the event of a border emergency; counting on '1,500 officers, as well as additional sea vessels, aircraft, vehicles and other equipment'. Returning to the issue of migration, as European media has been reporting over the past few years, Frontex is taking active part in 'search and rescue operations' of migrants, and numbers are very high; 'the saving of 33,000 lives in the Central and Eastern Mediterranean between January and November 2017 alone',[17] according to the message by its Executive Director.

Summing up EU law enforcement authorities and looking towards the future, it is fair to say that recent developments respond to two interwoven trends that constitute not only EU challenges but also global challenges; the tightly-knitted problem-complex of political and religious extremism, Islamist terrorism, violence, and forced migration. Despite its pressing urgency, the EU leaders were not able to come up with an agreement on a common asylum policy, but instead resorted to the short-sighted national interest accompanied by xenophobic overtones in some cases. In the absence of this, might an 'EU FBI Police' mitigate some of the negative effects from this problem-complex? It is interesting that the question about a common EU police with fully-fledged operational capacities has been discussed on and off in the past. For example, previous German Chancellor Helmut Kohl sought to push for this in the 1980s and 1990s. Coupled with the resistance from Member States' side, the European Parliament has rejected any transfer of coercive powers of such kind to Europol (Cocq and Galli, 2017: 132). Sweden has so far been very critical to deepening EU law enforcement cooperation in this direction since it would seriously jeopardise national sovereignty regarding law enforcement rights. But, the political pendulum in the EU might swing more forcefully to either side depending on the nature of global and European economic-political and security-migration critical junctures and the responses these generate from the EU leaders. So, perhaps one should not rule out the scenario where Europol in practice would have the right to provide directives to national police officers (*cf.* Bruggeman 2001: 286).

Sweden's Law Enforcement Policy

Generally speaking, law enforcement in Sweden in post-war times was regarded a national affair. Since the 1970s, there was a growing concern with shifting focus towards crime prevention with the overall

17 Frontex. 'Foreword' (Fabrice Leggeri, Frontex Executive Director), n/d, at https://frontex.europa.eu/about-frontex/foreword/.

goal of creating a safer society. In the 1974, the Swedish National Council for Crime Prevention (*Brottsförebyggande Rådet, Brå*) was created, functioning as the Swedish Government's agency of expertise and knowledge centre for the criminal justice system (under the Ministry of Justice), being 'responsible for the official criminal statistics and other statistics, which includes producing, following, analysing, and reporting on criminality and the criminal justice system's responses to crime.'[18]

After the end of the Cold War and the dismantling of the Soviet Union 1990/91 and a renewed national security debate, important shifts in law enforcement took place in Sweden. One of the main changes was the increased focus on prevention; that is, by means of employing intelligence gathering at an early stage and then analysing data, securing intervention in an illicit activity before it escalates. As mentioned earlier, compensatory measures introduced to curb increasing transnational crime were challenged by the elimination of internal borders between the Schengen countries. Therefore, it is not surprising that from Sweden's side there was a readiness for the changes in the making at the EU level, which it had to embrace from January 1, 1995 when becoming a full EU member. Besides, intelligence activities and sharing of such data between states has preceded the very covert operations undertaken by relevant authorities (*cf.* Berggren and Munck 2003:34). Clearly, changes in the Swedish police's organisation and working methods regarding law enforcement in a more preventive and problem-oriented direction meant that working methods increasingly turned to intelligence-driven police work and coordinated cooperation with other European partners (Colvin 2002:87; Flyghed 2000:179–190). As mentioned previously, NOA plays a vital role as 'national point of contact for the Swedish Security Service [*Säkerhetspolisen – SÄPO*], the Swedish Armed Forces and the National Defence Radio Establishment', and it is also 'responsible for managing sensitive information relating to terrorism and signals intelligence' as well as 'coordinating, planning and monitoring the special efforts undertaken by several authorities against serious organ-

18 Brå, 'About Brå', n/d, at https://www.bra.se/bra-in-english/home/about-bra.html.

ised crime'.[19] Importantly, NOA 'does not conduct any self-initiated operational activities but supports the police regions in their different activities' but it directs and supervises police operations and resources. According to the National Centre for Terrorist Threat Assessment (NTC), the terrorist threat level in Sweden has been constantly at level 3 (out of 5) since the failed terrorist attack in Stockholm in 2010, which implies that this threat is 'elevated'. The National Counter Terrorism Council, affiliated with NOA, is on permanent guard in the event of any changes with regard to this kind of threat.[20] Put differently, one could well argue that Sweden's counterterrorism policy is situated between prevention and mitigation (*cf.* Strandh and Eklund, 2015). As an example, the government has recently proposed a new act to facilitate for the Police Authority and Security Service 'to use camera surveillance without a permit for a three-month period to counter terrorist crime, serious violent crime and the drug trade'.[21]

As EU member, Sweden participates in the Council machinery; from working groups, via Permanent Representatives (Coreper) to the Council of Ministers. In the case of JHA, around 20 Council Working Groups deal with issues that affect Swedish Police activities, where experts from the Swedish Police Authority participate or officials from the Ministry of Justice (for example, since summer 2016, the Security Service has a contact person at Europol who participates regularly in the Council working procedures). The Swedish position is crafted by the Swedish National Police Board and/or the Ministry of Justice in tight dialogue with corresponding authorities.[22] For example, the Security Service represents Sweden in the EU Terrorism Working Group (TWG), the Police Working Group on Terrorism (PWGT) and Europol.[23]

19 Polisen. 'The Swedish Police Authority', n/d, at https://polisen.se/en/the-swedish-police/the-swedish-police-authority/.

20 Polisen. 'Raising general awareness of terrorism', n/d, at https://polisen.se/en/the-swedish-police/Raising-general-awareness-of-terrorism-related-issues/.

21 Government Offices of Sweden. 'New act to increase opportunities for camera surveillance', March 8, 2018, at https://www.government.se/press-releases/2018/03/new-act-to-increase-opportunities-for-camera-surveillance/.

22 Polisen. 'Council Working Groups', n/d, at https://polisen.se/en/the-swedish-police/international-cooperation/cooperation-in-europe/council-working-groups/.

23 Säkerhetspolisen. 'National and international cooperation', n/d, at http://www.sakerhetspolisen.se/en/swedish-security-service/counter-terrorism/national-and-international-cooperation.html.

In the fight against politically and religiously motivated terrorism, the Swedish Police Authority is supported by the Security Service and the National Centre for Terrorist Threat Assessment (NCT), which is a permanent working group within the Swedish Counter-Terrorism Cooperation Council producing annual assessments of terrorist threats to Sweden.[24] In 2011, the government launched the 'Action plan to safeguard democracy against violence promoting extremism', focusing on 'Preventing individuals from joining violent extremist groups and supporting defectors', 'Countering the breeding grounds for ideologically motivated violence', and 'Deepening international cooperation'.[25] In addition, the government designed a National Coordinator for Protecting Democracy against Violent Extremism in June 2014.

As a means to step up the fight against organized crime, lately the Government proposed a simplified procedure to intercept electronic communications. The current system is cumbersome as each time a criminal changes anonymous sim cards or phones, then a new decision on secret interception must be notified involving the courts. The Government's proposal, which has been referred to the Council on Legislation for consideration, implies a simplified procedure for certain secret interception decisions, leaving out the court's hearing on the matter. This new procedure may be used if there is already a valid interception permit, that is, a court hearing has been held, and it must also refer to a new telephone number, address or other electronic communication equipment pertaining to the same person and has to be based on the same circumstances as the previous permit. It is hoped that this new procedure will come into force on July 1, 2020.[26]

24 Nationellt Centrum för Terrorbedömning. 'One-year assessment. Assessment of the terrorist threat to Sweden in 2018', n/d, at http://www.sakerhetspolisen.se/download/18.5915abb616392094cf73b9/1529503049895/NCT-one-year-assessment-2018.pdf.

25 Government Offices Sweden. 'Action plan to safeguard democracy against violencepromoting extremism', Government communication, 2011/12:44, at https://www.government.se/contentassets/b94f163a3c5941aebaeb78174ea27a29/action-plan-to-safeguard-democracy-against-violence-promoting-extremism-skr.-20111244, pp. 8-9.

26 "Effektivare brottsbekämpning genom ett enklare beslutsfattande om hemlig avlyssning." Press release from the Swedish Department of Justice. Published Feb. 27, 2020. https://www.regeringen.se/pressmeddelanden/2020/02/effektivare-brottsbekampning-genom-ett-enklare-beslutsfattande-om-hemlig-avlyssning/

On June 22, 2017, the government decided to commission a special investigator with the task of investigating and proposing changes to the rules on confidentiality and information exchange that apply, *inter alia*, to the Police Authority, Social Services and Transport Agency in the fight against terrorism, thereby facilitating for effective, yet law-proof information exchange in the view of enhanced cooperation against terrorism. This proposal presented in the Swedish Government Official Reports in August 2018 motivates that a statement or information about an individual who is not 21 years of age can be sent from an authority within the social authorities to the Security Service for crime prevention purposes.[27] It then became a proposal referred to the Council on Legislation for consideration, with the ambition to enter into force as new law, on July 1, 2020. This clearly shows the rather lengthy legislative procedure to facilitate an urgent need for swift cooperation between authorities.[28] In recent years, Swedish media has put focus on the radicalisation of mostly young adults seeking to participate in the war in Syria, for or against the Islamic State. Obviously, this trend has contributed to closer cooperation between Member States' intelligence services. In 2015, it was estimated that some 300 Swedes had left for Iraq or Syria for *jihad* with the Islamic State, or to fight against it. Also, the Islamic State sought to strengthen its presence in Sweden (and the Nordic countries) through social media, in particular, urging intensified cooperation between EU countries. The uncertainty regarding the so-called returnees from conflict areas is one of the factors contributing to why the assessment of threats to Sweden from Islamist-motivated terrorism remains at a rather critical level.

27 Statens Offentliga Utredningar. (SOU 2018:65) *Informationsutbyte vid samverkan mot terrorism. Betänkande av Utredningen om informationsutbyte vid samverkan mot terrorism. Stockholm 2018*, at https://www.regeringen.se/4a36b8/contentassets/6b608132aaf84e1985fb180a45c99dc8/informationsutbyte-vid-samverkan-mot-terrorism-sou-201865. Utlämnande av sekretessbelagd information från socialtjänsten, pp. 200–201.

28 "Ett effektivare informationsutbyte mellan polis och socialtjänst vid samverkan mot terrorism." Press release from the Swedish Department of Justice. Published Feb. 21, 2020. https://www.regeringen.se/pressmeddelanden/2020/02/ett-effektivare-informationsutbyte-mellan-polis-och-socialtjanst-vid-samverkan-mot-terrorism/

The Fit Between Institutional Arrangements at National and EU Level

Regarding the issue of the degree of fit between EU institutional arrangements and Swedish authorities' law enforcement arrangements, for the outside observer it may seem a rather good match and quite a smooth Europeanisation process regarding internalising pressure for legal and organisational changes. It is important, though, to note that Sweden has not been one of the frontrunners but rather a cautious team player in EU law enforcement. In other EU policy areas, Sweden keeps a higher profile but in general, it has come out as a 'constructive' EU member, one that does not adopt an obstinate attitude in negotiations. Also, the socialisation process with EU law enforcement bodies seems to have worked out quite well over the years ('indirect Europeanisation'). However, the largest proportion of Europeanisation of 'direct' nature is about legal requirements for adapting national rules and regulations and organisations rather than norms and practitioners' behavioural repertoire.

Looking at 'direct' Europeanisation of national policy, the example of Sweden's interpretation and implementation of the Data Retention Directive (2006/24/EC) issued in February 2006 is quite revealing, which generated friction with the Court of Justice of the European Union (CJEU). Anything but a smooth transposition of an EU directive into national legislation, it turned out. The European Parliament and the JHA Council had decided that all companies offering Internet or telephone must save all traffic of data for at least six months and two years, at the most. At the heart of the debate was the issue whether this equated an effective means of law enforcement or rather a threat to personal integrity contributing to the so-called 'surveillance society'. While advocates claimed that a certain measure of intrusion into our privacy to fight increasingly more advanced cross-border crime is inevitable, critics sustained that no-one can guarantee that information is not abused. The debate in Sweden on this issue was infectious and the implementation of the directive was delayed until May 1, 2012 after Sweden had been fined by the CJEU for feet-dragging. On April 8, 2014, the CJEU declared the directive invalid for violating fundamental rights of EU citizens. Nevertheless, some EU member states, including Sweden and the U.K., actually continued obliging telecommunications providers to generally retain data under their national laws. But the company Tele2 Sverige protested with the CJEU, consequently, after the Administrative Court of Appeal (*Kammarrätten*) had requested a preliminary ruling, it became a landmark decision in favour of the EU Charter of Fundamental Rights while at the same time it left some ambiguous wordings that have made possible administrative policing for the sake of preventing threats to public safety. Critical voices pointed to the disparate interpretations among EU countries regarding this directive and what measures were taken to make it harmonise with existing laws and fundamental rights. Britain, for example, decided on more far-reaching data storage and a more generous use of the same than Sweden (Burén 2014). The 'minimum'/ 'maximum' time for data retention was criticised in Sweden besides the fact that this retention procedure happened irrespective of criminal offense (authorities were able to extract information relating to lower levels of crime suspicion and minor crimes that do not imply prison sentence). Years later, in May 2018, entered into force the EU General Data Protection Regulation (GDPR) (adopted by the European Parliament and the Council in April 2016), which replaces the Data Protection Directive 95/46/EC. The purpose is to harmonise data privacy laws in the EU, to protect EU citizens' data privacy and set a standard for how different commercial agents and organisations approach data privacy (the Facebook scandal with Cambridge Analytica starting in 2014, revealed during spring 2018, became a timely reminder of what can go wrong when profits overtake ethical principles regarding users' sensitive, private data). The efficacy of this new regulation on crime prevention in Sweden and the EU will play out in the forthcoming years and has to be judged by competent authorities and expertise.

On the other side, on April 17, 2018, the European Commission announced the e-Evidence Initiative, enabling for Member States to access content data and metadata (lumped under the term 'e-evidence') across national borders for criminal investigations. The conspicuous element in this is that EU law enforcement authorities will be given the mandate to obtain data directly from providers – including providers based outside the EU (Facebook, Google) – and much faster than the procedure applied hitherto. The regulation implies two new legal instruments: a European Production Order (EPO) and a European Preservation Order (EPrO). 'The provider must respond to an EPO within 10 days, or within 6 hours where there is 'imminent threat to life or physical integrity of a person or to a critical infrastructure,' subject to certain exceptions. Authorities may issue an EPO for subscriber or access data for all criminal offenses, but for content or transactional data only for serious offenses (*i.e.*, those with a minimum of a three-year sentence in the issuing Member State, or certain cyber and terrorism-related crimes).'[29] In fact, several Member States have expressed the wish for a more comprehensive act that would also include so-called instant access and real-time listening.[30] The JHA Council will deliberate on this issue over the forthcoming months.

An example of indirect Europeanisation is the EU Policy Cycle (EMPACT), a specific methodology taken into use in 2010. The purpose is to encourage EU countries to work jointly and more efficiently against organised crime together with the EU institutions, EU agencies, and 'relevant third parties'. Every four years, the JHA ministers create a new common list of areas to be prioritised, based on the lessons learned from the evaluation of the previous cycle.[31] The EU policy cycle contains four steps (this one below covers the period 2018–2021):[32]

29 Covington. Inside Privacy. Updates on developments in data privacy and cybersecurity. 'EU Releases e-Evidence Proposal for Cross-Border Data Access', by Lauren Moxley, May 8, 2018, at https://www.insideprivacy.com/uncategorized/eu-releases-e-evidence-proposal-for-cross-border-data-access/.

30 Regeringskansliet. Justitiedepartementet. EU-enheten. 'Kommenterad dagordning för rådets möte för rättsliga och inrikes frågor (RIF) den 4–5 juni 2018', May 28, 2018, at https://www.regeringen.se/49c2f4/contentassets/0adbf0da9c1242d795935d6180953d8f/kommenterad-dagordning-rif-radet-4-5-juni.pdf, p. 9.

31 Polisen. 'Europeiskt samarbete mot organiserad och grov brottslighet', latest reviewed on November 20, 2017, at https://polisen.se/om-polisen/internationell-verksamhet/verksamhet-inom-eu/europeiskt-samarbete-mot-organiserad-och-grov-brottslighet/.

32 n/a. Europol. 'EU Policy Cycle – EMPACT', at https://www.europol.europa.eu/crime-areas-and-trends/eu-policy-cycle-empact.

- Step 1: The serious and organised crime threat assessment (SOCTA)

The SOCTA emanates from Europol, it contains recommendations based on the 'intelligence-led approach' characterising EU law enforcement (drawing from Member States' intelligence services and databases, and other EU agencies like Frontex and Eurojust).

- Step 2: Strategic plans

Multi-annual strategic plans (MASPs) are elaborated on the basis of priorities defined in step 1, thus providing the strategic goals for tackling specific threats.[33]

- Step 3: European multidisciplinary platform against criminal threats (EMPACT)

The projects under EMPACT set out operational action plans (OAPs) to combat crime in the areas that have been assigned what is known as an EMPACT priority.

An OAP is designated for each objective, and Member States and EU organisations work in coordinated manner to implement each OAP.

- Step 4: Evaluation

Information on the OAPs is transmitted to Europol via its secure system, SIENA, for analysis. The intelligence derived from these investigations informs reviews by the Standing Committee on Operational Cooperation on Internal Security (COSI). The reviews are conducted on the basis of SOCTAs, *inter alia*, which evaluate efforts to tackle crimes in the EMPACT priority areas. Based on its reviews, COSI may recommend adjustments within one and another area.

33 'Since 2017 a Master MASP is developed, before all other MASPs, which describes the horizontal goals for all the threats.' EUCPN. 'EU Policy Cycle: what is it, how does it work and what is the role of prevention?!', n/d, p. 2, at https://eucpn.org/sites/default/files/content/download/files/the_eu_policy_cycle.pdf.

The priorities established by the Council decision from May 18, 2017 for the time period 2018–2021 are: 'cybercrime, drugs, facilitating illegal immigration, organised property crime, trafficking in human beings, excise & missing trader intra community fraud, firearms, environmental crime, criminal finances & money laundering, document fraud.'[34]

During the period 2014–2017, the Swedish Police Authority participated in virtually all of the prioritized areas. Additional examples of indirect Europeanisation in the JHA area and EU law enforcement in particular take place in exchanges of information and practical cooperation between Swedish police officials, prosecutors, and their counterparts from the EU countries. Precisely, it has to do with socialisation, this cognitive process that was frequently explored in the EU literature with a social constructivist approach from the mid-1990s until the early 2000s (*cf.* Christensen *et al.*, 2001; Checkel, 2005). The interaction with colleagues sharing knowledge and then together pushing forward the EU's frontiers in law enforcement matters is a distinct form of Europeanisation looking for greater security for EU countries and citizens by fighting organised crime and terrorism. At the same time, Swedish officials are well aware that situations may require the special Swedish 'hat' to be put on, on occasions when there is a special need for underscoring Swedish interests, priorities or perspectives.

The Fight Against Terrorism and Cross-Border Crime

Following the Al-Qaeda-led terrorist attacks in the United States in 2001 (9/11), the EU reacted swiftly; at the extraordinary European Council meeting on September 21, 2001, the heads of state and government set up an action plan for its response to international terrorism. Moreover, the Council adopted a Common Position (2001/931/CFSP) with a list of persons, groups and entities affiliated with terrorist acts and subject to restrictive measures. On June 13, 2002,

34 EUCPN. 'EU Policy Cycle: what is it, how does it work and what is the role of prevention?!', n/d, p. 4, at https://eucpn.org/sites/default/files/content/download/files/the_eu_policy_cycle.pdf.

the JHA ministers adopted the Framework Decision on combating terrorism (2002/475/JHA). It established a common definition of terrorism and what actions should fall under terrorist crime, besides acknowledging that it should be punishable to invite, recruit or train others to commit terrorist acts. This Framework Decision was turned into a Swedish Law in Act 2003:148, §2, on Criminal Responsibility for Terrorist Offences. Moreover, the Framework Decision regarding the European Arrest Warrant (EAW) was endorsed by the Swedish Parliament in May 2002 and subsequently adopted on June 13 by the JHA Council of Ministers (2002/584/JHA). Recalling the debate in Sweden around that time, criticism against the initiative focused primarily on two aspects. For instance, the Swedish Council on Legislation (*Lagrådet*) argued that the substance in the EAW might threaten Swedish rule of law; Swedish citizens could be extradited to another EU country even if they had not committed a criminal offense under Swedish law, but, for example, in their capacity as members of a political party or an organisation labelled as illegal or associated with crime in the country requesting extradition. Besides, the Council on Legislation expressed concerns that resorting to Framework Decisions might produce mindless laws in Sweden. In public opinion, concern was raised that new legislation would not be democratically anchored because concrete proposals would be 'top-down' in nature; from the JHA Council with lack of transparency and open discussion with stakeholders.

Some additional measures should be mentioned: Soon after 9/11, the EU followed suit on UN Security Council resolutions against black-listed persons or entities (then mostly associated with the Al-Qaeda network). The EU also concluded an agreement with the United States about mutual legal assistance and extradition of suspected terrorists.[35] Finally, Directive 2005/60/EC of the European Parliament and of the Council of 26 October 2005 imposes on the banking sector the obligation to ensure their systems are not used for money laundering or financing of terrorism activities. The so-called

35 European Council. Council of the European Union. n/d, 'EU counter-terrorism strategy', at http://www.consilium.europa.eu/en/policies/fight-against-terrorism/eu-strategy/.

'Prüm Decision' should be mentioned here as well, a corollary to the Council decision (2008/615/JHA) adopted on June 23, 2008, 'on the stepping up of cross-border cooperation, particularly in combating terrorism and cross-border crime', which aims at mandating the exchange of DNA, fingerprint and vehicle registration data (VRD) between the Member States.

The EU's fight against terrorism and cross-border crime has its 'natural residence' in the JHA Council, which includes different working groups; some of these are specialised on organised crime and terrorism consisting of experts from the corresponding authorities in the EU countries. Since 2007, the EU has a special Counter-Terrorism Coordinator, located in the General Secretariat of the Council. This trend has created a political push for increased cooperation focusing on enhancing security in other policy areas, for example, Common Foreign and Security Policy, transport, energy, employment, and social issues. Besides, few cooperation initiatives that have added to the stated purpose to fight terrorism are, strictly speaking, purely anti-terrorist measures; their scope reaches out to combat other types of crime, for example, drug trafficking. The EU counter-terrorism strategy came about as a result of the terrorist attacks in Madrid on the commuter train system, on March 11, 2004, only a few days before general elections, with almost 200 dead and more than 2,000 non-fatally injured. Then, on July 7, 2005, the London subway and bus system was hit; leaving some 50 killed and many wounded. The strategy was adopted by the Council in 2005 and has four main axes:[36]

- PREVENT: Addressing the causes of radicalisation and terrorist recruitment is a key priority for the EU. To this end, the Council adopted an EU strategy for combating radicalisation and recruitment to terrorism in 2008. The strategy was revised in June 2014 in light of evolving trends, such as lone-actor terrorism, foreign fighters, and the use of social media by terrorists.

36 European Council. Council of the European Union. n/d, 'EU counter-terrorism strategy', at http://www.consilium.europa.eu/en/policies/fight-against-terrorism/eu-strategy/.

- PROTECT: Protecting citizens and infrastructure and reducing vulnerability to attacks is the second priority of the EU counter-terrorism strategy. This includes securing external borders, improving transport security, protecting strategic targets and reducing the vulnerability of critical infrastructure. In this area, the EU adopted a directive regulating the use of passenger name record (PNR) data in April 2016. Member states will have to comply with the new rules within two years.
- PURSUE: The EU is working to hinder terrorists' capacity to plan and organise, and to bring these terrorists to justice. To achieve these goals, the EU has focused on: strengthening national capabilities improving cooperation and information exchange between police and judicial authorities tackling terrorist financing depriving terrorists of their means of support and communication. In May 2015, the Council and the European Parliament adopted new rules to prevent money laundering and terrorist financing.
- RESPOND: Preparing, managing and minimising the consequences of a terrorist attack is the fourth objective of the EU counter-terrorism strategy. This is done by improving capabilities to deal with the aftermath, the coordination of the response, and victims' needs.
  Priorities in this area include: developing EU crisis coordination arrangements, revising the civil protection mechanism, developing risk assessment tools, sharing best practices on assistance to victims of terrorism.
  Priorities in recent years have included: defining the arrangements for the implementation by the EU of the solidarity clause, through a Council decision adopted in June 2014, reviewing the EU emergency and crisis coordination arrangements, replaced by the EU integrated political crisis response arrangements (IPCR) in June 2013, revising EU civil protection legislation at the end of 2013.

Across these pillars, the strategy recognises the importance of cooperation with third countries and international institutions. Unlike other policy areas studied in this book, the development of new provisions for EU and thereby Swedish law enforcement measures is a direct result of the spread of Islamist terrorism globally, which has generated the worst refugee disaster the world has experienced since the Word War II. The countless and distressing human suffering is also coloured by organised and cross-border criminal networks who are the ones providing organised escape routes into Europe. Trafficking in people (especially women and children and children), human organs and cultural artefacts is used for to finance terrorist acts. According to a study by Europol, published in January 2016, cited in *The Guardian*, about 10,000 unaccompanied refugees has disappeared in Europe, and many of them are exploited in the sex industry and slave-like conditions of criminal networks (Townsend 2016).

One could say that the spark was set with the attack against the French satirical weekly newspaper Charlie Hebdo in Paris on January 7, 2015, where 12 people got killed. On January 9, another terrorist killed four hostages at a Jewish supermarket. Later this same year, on November 13, a suicide bombing at the Stade de France stadium were followed by more coordinated explosions and shootings at popular bars and restaurants in Paris. The terrorists also opened fire at Bataclan concert hall and killed spectators for a show with a Death Metal band. More than 130 people lost their lives and hundreds of others were injured. In Belgium, the Brussels bombings on March 22, 2016 killed 32 people and wounded more than 300 other victims in coordinated bombings at Brussels Airport and another bombing at Maalbeek, the bustling metro station in the heart of the EU headquarter. Counterintelligence cooperation between Belgium and France made clear that there were links between the two terrorist cells perpetrating these two attacks, both affiliated with the Islamic State (or, Islamic State of Iraq and the Levant (ISIL). Back to France, on the eve of the celebration of the Bastille Day on July 14 that same year, in Nice, a lone terrorist mowed down people who had gathered on the promenade by the seaside, killing 84 people and injuring hundreds of others. On July 26, a group of terrorists slit the throat of a priest and took several others hostage after storming a church during mass in Normandy. There were also four sporadic terrorist attacks in Germany during July 2016, with few civilian victims. On December 19, a lone 'copycat' terrorist drove a truck into a packed Christmas market, killing 12 people and injuring more than 60, in Berlin. Then in 2017 more attacks followed: In Paris on February 3, an attempt was avoided when policemen shot down a knifeman who sought to enter the Louvre Carrousel shopping centre. On April 20, 2017, a policeman was shot dead on the Champs-Élysées a few days before the presidential election.

Britain had not experienced Islamist terrorism since the July 2005 London bombings. Then, on March 22, 2017, a lone terrorist mowed down pedestrians on Westminster Bridge, killing four people and injuring many others. He then crashed his car into the railings outside Parliament, ran up to the New Palace Yard where he stabbed a police officer to death. At the concert in the Manchester Arena featuring Ariana Grande on May 22, terrorists killed at least 22 people and injured 59 others, many of them children and adolescents. On June 3, terrorists killed eight people and injured many others on London Bridge and in nearby Borough Market.

In Barcelona, on August 17, a terrorist rammed crowds of people at the popular pedestrian street Las Ramblas, killing 13 people and injuring more than a hundred. A few hours later, police shot dead more terrorists in Cambrils, a town southwards of Barcelona, after they had rammed into another street.

In Stockholm, on April 7, a lone terrorist used the same strategy as in Nice and Berlin; stealing a truck and mowing down people on the pedestrian street Drottninggatan, killing five people and injuring well over a dozen others. The perpetrator, Rakhmat Akilov, a failed asylum seeker from Uzbekistan, declared he had sympathies for the Islamic State. He was sentenced to life for terrorist crimes in June 2018 and has decided not to appeal the verdict. It should be said that what has been described as the first suicide attack in the Nordic countries linked to Islamist terrorism took place in central Stockholm, near the Parliament, on December 11, 2010, but it was a failed attempt since only the terrorist died.[37]

37 Express (Home of the Daily and Sunday Express), 'Terror attacks timeline: From Paris and Brussels terror to most recent attacks in Europe', by Alice Foster, August 18, 2017, at https://www.express.co.uk/news/world/693421/Terror-attacks-timeline-France-Brussels-Europe-Isis-killings-Germany-dates-terrorism.

Summing up: the role of the EU is to support national law enforcement authorities, and while the EU has no direct operational law enforcement 'muscles' in the form of a European Police Force or a European Intelligence Agency, it can still decide on common rules and steer legislation quite firmly into tighter cooperation in this area, hence procuring more Europeanisation in EU law enforcement and fight against terrorism. Since 2006, Europol issues annual reports with statistics concerning 'foiled, failed or completed terrorist attacks' in the EU. For example, the EU Terrorism Situation and Trend Report (TE-SAT) 2018 detailed that the threat level of religiously motivated terrorism in Europe remains high in several Member States.[38] In the end of the day, the main responsibility for combating terrorism-related crimes lies still with the Member States, the challenge being that 'it is one thing for Europe's policymakers to make public promises to improve the fight against terrorism via better intelligence sharing across Europe, and quite another thing for them to persuade the relevant national agencies to comply' (Bureš, 2016: Abstract).

Conclusion

Assuming Europeanisation denotes an adaptive response of different national political actors towards a changing supranational political context and a certain EU-jargon manifested in discourses on EU law enforcement, then, concerning purely formalised and organisational aspects, since 2001, the Swedish police system has handled both indirect and direct Europeanisation 'pressures'. As for the indirect effects, new norms and exchanges between expertise are on the social side whereas new organisational changes (for example, liaison structures between Europol and units in the Swedish police system) and political impetus from the EU Policy Cycle have led to new policy contents in Sweden's law enforcement procedures. Regarding direct effects, new directives in EU law enforcement has required legislative adaption/

38 Europol. 'Terrorist Threat in the EU Remains High Despite the Decline of IS in Iraq and Syria', Press Release, June 20, 2018, at https://www.europol.europa.eu/newsroom/news/terrorist-threat-in-eu-remains-high-despite-decline-of-in-iraq-and-syria.

incorporation into Swedish law, which has not always been smooth as the case of the data retention directive illustrates. Another way of capturing this change is to talk in terms of progressive vs. regressive Europeanisation, although, it should be said, what counts for what is often a strictly personal judgement. Arguably, the progressive kind has become visible in new and more efficient forms of cooperation, such as the EU Policy Cycle, whereas the regressive one is visible in the diminishing of personal integrity that the data retention directive illustrates. It used to be rather easy to say that the Europeanisation effect is relatively sparse in this policy area in comparison with competition policy or agricultural policy. However, what used to be a clearly intergovernmental approach has morphed into a tight cooperation dynamic with supranational connotations. But the EU remains still far from the idea of creating a EU Police Force or European Intelligence Agency; the issue is way too sensitive regarding national sovereignty and since it is not contemplated in the EU treaties, it would require a major revision and, hopefully, public debate, if the heads of state and government should consider this a desirable path for safeguarding security and fighting cross-border crime.

The public debate in Sweden about the Europeanisation of its national law enforcement authorities and measures has been characterised by a certain ambiguity and politicians from all political parties could well do more to explain the implications of tighter EU cooperation in this area for enhancing State and individual security, but not shying away from pointing out some of the controversial implications for fundamental rights and freedoms. Media has an important role to play as well; if media does not specify the EU dimension in a particular ongoing criminal investigation, then, public opinion in Sweden will not get the point that Sweden's law enforcement is, inextricably, tied to EU law enforcement.

It is a widespread perception within the EU (negotiation system) that Sweden is a rather 'smooth' partner, quite apt at aligning national legislations with the EU's. In the domestic context, though, critics argue that Sweden has adapted too readily to a repressive, 'mainstream' view of law enforcement that has come at a high cost for the individual in terms of protection of fundamental rights and freedoms. As regards massive intelligence gathering, benefitting big companies in technology for communications, sceptics hold that this leads to uncontrolled monitoring and innocent people might suffer from this, not just those who are legitimately suspected of illicit activities. And, despite Member States and EU institutions efforts to safeguard personal integrity, for example, with the EU General Data Protection Regulation (GDPR) that entered into force on May 25, 2018, we simply have no guarantee that our personal information of strictly private nature will not be turned against us, which is a sensitive issue in this era of social media, digital revolution, and Artificial Intelligence.

In conclusion, although EU countries' cooperation in law enforcement is largely characterised by lack of transparency, control and clear accountability (Colvin 2002:88), the majority of EU citizens realise that increasing threats to democracy and the 'open society' characterised by civil liberties actually require stronger common efforts to uphold these shared values. Indeed, at the press conference following the Paris-Bataclan terrorist attack, the Swedish Prime Minister expressed that Sweden in the EU has a solidarity spirit and even self-interest in expressing support for EU law enforcement in this area.[39] Given the past three years of terrorist attacks in several EU countries, the question must be asked if we should not have more, rather than less, Europeanisation of Swedish law enforcement.

39 *Svt Nyheter*. 'Löfven: Ingen konkret hotbild mot Sverige', Maria Holmin, November 14, 2015, at https://www.svt.se/nyheter/inrikes/lofven-ingen-konkret-hotbild-mot-sverige.

References

Berggren, N.O. & J. Munck 2003. *Polislagen. En kommentar*, 4 ed. Stockholm: Norstedts Juridik.

Block, Ludo. 'Establishing trust despite the risk? An analysis of the need for trust in police cooperation', In: Hufnagel, Saskia & Carole McCartney (eds.). (2017) *Trust in International Police and Justice Cooperation*, Oxford and Portland, Oregon: Hart Publishing, Onati International Series in Law and Society.

Bossong, R. & M. Rhinard 2015. *Explaining EU Internal Security Cooperation. The Problem of Producing Public Goods*. London: Routledge.

Bruggeman, W. 2001. 'International Law Enforcement Co-operation: A Critical Assessment', *European Journal on Criminal Policy and Research*, 9(3).

Bruggeman, W. & M. Den Boer 2007. 'Shifting Gear: Europol in the Contemporary Policing Era'. *Politique Européenne*, 23(3).

Brå, 'About Brå', n/d, at https://www.bra.se/bra-in-english/home/about-bra.html.

Burén, J. 2014. 'Brottsbekämpning eller skydd för privatlivet – den infekterade debatten om datalagring lever vidare.' Kaliber. Sveriges Radio P1. November 16, 2014.
http://sverigesradio.se/sida/avsnitt/460237?programid=1316

Bureš, Oldřich. 'Intelligence Sharing and the Fight against Terrorism in the EU: Lessons Learned from Europol', *European View*, First Published June 1, 2016, DOI: https://doi.org/10.1007/s12290-016-0393-7

Casale, D. 2012. Role of an International Organization in Homeland Security against Terrorism: The European Union, in J. Charvat (ed.) *Homeland Security Organization in Defence Against Terrorism*. Amsterdam: IOS Press BV.

Carrapico, H. 2013. 'The External Dimension of the EU's Fight against Organised Crime: The Search for Coherence between Rhetoric and Practice'. *Journal of Contemporary European Research*, 9(3).

Checkel, J. T. (2005). International Institutions and Socialization in Europe: Introduction and Framework. *International Organization*, 59(4), 801–826.

Christiansen, T., K. E. Jorgensen & A. Wiener 2001. 'Introduction'. T. Christiansen, K. E. Jorgensen & A. Wiener (eds.), *The Social Construction of Europe* (pp. 1–19). London: Sage Publications.

Cocq, Celine and Francesca Galli. 'The evolving role of Europol in the fight against serious crime: current challenges and future prospects', In: Hufnagel, Saskia & Carole McCartney (eds.). (2017) *Trust in International Police and Justice Cooperation*, Oxford and Portland, Oregon: Hart Publishing, Onati International Series in Law and Society.

Colvin, M. 2002. 'Emerging Integration in: Policing and Criminal Justice', In: M. Farrell, S. Fella & M. Stefano (eds.) *European Integration in the 21st Century. Unity in Diversity?* London: SAGE.

Covington. Inside Privacy. Updates on developments in data privacy and cybersecurity. 'EU Releases e-Evidence Proposal for Cross-Border Data Access', by Lauren Moxley, May 8, 2018, at https://www.insideprivacy.com/uncategorized/eu-releases-e-evidence-proposal-for-cross-border-data-access/.

Den Boer, M. 2001. 'The Fight Against Organised Crime in Europe: A Comparative Perspective', *European Journal on Criminal Policy and Research*, 9(3).

— 2002a. 'Intelligence Exchange and the Control of Organised Crime: from Europeanisation via Centralisation to dehydration?', In: M. Anderson & J. Apap (eds.), *Police and Justice Co-operation and the New European Borders*. The Hague: Kluwer.

— (ed.) 2002b. *Organised Crime: A Catalyst in the Europeanisation of National Police and Prosecution Agencies?* Maastricht: European Institute of Public Administration.

— (ed.) 2003. 'The EU Counter-terrorism Wave: Window of Opportunity of Profound Policy Transformation?', In: M. van Leeuwen (ed.), *Confronting Terrorism: European Experiences, Threat Perceptions and Policies*. The Hague: Kluwer Law International.

— (ed.) 2011. 'Technology-led Policing in the European Union: An Assessment', In: E. De Pauw, P. Ponsaers, K. van der Vijver & K. Bruggeman (eds.). *Technology-led policing*. Antwerpen, Belgium: Maklu.

Den Boer, M. & F. Doelle 2002. 'Converge or not to converge... that's the question: a comparative analysis of Europeanisation of National Police trends in criminal justice organisations', In: M. Den Boer (ed.) *Maastricht Journal of European and Comparative Law*. Maastricht.

ELSJ. Reséau universitaire européen. 'The Paris Terrorist Attacks: Failure of the EU's Area of Freedom, Security and Justice?', P. de Bruycker, D. Watt, H. Labayle, A. Weyembergh, C. Brière, January 8, 2016, at http://www.gdr-elsj.eu/2016/01/08/cooperation-judiciaire-penale/the-paris-terrorist-attacks-failure-of-the-eus-area-of-freedom-security-and-justice/.

EUCPN. 'EU Policy Cycle: what is it, how does it work and what is the role of prevention?!', n/d, p. 2, at https://eucpn.org/sites/default/files/content/download/files/the_eu_policy_cycle.pdf.

EUR-Lex. Treaty on the Functioning of the European Union, at https://eur-lex.europa.eu/legal-content/EN/TXT/PDF/?uri=CELEX:12012E/TXT&from=EN.

EUR-Lex. Consolidated version of the Treaty on European Union – Title V: General Provisions on the Union's External Action and Specific Provisions on the Common Foreign and Security Policy – Chapter 2: Specific provisions on the common foreign and security policy – Section 2: Provisions on the common security and defence policy – Article 42 (ex Article 17 TEU), at https://eur-lex.europa.eu/legal-content/EN/TXT/?uri=CELEX%3A12008M042.

europa.eu. 'Eurojust', Overview, at https://europa.eu/european-union/about-eu/agencies/eurojust_en.

European Commission. Migration and Home Affairs. 'Schengen Information System.' Last update: 28/08/2018. At https://ec.europa.eu/home-affairs/what-we-do/policies/borders-and-visas/schengen-information-system_en.

European Council. Council of the European Union. n/d, 'EU counter-terrorism strategy', at http://www.consilium.europa.eu/en/policies/fight-against-terrorism/eu-strategy/.

Europol. n/a. 'The Council of the EU Appoints Catherine De Bolle as new Executive Director of Europol', Press release, March 08, 2018, at https://www.europol.europa.eu/newsroom/news/council-of-eu-appoints-catherine-de-bolle-new-executive-director-of-europol.

Europol. 'Europol Analysis Projects', n/d, at https://www.europol.europa.eu/crime-areas-trends/europol-analysis-projects.

Europol. n/a. 'Governance & Accountability', at https://www.europol.europa.eu/about-europol/governance-accountability.

Europol. n/a. 'EU Policy Cycle – Empact', at https://www.europol.europa.eu/crime-areas-and-trends/eu-policy-cycle-empact.

Europol. 'Terrorist Threat in the EU Remains High Despite the Decline of IS in Iraq and Syria', Press Release, June 20, 2018, at https://www.europol.europa.eu/newsroom/news/terrorist-threat-in-eu-remains-high-despite-decline-of-in-iraq-and-syria.

Europol. 'European Counter Terrorism Centre – ECTCn', n/d, at https://www.europol.europa.eu/about-europol/european-counter-terrorism-centre-ectc.

Express (Home of the Daily and Sunday Express), 'Terror attacks timeline: From Paris and Brussels terror to most recent attacks in Europe', by Alice Foster, August 18, 2017, at https://www.express.co.uk/news/world/693421/Terror-attacks-timeline-France-Brussels-Europe-ISIS-killings-Germany-dates-terrorism.

Felia, A. & M. Den Boer 2013. 'United We Stand? Conceptual Diversity in the EU Strategy against Organised Crime'. *Journal of European Integration,* 35(2).

Frontex. 'Foreword' (Fabrice Leggeri, Frontex Executive Director), n/d, at https://frontex.europa.eu/about-frontex/foreword/.

Government Offices of Sweden. 'New act to increase opportunities for camera surveillance', March 8, 2018, at https://www.government.se/press-releases/2018/03/new-act-to-increase-opportunities-for-camera-surveillance/.

— 'Action plan to safeguard democracy against violencepromoting extremism', Government communication, 2011/12:44, at https://www.government.se/contentassets/b94f163a3c5941aebaeb78174ea27a29/action-plan-to-safeguard-democracy-against-violence-promoting-extremism-skr.-20111244.

Helmius, I. 2000. *Polisens rättsliga befogenheter vid spaning.* Uppsala: Iustus förlag.

Hufnagel, Saskia & Carole McCartney (eds.). (2017) 'Introduction', In: Hufnagel, Saskia and Carole McCartney, *Trust in International Police and Justice Cooperation*, Oxford and Portland, Oregon: Hart

Publishing, Onati International Series in Law and Society.
Lodge, J. 2002. 'Sustaining Freedom, Security and Justice – From Terrorism to Immigration', *Liverpool Law Review*, 24(1-2).
— 2004. 'EU homeland security: citizens or suspects?', *Journal of European Integration,* 26(3).
— 2009. 'Security and Liberty in the European Union: Foreword'. *Journal of Contemporary European Research,* 5(2):140–147.
Nationellt Centrum för Terrorbedömning. 'One-year assessment. Assessment of the terrorist threat to Sweden in 2018', n/d, at http://www.sakerhetspolisen.se/download/18.5915abb616392094cf73b9/1529503049895/NCT-one-year-assessment-2018.pdf.
O'Neill, M., K. Swinton & A. Winter (eds.) 2013. *Internal Security Strategy. New Challenges for the EU.* Newcastle upon Tyne: Cambridge Scholars Publishing.
Paoli, L. 2014. 'How to Tackle (Organized) Crime in Europe? The EU Policy Cycle on Serious and Organized Crime and the New Emphasis on Harm', *European Journal of Crime, Criminal Law and Criminal Justice*, 22 (1):1–12. DOI: 10.1163/15718174-22012036
Polisen. 'Council Working Groups', n/d, at https://polisen.se/en/the-swedish-police/international-cooperation/cooperation-in-europe/council-working-groups/.
— 'The Swedish Police Authority', n/d, at https://polisen.se/en/the-swedish-police/the-swedish-police-authority/.
— 'Raising general awareness of terrorism', n/d, at https://polisen.se/en/the-swedish-police/Raising-general-awareness-of-terrorism-related-issues/.
— 'Europeiskt samarbete mot organiserad och grov brottslighet', latest reviewed on November 20, 2017, at https://polisen.se/om-polisen/internationell-verksamhet/verksamhet-inom-eu/europeiskt-samarbete-mot-organiserad-och-grov-brottslighet/.
Regeringskansliet. 'Regeringen ser över regelverk för att öka skyddet mot säkerhetshot', August 24, 2018, at https://www.regeringen.se/pressmeddelanden/2018/08/regeringen-ser-over-regelverk-for-att-oka-skyddet-mot-sakerhets-hot/.
— Justitiedepartementet. EU-enheten. 'Kommenterad dagordning för rådets möte för rättsliga och inrikes frågor (RIF) den 4–5 juni 2018', May 28, 2018, at https://www.regeringen.se/49c2f4/contentassets/0adbf0da9c1242d795935d6180953d8f/kommenterad-dagordning-rif-radet-4-5-juni.pdf.
— 'Nordiskt polissamarbete fördjupas', June 1, 2018, at https://www.regeringen.se/pressmeddelanden/2018/06/nordiskt-polissamarbete-fordjupas/.
Riksdagen. 2017. Statens Offentliga Utredningar. Datalagring – brottsbekämpning och integritet. Delbetänkande av Utredningen om datalagring och EU-rätten. Stockholm: Elanders Sverige AB. At https://data.riksdagen.se/fil/3FF311F7-85AF-4595-A365-04B0D595378D.
Schalken, T. & M. Pronk. 2002. 'On Joint Investigation Teams, Europol and Supervision of Their Joint Actions', *European Journal of Crime,*

Criminal Law and Criminal Justice, Vol. 10(1).

Scherrer, A., J. Jeandesboz & E-P. Guittet 2011. *Developing an* EU *Internal Security Strategy, Fighting Terrorism and Organised Crime.* PE 462.423. Brussels: European Parliament.

Smyrl, M. 2007. 'European Anti-Terrorism Policy: A Trans-Atlantic Perspective.' *Politique Européenne*, 23.

Spapens, T. 'Building trust and more: the importance of police cooperation networks in the European Union', In: Hufnagel, Saskia & Carole McCartney (eds.). (2017) *Trust in International Police and Justice Cooperation*, Oxford and Portland, Oregon: Hart Publishing, Onati International Series in Law and Society.

Statens Offentliga Utredningar. (SOU 2018:65) 'Informationsutbyte vid samverkan mot terrorism. Betänkande av Utredningen om informationsutbyte vid samverkan mot terrorism. Stockholm 2018', at https://www.regeringen.se/4a36b8/contentassets/6b608132aaf84e1985fb180a45c99dc8/informationsutbyte-vid-samverkan-mot-terrorism-sou-201865.

Strandh, V. & N. Eklund. 2015. 'Swedish Counterterrorism Policy: An Intersection Between Prevention and Mitigation?', *Studies in Conflict & Terrorism*, 2015, 38 (5): 359–379. DOI: https://doi.org/10.1080/1057610X.2015.1009799.

Svt Nyheter. 'Löfven: Ingen konkret hotbild mot Sverige', Maria Holmin, November 14, 2015, at https://www.svt.se/nyheter/inrikes/lofven-ingen-konkret-hotbild-mot-sverige.

Townsend, M. 2016. '10,000 refugee children are missing, says Europol.' *The Guardian*, January 30, 2016, at http://www.theguardian.com/world/2016/jan/30/fears-for-missing-child-refugees.

11. Foreign and Security Policy

Sweden's Path from Non-Alliance to a Solidarity Doctrine

Fredrik Bynander

> 'Sweden's security policy remains firmly in place. Our non-participation in military alliances serves us well and contributes to stability and security in northern Europe.'
>
> 'Sweden will not remain passive if another EU Member State or a Nordic country suffers a disaster or an attack. We expect these countries to act in the same way if Sweden is affected. We must therefore be able to both give and receive support, civilian as well as military.'

This is what the Swedish Foreign Declaration of 2019 states regarding the country's security policy. The Declaration, traditionally delivered by the Foreign Minister in February of each year, was previously markedly different.[1] Today's wording clearly points to the change that Swedish foreign and security policy has undergone since the great upheavals of 1989–91 and the end of the Cold War. A doctrine (the policy of neutrality), which was mechanically repeated as the main label of the country's grand strategy, has now been truncated and supplemented by the declaration of solidarity that Sweden embraced with the Lisbon treaty of 2007 (Murray *et al.* 1994; Westberg 2016). In Swedish alliance strategy, the country's Union affiliation has strongly influenced external relations to the extent that no position is taken in an important foreign or security policy without regard to the European Union (EU) as an enabler, a constraint and the pivotal decision-making arena. The other member states' respective positions both seem to empower and restrain Swedish maneuverability and a

1 Government Declarations and Foreign Declarations used to express variants of the phrase 'freedom of alliance in peace aimed at neutrality in war'.

successful Brussels process promises significantly increased influence on global and regional problems for Sweden. The Common Foreign and Security Policy (CFSP), as well as the Common Security and Defence Policy (CSDP), are governed by national competencies, but all major international commitments relating to several Member States are handled in the EU and often decisions are made within the framework of the EU.

What does Sweden aim for as a political actor in the international arena that the country through membership and active involvement harmonized its foreign and security policy with the EU? What country has the country chosen during the Cold War and what does it mean for the country's ability to exert international influence in an increasingly tense world situation, which implies a new set of threats and opportunities? How does the domestic policy arena affect these issues over time? The chapter analyzes these issues and tries to draw relevant conclusions about developments in Swedish foreign and security policy since EU membership.

Analyzing Swedish foreign and security policy after EU membership is a paradoxical exercise that revolves around a question of origin – whether the changes it has made since January 1, 1995 are the results of membership or if the entire integration process to the EU is a result of the cold war's abrupt ending. This question is fundamental (because it places geopolitical factors against institutional) and instrumental (since it affects the driving forces behind Swedish policy that can give us benchmarks for future choices). On the other hand, it is too complex and too digital as an overall analytical question for a shorter presentation such as this. It is more appropriate to descriptively capture the changes and how they, in turn, can be seen to have affected the traditionally quite slow moving Swedish foreign and security policy formation.

This chapter will in turn deal with a number of aspects of foreign and security policy – how it is organized and managed, and what it contains in terms of political programs, strategies and doctrines. The chapter will discuss what logic can be found behind the changes that have taken place and the additional element of complexity that has emerged with EU membership. In conclusion, a discussion follows on the relationship between Swedish foreign and security policy, on the one hand, and the external relations of the EU and the Common Foreign and Security Policy (CFSP).

The End of the Cold War and EC Application

In his dissertation from 1998, Jacob Gustavsson describes how the social-democratic government under domestic political turmoil deviates from its traditionally sceptical attitude to membership in the European Community (EC) and relatively quickly guides the country towards a membership application (see also Sundelius 1994). The declared reason against membership had previously been strongly linked to the country's neutrality policy: 'Non-participation in military alliances in peace aiming for neutrality in war'. Sweden had drawn diametrically different conclusions from the experience of World War II compared to the geographically and culturally adjacent Norway and Denmark. In Sweden, a policy of neutrality was still a recipe for success, and during some years after the end of the war, the Swedish government sought to 'extend the Swedish neutrality to the rest of Scandinavia' (Noreen 1994). When the negotiations on a Scandinavian defence federation finally broke down, the clean neutrality line in front of Sweden was seen as the only politically viable option.

In the years that followed, Western Europe rose from the ashes, partly as a result of the co-operation that began with the coal and steel union of 1952. After some discussion, Sweden's position stating that participation in emerging European cooperative structures was incompatible with the neutrality line (Molin 1991; Misgeld 1990). The national political endorsement of this policy was mainly strong. It is appropriate to talk of an operational consensus – a compromise on the main pillars of a policy, which has been arrived at for differing reasons, but is held together by the need for stability in the interface with domestic policy (Sundelius *et al.*, 1997). In Sweden, a policy of neutrality meant a need for a strong defence, creating and maintaining diplomatic and political freedom of action, and overcoming ideological differences on foreign policy – something that satisfied a number of key actors in Swedish foreign and security policymaking. From this perspective, the EU accession issue was pivotal, as it could put national consensus in question. The implication of intimate economic and political cooperation with the members of one of the two global power blocs was considered by some as too challenging for the non-aligned states of the Cold War. Being dependent on the West (especially the United States) for a number of security related policies, apparently, did not signal the same level of alliance commitments as NATO membership would, for those who defended the policy of neutrality (see SOU 1994: 11; SOU 2002: 108).

The Swedish foreign and security policy during the Cold War has been described as functioning according to two distinct lines. First, an active foreign policy, expressed in a global commitment that was designed to rarely lead to criticism of the great powers but rather support for states in the global periphery. The second line was a regionally focused security policy that was rigid, self-serving and tightly linked to the dictates of non-alliance (see Zetterberg 1997, Hallenberg 2000). During certain periods it was difficult to combine the two action patterns, as during the submarine incidents in the nineteen eighties that caused friction with Prime Minister Olof Palme's commitment to 'common security' within the UN framework. The relation of the foreign policy debate with the domestic policy arena was complicated during many periods of the Cold War, and moral or ideological arguments were combined with practical ('realist'), economic and cultural ones in order to reshape the balance between the two lines.

With the end of the Cold War, a redirection was possible. For a trade-dependent, small state such as Sweden, an opportunity emerged to eliminate the threat of isolation that could undermine the country's economic and political well-being (Gustavsson 1998; Sundelius 1994). Security policy, however, was still a balancing act. The policy of neutrality had been cemented as a 'meta narrative' for Swedish foreign policy, just as rooted in political culture as parliamentary democracy and representative monarchy (see Bjereld 2002). Successive governments faced the problem of changing policies but not rhetoric – releasing the seemingly compelling logic of neutrality without approaching binding security policy cooperation too quickly or too clearly.

The security policy doctrine

Following the failure of the Scandinavian Defence Federation in 1948, Sweden was on its own for the post-war period. Membership in NATO was never a realistic option when neutrality had 'served the country well' (see UD 2003) during World War II, and it was now necessary to define it as a consistent policy line even in peacetime. In 1950, they formulate the central doctrine that, with a slightly different wording, would be repeated as a mantra until the beginning of the 1990s: 'The foreign policy, which Sweden wishes to follow in future, is intended to allow neutrality in the event of a general conflict.'[2] Alliance freedom was used to pursue this policy and it was being a dominant aim for many years to come. The link between the two policy elements, alliance freedom in peace aimed at neutrality in the event of armed conflict, was considered to be in the credibility that the country could create around its doctrine. Weakness – political or military – could be seen as a sign that the country would not live up to its obligations, such as under pressure as in World War II, or experienced insecurity that could lead to a Western orientation of security policy (see Hakovirta 1988; Goldmann 1991; Agrell 1991). The models for creating this credibility were many and aimed, inter alia, at building military force and in-house consensus on the central features of the doctrine.

The accelerated upheavals in world politics 1989–1991 coincided with the change of government in 1991, which brought Carl Bildt to the premiership. Those who counted on radical changes in the security policy doctrine, instead, witnessed a continued consensus. A large part of the explanation for this continuity was that the overriding goal that the government shared with the largest opposition party was Sweden's membership in the EC/EU. No security policy risk-taking could be allowed to break the broad parliamentary front by reintroducing the neutrality policy in the debate and questioning EU membership based on the classic objection.[3] The traditional

2 Statement in the Riksdag 22 March 1950 on Sweden's foreign policy.

3 The events in the Baltic states in connection with the collapse of the Soviet Union sharpened this requirement. Sweden's position was, after all, a cautious support for freedom efforts, but 'pace and firmness' was required to not further destabilize the situation in the northern Baltic Sea area. See Andrén 2002.

security policy was eliminated in this process, which led to the gradual abandonment of neutrality policies (see Andrén 2002). Rhetorically, a rather empty shell was maintained stating: 'Military alliance freedom and neutrality ambitions in a conflict in the immediate area'. In practice, however, the Cold War's neutrality policy was abandoned in 1992 and Sweden had resorted to a security community based in Western Europe, but with strong ties to other structures of global scope (more about this in the Common Foreign and Security Policy section). A multipartisan deal was made in 2002 in a proposal for a new security doctrine stated 'Sweden is militarily non-aligned' and that this 'security policy, with the option of neutrality in conflicts, has served us well' (UD 2003). This made evident that Sweden's security policy position had shifted significantly. Instead of declaring a long-term consistent policy, one finds a softer ambition, but with a suggestion that it may have played its political role. As a doctrine, the phrase can only be termed as non-compulsory in the longer term. Completion of the new security policy line came after 2009 in the consolidation of an integrated foreign policy – let's call it the *solidarity doctrine* following Sweden's unilateral declaration of solidarity with the EU and neighbouring countries.[4] Sweden's initially very sceptical attitude to a common foreign and security policy had been replaced in full-throated support, which also became a cornerstone of national politics.

Foreign policy focus

The Swedish experience from the post-Cold War era demonstrates the abandonment of 'neutrality' and unilateralism in favour of diplomatic collaboration. In many cases, Sweden has chosen to seek the intergovernmental compromise as opposed to unilateral perfectionism. The political pattern in responding to conflicts in Bosnia 1992–95, Kosovo 1999, Afghanistan 2002–2014 and Libya 2011 have demonstrated

4 'Sweden will not be passive if a disaster or attack would affect another EU member state or Nordic country. The government expects these countries to act in the same way if Sweden is affected. Sweden should have the ability to provide and receive military support. 'Prop. 2008/09: 140, p. 29.

how destructive a breakdown in the Western Security Community may be for effective conflict resolution. A united front of western states, which is important especially from a small state perspective, can reinforce the structure and stability of the international system (Goetschel 2013). Discord and lack of political commitment leads to situations like those in Bosnia and Syria, where western paralysis allowed outbreaks of extensive ethnic fighting and diffusion of the original conflict.

From a historical-psychological perspective, it is often stated that a nation's foreign policy is guided by dominant analogies – historical events that form national decision makers' ways of seeing their state's role in world politics, identify the threats and opportunities in the world and decide how to deal with them (Khong 1992; Brändström *et al.* 2003). Sweden's foremost security policy analogy long remained the 'Midsummer crisis' of 1941 (when Sweden was pressured by Germany to allow troop transit from Norway) and other situations where armed neutrality was challenged but seen to be effective. The examples of international efforts (or lack of such) in the post-Cold war era have increasingly served as guiding analogies for Swedish foreign policy. These situations have shown how serious political problems originate (and require cooperation) across borders, and that solutions can only be found beyond classical, often heavy-handed diplomacy.

The more intimate institutionalized EU cooperation can be seen as a model and platform for Swedish leaders who have found new ways to influence world policy. The UN has long since ceased to be the predominant arena for Swedish security policy influence. In addition, meaningful UN mandates are vulnerable to the structural problems of the Security Council with recurring veto threats stopping concerted action. CFSP and informal cooperative structures at the highest level within the EU have become the path to political influence over regional security.

Since EU accession, it has also become increasingly evident that Sweden, more than larger states, has everything to gain from European/Western Consensus. The reasons for this are predominantly the weaker influence of small states in foreign policy disputes between parties that normally cooperate. By siding with stronger states, the small state can marginally affect policy outcomes and create its own freedom of action – something that becomes impossible when the great powers jostle for position and relegate smaller states like Sweden to the sidelines.[5] The loss of a regular ally, the United Kingdom with Brexit, makes Sweden's position increasingly difficult as the power balance in the European Council will shift further away from the north European perspective often supported by the UK.

However, the domestic-foreign policy divide plays a central role. In a political climate that is largely characterized by the mindset of neutrality and a historical legacy of 'active foreign policy', obviously, power politics or stability-oriented approaches can easily be vilified. This is a problem for the Swedish Social democrats because of a latent contradiction of foreign policy principles that runs within its own party (see Ohlson 2014). If a Social Democratic government can show EU endorsement of the line advocated nationally, it can mitigate both parliamentary criticism and internal party divisions. Furthermore, EU consensus often works galvanizing for decisions taken within the UN system, which provides further internal credibility. Western unity during the Kosovo crisis in 1999 and the struggles in the UN Security Council over the intervention in Iraq in 2003 set the perfect contrast between a successful and a failed diplomatic effort (Davidson 2011). The traditional Swedish emphasis of international law as part of the active foreign policy was completely eliminated (Kosovo), or was reclaimed only when the battle of unity was already lost after the US-British invasion of Iraq.

Sweden and the CFSP

The EU membership has meant a dramatic change in focus for Swedish foreign policy, from principled global perspective towards the EU and its neighbourhood (particularly to the ENP countries, see Chapter 12). Sweden's political position is now so closely linked to EU policy shaping processes that they can no longer be separated. Finding allies within the Union is now the prime criteria for promot-

5 This is referred to in the theoretical literature as the 'Bandwagon effect', which means that weaker states join behind the stronger to gain benefits and not risk contradictions. See, for example, Jervis & Snyder, 1991.

ing a certain policy line internationally. But Sweden is in many ways a disproportionately successful country in terms of influencing common policies.[6]

Previously, Sweden acted jointly with other countries, including Western Europeans, only if it would preserve the foundation of non-alliance. *E.g.* Olof Palme's cooperation with Willy Brandt 's West Germany in the 70's and 80's was acceptable because it could be portrayed as a 'third position' with disapproval targeting both superpowers. On the other hand, to take a clear position on Finland's response during the so-called note crisis of 1961, when the Soviet Union pushed Finland's policy positions by invoking the so-called Friendship, Cooperation and Development Pact (VSB), was virtually unthinkable. Sweden's line was aimed at preserving its policy of neutrality, and arguably indirectly easing the pressure on Finland.

Security policy after 1991 is devoid of this dimension. The Maastricht Treaty of 1993 established a Common Foreign and Security Policy (CFSP) as the Union's second pillar. Following the 1999 Council Decision on the European Common Security and Defence Policy (CSDP), Swedish ministers were skeptical and trivialized the importance of the agreement. However, soon a national political insight materialized the effect that the CFSP and CSDP were the ultimate tools for a small state to become part of cooperation in the difficult security policy issues while renouncing a future NATO membership. Sweden participated in the French-led Operation Artemis, which was a peacekeeping initiative in Congo 2003 (Strömvik 2005). In 2004, it participated in the development of the EU's new Battle Group concept by setting up a Nordic force that was in preparation for the first half of 2008 and later 2011 and 2015. When the most ambitious and defence-oriented EU initiative to date, the permanent Structured Cooperation (PESCO) went operational, Sweden participated in three of the 17 projects with options suggesting it may join additional projects in the near future.

The commitment to joint solutions is also illustrated by participation in the co-operation on military equipment launched in 2001. The

6 See for example The European Foreign Policy Council's ranking of the *European Foreign Policy Scorecard* (2016).

cooperation concerns: '… security of supply, transfer and export procedures, security of confidential information, defence related research and technology, processing of technical information, harmonization of military requirements and protection of commercially sensitive information '(Prop. 2001/02: 10). This program is far-reaching and contains promises for a war-time cooperation that would be incompatible with a declaration of neutrality if a participating state would be in armed conflict. However, this relationship has only been sparsely publicized and has been the subject of little debate (see the OAG 2004). This indicates that the European dimension of security policy is only in exceptional cases controversial and that, in such cases, the questions tend to revolve around the relationship with NATO rather than cooperation within the EU framework.

The exceptions to this 'rule' has consisted of the statements on a future common defence which occurred in the Treaties of Amsterdam and Nice which suggested a constitution for the EU, but that did not survive ratification in the Lisbon Treaty. The debate made clear that security is still a potentially divisive force in Swedish domestic policy. Swedish EU skeptics used these stated ambitions to warn of the 'slippery slope' towards alliance commitments they consider consecutive governments to only mildly oppose by accepting the development of the CSDP (Schlaug 2013) .

Several Governments have therefore chosen to make a commitment to European security within the Union's framework overt and outspoken, as a strategy for continued military non-alliance. The alternative would be to take the plunge and abandon nonalliance and open to broader commitments in the EU as well as in the increasingly intimate cooperation with NATO structures developed. During 2015 all four center-right Alliance parties of the Swedish parliament had adopted a pro-NATO accession stance. This has polarized the domestic debate on security policy, and caused the Social democrats, the senior government partner since 2014, to pursue bilateral cooperative agreements that are designed to deflate the urgency that the centre-right is trying to inject into the NATO accession debate.

There is a divide in Swedish parliamentary parties' views on the security policy relationship between EU membership and a future NATO membership. Proponents of the current government's approach, based on the declaration of solidarity with the EU, see European security policy cooperation as a 'NATO light', which together with deeper integration with NATO structures, suffices to avoid security policy isolation. Isolationists believe that the declaration of solidarity risks entangling Sweden in future conflicts, but has very few benefits in terms of guarantees that other states will come to the rescue. Ironically, they share this view with many NATO advocates who believe that only the binding Article V of the NATO Charter can provide a basis for a defence doctrine based on cooperation with other states in war as well as in peace.

What is Sweden trying to achieve within the framework of EU foreign policy cooperation? The stability ambition has been mentioned as a major priority in terms of most common issues of foreign and security policy importance that are being dealt with within the EU. This should be seen primarily as the small state's means of exercising influence and ensuring space for action. Sweden has fought for a number of policy goals over the years and has generally been fairly successful. They advocated that the enlargement to the east should be as broad as possible, rapidly concluded and comprehensive in the sense that the new members should quickly enjoy all aspects of European cooperation. Sweden's goal was clearly creating a stronger community between the Baltic Sea states, as is also apparent in its promotion of the Council of Baltic Sea States (CBSS).

Sweden has long sought further liberalization of international trade by strengthening the common market, but primarily through a programmatic extension of the European free trade policy with common positions in the framework of the World Trade Organization (WTO) and other international events in the area. The Eastern Partnership (see chapter 12) was a flagship for Sweden and its failure has put the entire Swedish solidarity doctrine in question . The Russian annexation of the Crimea and its proxy war in eastern Ukraine shows the constraints of the EU's common foreign policy (as well as other Western co-operation). The fact that the EU and the United States has been able to create a sanctions regime against Russia in the Crimean issue is absolutely crucial for maintaining credibility of the Swedish political line. EU's common front, however fragile, particularly in light of enlargement and increased political division in the European

Council has been crucial for continued Swedish commitment to EU as its main foreign policy arena. The recurrent and prolonged financial crises that have affected parts of the Eurozone and the 2015 refugee crisis (see chapter 9) has put the cohesion in question, which fuels concern about CFSP as well.

The conclusion of many political actors in Sweden has been to disregard EU mandates for security forces in the light of developments in the immediate area and actively propagate for a NATO membership. The NATO advocates believe that it is a natural extension of a policy that is increasingly seeking common Western/European solutions and that NATO thus is a complement to the EU within a wider policy area, rather than a revolutionary change (Aggestam & Hyde-Price 2016). The debate takes place against a backdrop of increased Russian ambitions in the region that are characterized by enhanced military presence and large-scale exercises, qualitative and quantitative military rearmament, the use of natural resources as coercive means and a stronger global claim to power through the intervention in Syria.

Together with Finland, Sweden launched the Petersberg tasks (humanitarian and peacekeeping missions) as a vital part of the EU's Common Foreign and Security Policy for the Amsterdam Treaty in 1999. This capacity was incorporated into the treaty, and for the non-NATO states, there was thus a 'back door' to international missions under NATO leadership (see Aggestam & Hyde-Price 2016) . These efforts should have a UN mandate, but as demonstrated by the Kosovo crisis 1998–1999, one can consider 'humanitarian interventions' when the UN Security Council is dead-locked and it would probably be possible to invoke the provisions of the Amsterdam Treaty for participation in such an operation also for the non-aligned. The purpose of the Finnish-Swedish initiative was to create a kind of NATO 'à la carte', where non-members of NATO can play a role in peacekeeping operations linked to NATO without alliance commitments. This increased its influence and ability to engage in a time (1999) when NATO reemerged as the dominant security policy organization in Europe. At the same time, however, the activation of this mechanism is dependent on NATO's approval in each case, which is a significant factor of uncertainty in the ambition to choose the degree of commitment in each individual question. Sweden and Finland managed to open an institutional window to voluntary participation, but establishing a practice of regular cooperation would be a more demanding task, especially after NATO's political breakdown over Iraq.

In the ISAF initiative in Afghanistan, which began for Sweden in 2002, it supplied a relatively large number of troops until 2014, committed by governments from both sides of the political aisle. Security responsibilities were shouldered for four provinces in northern Afghanistan, with headquarters in Mazar-e Sharif. By demonstrating extensive commitment to a US-led effort, it became possible to get a prominent role as a de facto 'framework nation' in NATO (Andersson 2013). The process has resulted in a further deepening of the cooperation and in May 2016, the Swedish parliament ratified a host country agreement with NATO that creates legal conditions for NATO troops based on Swedish soil and far-reaching joint exercises. The approach to NATO is both a result of, and a response to, EU cooperation. Swedish governments have seen its advantages, but also its limitations. It has been discovered that the maximum impact on efforts and planning requires influence in both intergovernmental organizations.

The broader concept of security

When the British researcher Barry Buzan in 1982 published his *People, States, and Fear* a debate started that has come to mould both the study and practice of security policy, in Sweden and in Europe. Buzan argues that the traditional, military-focused concept of security can, (and even should) be complemented by other social and political considerations for the well-being of citizens. This means that society's security needs can be divided into sectors to meet threats in the economic, ecological, political and social sectors, as well as the traditional military ones. The citizen is entitled to protection from existential threats in all these areas, which forces the state in Buzan's reality to broaden its security repertoire to face a wider range of threats. These thoughts have penetrated government policy, mainly in the western world's mature democracies, and especially in Scandinavia. A Swedish legal bill (1996/97: 11) stated:

> Just observing security from a military perspective is a perverted approach. Instead, we now proceed from an expanded security concept. Interruptions in power supply, environmental disasters and accidents at nuclear power plants are examples of events that can have major consequences for both the country and its population. International terrorism acts ruthlessly and does not hesitate to exploit the vulnerabilities of modern society. War, oppression and poverty often lead to major refugee displacement and even relocations. Natural disasters can cause severe strains.

It links to an old Swedish idea of total defence – the ambition to engage every part of society for a possible war effort. The security policy approach that started with the legal initiative cited above, in which societal functions are integrated into a broader societal defence, provided the Armed Forces with new tasks and focuses on vulnerabilities of society and established preparedness for a number of severe peace-time stresses (Ds 2003:34). The idea of creating a civilian crisis management capacity to meet these strains led to a widespread expansion of the security policy focus that previously only included the armed attack. However, as Russia's illegal annexation of Crimea demonstrated the recurrence of war on the European continent, the pendulum started swinging the other way. As of 2015, the Swedish government, with significant multipartisan support, is rebuilding a territorially focused armed forces and the brunt of a civil defence that was decommissioned in the nineteen nineties.

The change that was imposed on security policy thinking obviously affected the traditional defence sector, which saw its core functions extended to peace-time threats and international missions to a greater extent than before. Another, and perhaps equally important consequence, was that other sectors of society were included in security policy practice and were assigned functional responsibility for key policy areas to address vulnerabilities and threats (MSB 2014). In 2009, the Swedish Contingencies Agency (MSB) was established. It was given national responsibility for coordinating issues of civilian crisis management and the protection of society's vital resources. The idea that Sweden only seemed to face temporally distant or marginal threats allowed state power to expand its ambition to counteract threats to society and broadened its repertoire to meet them. As Russia started to regain its military capabilities and act more belligerent, revolts in the Middle East turned into civil wars in Libya and Syria and led to IS expansion in Syria, Iraq and Libya. Sweden's and the EU's response to these challenges has not been convincing in all respects.

A parallel development can be seen at EU level. In 2003, the *European Security Strategy* was adopted and followed in 2010 by an *Internal Security Strategy*. The most significant development from a security perspective was the solidarity clause in the Lisbon Treaty (Art. 222). It states that 'The Union and its Member States shall act jointly in a spirit of solidarity if a Member State is the object of a terrorist attack or the victim of a natural or man-made disaster. The Union shall mobilise all the instruments at its disposal, including the military resources made available by the Member States' (Lisbon Treaty 2008). In order to mobilize EU member resources in the event of crises and disasters, there are a number of coordination and alert functions: the Commission's Civil Protection Mechanism and its Rapid Response Mechanism and, in particular, the Emergency Response and Coordination Center (ERCC). Sector-dependent interventions can be controlled by authorities under the Commission, such as FRONTEX regarding border issues or ECDC in the area of decease control. In the field of foreign and security policy there are mechanisms for military crisis management, civilian crisis management and conflict prevention measures (Boin *et al.*, 2013). Willingness to ask and offer help varies, and is linked to political positions and connected other political collaboration. If you are, like Sweden, a net contributor to the EU budget, it is common to advocate restraint regarding the use of common crisis management resources. Tensions about the use of common capabilities exist throughout the field of Union activity, and especially in the field of foreign and security policy, and they risk undermining the credibility of the collective commitment.

The most comprehensive co-operation on crisis management in foreign and security policy is the Council's Integrated Political Crisis Response Arrangements (IPCR). The IPCR came into force in 2015 and is a further development of the Crisis Coordination Arrangement (CCA), which originated from the perceived lack of political coordination following the terrorist attacks in Madrid and London, as well as the tsunami disaster in Southeast Asia 2004 and

2005. IPCR aims to rapidly activate the proper Council constellation to produce a common response in serious crises. The presidency has left a strong mandate to activate IPCR and push forward a common line. CCA was activated on three occasions in so-called 'information sharing mode', as was the case with IPCR during the refugee flows in autumn 2015. Considering the many difficult situations the EU faces in the future, the tools available to the Union have been refined and made substantial, while the will to use them for common purposes seems to slowly erode.

An increasingly integrated foreign policy?

Where is Sweden headed as a member of the EU in its foreign and security policy role? As noted above, this largely depends on the development of the EU as an organization and the credibility of its common frameworks for foreign and security policy. Today, the internal fragmentation within the EU includes leading nations within the Union, sometimes moving away from political priorities that have previously been sources of unity. Some estimates suggest that the disruption of refugee reception along with the difficulty of enforcing sanctions against Russia undermines the credibility of the Union's foreign policy for a long time to come (Ashford 2016; Lehne 2016). The drivers of the Union's common interests during the previous commission, Commission President Jean-Claude Junker, Council President Donald Tusk and High Representative Federica Mogherini were often marginalized when security issues touched upon the interests of the major member states and had more narrow space for action when the disagreement locks the council structures. Brexit puts additional burdens on the political forces that drive long-term solutions to these urgent problems. However, it can be noted that the EU's development towards further integration and stronger political coordination has been driven by worsening crises – the members have brought each other to the precipice, to the brink of a common defeat, only to pivot and create stronger cooperative structures and deeper integration.

Sweden's position in this process is likely to drive integration-oriented solutions, as its recent modus offer. The alternatives to such a development are detrimental to the small state – a continued fragmentation right through the core of the Union on foreign and security policy would greatly reduce Swedish influence over broad political fields. When the leading EU states are in conflicts of interest and thus more overtly push their national agendas in the EU, smaller states are robbed of leverage and cannot use compromises in the Council to move forward their positions.

For Sweden, this involves the complicated relationship between foreign and domestic policy. The steps towards a regional security policy commitment are surrounded by strong national interests and problematic internal divisions in the leading political parties, not the least in the Social Democratic Party. Choosing the EU path over NATO towards enhanced security policy cooperation is in this light considerably more attractive for maintaining a measure of national consensus. Crucial to the attraction of this option is the demonstrated ability to find long-term solutions to genuine European problems. The inclusion of neighbouring states in a positive political development, managing refugee flows that will continue across the EU's external border, and not least the strained relations with Russia, are all crucial for EU cooperation as a major security policy instrument for the Member States. It can be argued that these tasks are a big ask of any organization that is so loosely composed and internally divided as the EU, but it has delivered long-term institutional sustainability before and might surprise its detractors again.

Conclusions

Sweden is a state which for historical and geopolitical reasons existed in Europe's political periphery during the Cold War. When the political upheavals in eastern Europe began in 1989, the country's prerequisites for pursuing its foreign and security policy changed significantly as the threat from the East was disrupted. The states who had lived under Soviet domination drew immediate consequences of this and undertook radical internal and external reorientations and sought reassurances for the security policy in case the 'strategic time-out' were to end. When NATO members also realigned their security perspective beyond Europe, the non-aligned states entered a period of confusing self-examination.

Movements towards the EU came quite quickly in the wake of a growing economic crisis in 1991–92, while more far-reaching discussions about Sweden's security policy choices were sidelined. The EU was considered to be an opportunity for greater economic prosperity and political involvement in European political structures, without restricting the country's security policy freedom of action. This process was expedited mainly for domestic reasons, as there were strong latent opposition on this issue – especially within the single party government itself.

As member, Sweden has since then increasingly adopted a new role of the fully committed participant of the Brussels arena, as an equal player in the European political landscape with the ability to muster support for political solutions at the political level. The various governments have favoured the European Union increasingly in international issues because of the simple reason that the total weight of the Member States can really shift political structures at a global level, while the small state has few instruments of power. The problem has rather been not to put too many of the foreign and security policy eggs in the European basket. In the event of a collapse in the consensus on sanctions against Russia, few effective unilateral Swedish tools remain. Such a community failure would for Sweden trigger an awakening from the beautiful world of the common security strategies and would risk throwing the political debate in an isolationist direction. It's not easy to be a small country on a troubled continent.

References

Aggestam, L. & A. Hyde-Price 2016. 'A Force for Good: Paradoxes of Swedish Military Activism', In: J. Pierre (ed.) *Oxford Handbook of Swedish Politics*, Oxford: Oxford University Press.

Agrell, W. 1991. *Den stora lögnen: ett säkerhetspolitiskt dubbelspel i alltför många akter* [The Big Lie: A Security Policy Doubles Game in too Many Acts]. Stockholm: Ordfront.

Andersson, J. J. 2013. 'A New Swedish Defence for a Brave New World' In: J. M. Haaland & Ø. Østerud (eds.) *Denationalization of Defence: Diversity and Convergence*. Farnham: Ashgate

Andrén, N. 2002. *Säkerhetspolitik: analyser och tillämpningar* [Security Policy: Analysis and Applications], 2nd ed. Stockholm: Norstedts Juridik.

Ashford, E. 2016. 'Non-So-Smart Sanctions: The Failure of Western Restrictions Against Russia' *Foreign Affairs*, 95 (1).

Bjereld, U. 1997. *Hjalmarsonaffären: ett politiskt drama i tre akter* [The Hjalmarson Affair: A Political Drama in too Many Acts], (Gothenburg Studies in Politics). Stockholm: Nerenius & Santérus

— 2002. 'New survey on Swedes 'attitude towards NATO:' record resistance against connection' *Dagens Nyheter* 2002-03-05, p. 4

Black, D. 1948. 'On the Rationale of Group Decision Making', *Journal of Political Economy*, February 1948.

Boin, A., M. Ekengren & M. Rhinard 2013. *The European Union as Crisis Manager*. Oxford: Oxford University Press.

Brändström, A., F. Bynander & P. 't Hart 2004. 'Governing by Looking Back: Historical Analogue and Contemporary Crisis Management,' *Public Administration*. 82 (1): 191–210

Buzan, B. 1982/1991. *People, States, and Fear: An Agenda for International Security Studies in the Post-Cold War Era*. Hemel Hempstead: Harvester Wheatsheaf.

Buzan, B. O. Wæver & J. de Wilde, 1998. *Security: A New Framework for Analysis*. Boulder: Lynne Rienner.

Bynander, F. 2003. *The Rise and Fall of the Submarine Threat: Threat Politics and Submarine Intrusions in Sweden 1980–2002*. Thesis. Uppsala: Acta Universitatis Uppsaliensis.

Davidson, J. W. 2011. *America's Allies and War: Kosovo, Afghanistan, and Iraq*, Houndmills: Palgrave.

Downs, A. 1957. *An Economic Theory of Democracy*, New York: Harper & Row.

Ds 2003: 34. *Vårt militära försvar – vilja och vägval : försvarspolitisk rapport* [Our military defence: will and choice. Defence Policy Report from the Defence Committee]. Stockholm: Fritzes.

European Council on Foreign Relations. 2016. *European Foreign Policy Scorecard*. https://www.ecfr.eu/scorecard/2016

Goetschel, L. 2013. *Small States Inside and Outside the European Union: Interests and Policies*. Boston: Kluwer Academic Publishers.

Goldmann, K. 1991. 'The Swedish Model of Security Policy' *Western European Politics*, 14 (3).

Gustavsson, J. 1998. *Politics for Foreign Policy Change: Explaining the Swedish Reorientation on EC Membership*. Lund: Lund Political Studies.

Hakovirta, H. 1988. *East-West Conflict and European Neutrality*. Oxford: Clarendon.

Hallenberg, J. 2000. 'Swedish Foreign and Security Policy', In: L. Miles (ed.) *Sweden and the European Union Evaluated*. New York: Continuum.

Jervis, R. & J. Snyder (eds.) 1991 *Dominoes and Bandwagons: Strategic Beliefs and Great Power Competition in the Eurasian Rimland*. New York: Oxford University Press.

Johansson, A. W. 1995. *Herbert Tingsten och det kalla kriget: anti-kommunism och liberalism i Dagens nyheter 1946–1952* [Herbert Tingsten and the Cold War: Anti-Communism and Liberalism in Today's News 1946–1952]. Stockholm: Tiden.

Khong, Y. F. 1992. *Analogue at War: Korea, Munich, Dien Bien Phu and the Vietnam Decisions of 1965*. Princeton: Princeton University Press.

Lehne, S. 2016. *How the Refugee Crisis Will Reshape Europe*. Brussels: Carnegie Europe. http://carnegieeurope.eu/2016/02/04/how-refugee-crisis-will-reshape-eu/itj7

Misgeld, K. 1990. 'Swedish Social Democracy and Europe', In: B. Huldt & K. Misgeld (eds.) *Socialdemokratin och svensk utrikespolitik: från Branting till Palme* [Social Democracy and Swedish Foreign Policy]. Stockholm: Utrikespolitiska institutet [Swedish Institute for International Affairs].

Molin, K. 1991. *Omstridd neutralitet : experternas kritik av svensk utrikes-politik 1948–1950* [Controversial Neutrality: Experts' Critique of Swedish Foreign Policy 1948–1950] Stockholm: Tiden.

MSB 2014. *Common foundations for cooperation and management in social disturbances*. Stockholm: MSB.

Murray, W., M. Knox & A. Bernstein (eds.) 1994. *The Making of Strategy: Rulers, States, and War*. Cambridge: Cambridge University Press.

Mörth, U. & B. Sundelius. 1998. *Interdependens, konflikt och säkerhetspolitik : Sverige och den amerikanska teknikexportkontrollen* [Interdependence, conflict and security policy: Sweden and the US technology export control]. Stockholm: Nerenius & Santérus.

Noreen, E. 1995. *Brobygge eller block-bildning?: de norska och svenska utrikesledningarnas säkerhetspolitiska föreställningar 1945–1948* [Bridge Building or Block Formation]. Stockholm: Carlsson.

Ohlson, P. T. 2014. *Svensk politik*. [Swedish Policy]. Lund: Historiska Media.

Prop. 1996/97: 11. *Hot och risker i samhället: populärversion av regeringens proposition 1996/97:11* [Threats and Risk in Society]. Stockholm: Försvarsdepartementet.

Prop. 2001/02: 10. *Fortsatt förnyelse av totalförsvaret* [Continued Renewal of the Total Defence]. Stockholm: Riksdagens tryckeriexp.

Prop. 2008/09: 140. *Ett användbart försvar* [A Useful Defence]. Stockholm: Riksdagens tryckeri-exp.

Putnam, R. 1988. 'Diplomacy and Domestic Politics: The Logic of Two-Level Games' *International Organization*, 42 (3).

Government Declaration at the Foreign Policy Debate in Parliament,

Wednesday, February 12, 2003. Ministry of Foreign Affairs, 2003.
Government statement in Riksdag 22 March 1950 for Sweden's foreign policy. Ministry of Foreign Affairs, 1950.
Riker, W. 1962. *The Theory of Political Coalitions* . New Haven: Yale University Press.
National Audit Office 2004. *Material for Billions: A Review of Defence Material Supplies.* RiR 2004: 6, Stockholm: OAG.
Schlaug, B. 2013. *Defence Preparation on Sloping Plan.* http://schlaug.blogspot.se/2013/06/forsvars-beredning-pa-sluttande-plan.html
SOU 1994: 11. *Om kriget kommit: förberedelser för mottagandet av militärt bistånd 1949–1969* [If the war has come ... Preparations for receiving military assistance 1949–1969]. Stockholm: Fritzes.
SOU 2002: 108. *Fred och säkerhet: svensk säkerhetspolitik 1969–1989* [Peace and Security: Swedish Security Policy 1969–1989]. Report from the Security Policy Investigation. Stockholm: Fritzes.
Sundelius, B. 1994. 'Changing Course: When Neutral Sweden Chose to Join the European Community' In: W. Carlsnaes & S. Smith (eds.) *European Foreign Policy: The EC and Changing Perspectives in Europe.* London: Sage.
Sweden's security policy line, Ministry of Foreign Affairs, 2002. http://www.utrikes.regeringen.se/fragor/utrikespolitik/sakerhet/index.htm
Tsebelis, G. 1990. *Nested Games: Rational Choice in Comparative Politics.* Berkeley: University of California Press.
UD, 2003. *Government Declaration at the Foreign Policy Debate in the Riksdag,* Wednesday, February 12, 2003, Stockholm: Ministry of Foreign Affairs.
Zetterberg, K. 1997. 'Introduction' In: K. Zetterberg (ed.) *Hotet från öster : tre studier om svensk säkerhetspolitik, krigsplanering och strategi i det kalla krigets första fas 1945–1958* [The Threat from Öster: Swedish Security Policy, War Planning and Strategy 1945–1958]. Stockholm: Försvarshögskolan [Swedish Defence College].

12. The European Neighbourhood Policy

From Swedish Politics in the Baltic Sea to EU's Eastern Partnership

Martin Nilsson

Currently, the European Neighbourhood Policy (ENP)[1], which represents one of the most developed policy areas in foreign relations of the European Union (EU), deals with the EU's policy orientation toward the eastern post-Soviet countries of Georgia, Ukraine, Moldova, Armenia, Azerbaijan and Belarus. Foreign policy is, in practice, however, a competence area characterised by shared powers; the EU can impose a common policy, if all EU-member states agree, but each member state can still execute its own national foreign policy.[2]

From a Swedish perspective, the content of the Swedish policy towards neighbouring countries to the east have changed, partly after Sweden's EU membership and partly as the EU has expanded to the east. After the end of the Cold War and before EU membership, the Swedish government pursued active aid, trade, and other cooperative policies in relation to Estonia, Latvia, and Lithuania; in part, Poland, and the Ukraine; and, to some extent, Russia. However, after the Baltic countries and Poland approached the EU, initially through cooperative agreements in the 1990s, to request EU membership in

1 The EU's European Neighbourhood Policy (ENP), officially based on values such as democracy, the rule of law and respect for human rights is primarily bilateral in its application to relationships between the EU and 16 neighbouring states. The 16 target states are as follows: Algeria, Armenia, Azerbaijan, Egypt, Georgia, Israel, Jordan, Lebanon, Libya, Morocco, Moldova, Palestine, Syria, Tunisia, Ukraine and Belarus. The ENP is characterized by further development via multilateral regional cooperation initiatives to the east and south – such as the Eastern Partnership (2009–) and the Mediterranean Union (2008–).

2 Chapter 11 describes the EU, as a foreign policy player, in more detail.

2004, foreign relations between Sweden and its neighbours around the Baltic Sea have undergone a gradual change. After the respective 2004 and 2007 enlargements, to Eastern Europe and Central Europe, which included most countries within the formerly communist eastern bloc, except most of post-Soviet countries, Russia included, the EU's launched its next phase, in the form of the so-called European Neighbourhood Policy (ENP). Sweden's Baltic neighbours were now members of the EU, a reflection of the entire policy's eastward movement, which remained, however, within the EU-framework. As an EU member, Sweden actively promoted this Europeanisation, first through the eastern enlargement during the 1990s and 2000s, and then via the establishment and development of the new neighbourhood policy, aimed at countries even further east, geographically speaking.

First, this chapter describes the current neighbourhood policy, the gradual Europeanisation of Sweden's eastern policy; even before its 1995 EU membership, Sweden has been deeply involved in the geographical shift eastward and the power shift to EU institutions in accordance in EU development between 1995 and 2018. Thereafter, the chapter analyses the direct and indirect Europeanisation of Sweden's eastern Baltic policy; subsequent to this analysis is a section analysing the nature of the policy model that characterises the current neighbourhood policy.

Sweden's Neighbourhood Policy Before the Accession to the EU in 1995

Before its accession of the EU, Sweden's international activity, in relation to neighbouring countries, was determined primarily by the security policy. The Baltic States had been held in an iron grip by the Soviet Union since World War II. Like other countries in Eastern Europe, Poland's communist regime was bound, by force, to the Soviet Union, through a security package (Warsaw Pact) and a cooperative trade agreement (COMECON). When, for example, the Polish insurgency (as in 1970 and 1981) threatened to undermine the Polish communist regime, the Soviet Union was ready with a violent military response. Further, it should here be noted that Finland was, more or less, forced to sign a treaty pledging its friendship, cooperation and mutual assistance, with the Soviet Union that endured from 1948 until 1992. Sweden's practical relations with neighbouring countries, on the eastern Baltic Sea, were thereby limited.

However, as the Cold War was about to end, from 1988 to 1991, Sweden's foreign policy began to change (see Doeser 2008). A series of events changed Sweden's relationships with neighbouring countries. When the eastern bloc disintegrated, the formerly communist states were replaced, one by one, with democratically elected governments until, finally, the Soviet Union itself collapsed (Hallenberg 2002). In 1989, Poland was among the first states to elect and empower a non-communist government. Although American-Soviet relations were relatively relaxed by 1990, a major disarmament had yet to occur in Sweden's vicinity. When the Baltic region started liberating itself from the Soviet Union, the security policy context worsened further. When the remaining Soviet republics became independent states, the dissolution of the Soviet Union, formalised on December 31, 1991, followed. This represented the practical conclusion of the decades-long impending conflict – the Cold War – that had forced the United States (US), Western Europe and the North Atlantic Treaty Organisation (NATO) against the Soviet Union, Eastern Europe and the Warsaw Pact (Hallenberg 2002).

Given the security policy context that characterised early 1990, the Social Democratic government maintained Sweden's neutral status, thereby delaying Sweden's application for membership to the European Community (EC). A similarly unstable security policy context characterised the region neighbouring Sweden. The liberal and conservative opposition, under Carl Bildt's leadership of the Moderate Assembly Party, however, argued that Sweden should seek membership (Gustafsson 1998, Doeser 2008). When autumn of 1990 brought American-Soviet negotiations to a close via a comprehensive disarmament agreement, Sweden's Social Democratic government prepared itself for membership. At the same time, however, Sweden seemed inclined to maintain its policy of neutrality, even in the context of potential membership. In July 1991, Sweden, finally submitted its membership application to the EC (Gustafsson 1998, Doeser 2008).

After the Baltic States and Poland liberated themselves, a new spirit of cooperation was established between Sweden and its Baltic neighbours. When four decades of Cold War finally ended, the disintegration of the Soviet Union prompted the Baltic States, to approach the West, EU and NATO; in turn, this led Sweden to pursue a more active foreign policy, with regard to its neighbours.

Swedish policy was (Sida 2004), promoting military and economic aid- and cooperation. In terms of military cooperation, the neighbouring states provided Sweden with a so-called sovereignty support, which consisted of assistance, in the form of support for the civilian branch of defence; Sweden, at this time, was still not exporting arms to the Baltic countries, given the security situation. At this time, old Soviet troops remained in the area. In terms of trade cooperation, between 1992 and 1993, Sweden signed free trade agreements with Estonia, Latvia, Lithuania and Poland (Regeringens proposition 1991/92: 142; 1992/93: 146). Establishing free trade agreements aimed at, among other things, accelerating integration with and the accommodation of Western norms and values, embodied by the EC and the European Free Trade Association (EFTA). Bilateral aid, however, was initially quite modest and involved providing support for community development, democracy, environmental work, agriculture, as well as for the economic and social infrastructure, including the banking system (Regeringens proposition 1992/93: 100).

Finally, Swedish policy was arranged organically, through government proposals, discussions and preparations by the Foreign Affairs Committee and with parliamentary support. Most of Sweden's political parties agreed on the Swedish policy toward neighbouring Baltic countries, regardless of the specific constellation of government. To the extent that Swedish policy was also being conducted in tandem with intergovernmental organisations, such as EFTA and the Nordic Council, the Swedish Parliament, however, still made decisive and independent judgments (Svenska riksdagen 2015).

Following EU Membership: Baltic Sea Cooperation and Eastern Enlargement 1995–2004

Upon joining the EU, Sweden's autonomous policy against the Baltic countries changed. Following the Maastricht Treaty (in force 1993),

Sweden entered into a new political and economic union that was motivated by ambitions such as the development of its own currency (*i.e.*, the Euro) and foreign policy. Moreover, a potential enlargement toward Eastern and Central Europe rapidly began accelerating in the late 1990s. The enlargement process operated in tandem with all candidate countries, wherein the EU's new membership criteria, the so-called Copenhagen criteria (1993) were articulated and applied. Establishing membership criteria reflected a demand for compliance, by all new member states, with certain democratic and market economy principles and that, further, the countries had to absorb the existing *acquis communautaire* to accommodate new policy and enlarged community priorities. The European Council's adoption of the Copenhagen criteria coincided with the decision to grant the countries of Eastern and Central Europe future membership to the EU (European Council 1993).

Following Sweden's 1995 accession of the EU, it was evident that Sweden's policy toward the Baltic countries implied an indirect acceptance of Europeanisation and adaptation to EU policies in this area. Around 1997, Sweden began to emphasise the importance of a 'good neighbourhood' (Regeringens proposition 1997/98: 70; Sida 2004). Sweden's development cooperation became part of the broader Swedish voluntary aid cooperation with Central and Eastern Europe, focused on the Baltic Sea region, namely the Baltic States, Poland and, partly, Russia and the Ukraine (Regeringens proposition 1997/98: 70). The purpose of the new Swedish policy had already been articulated in 1995:

> ... The cooperation is aimed at strengthening security, democracy and sustainable development throughout Europe. The importance of the Baltic Sea region for creating a dynamic northern Europe is a basic element of the cooperation program ... (Regeringens proposition 1994/95-160: 6)

As the EU-East membership negotiations progressed in the 1990s, Swedish cooperation continued in tandem with EU programs, exemplified by Poland and Hungary: Assistance for Restructuring Their Economies (Phare), which had developed into a primary tool of integrating the Baltic States and Poland into EU policy objectives, across a wide range of areas (PAGE 2004). In the early 2000s, the eastern countries also gained access to other support schemes devised by the EU, such as the Special Accession Program for Agriculture and Rural Development (SAPARD) and the Instrument for Structural Policies for Pre-Accession (ISPA), which aimed primarily at developing agriculture (European Commission 2002). Sweden's development cooperation with the Baltic States and Poland was therefore implemented in co-existence with EU policies related to integration. The Swedish government even provided confirmation of this, in another bill:

> ...Compares the demands made by the EU on the future member states, the so-called The Copenhagen criteria, and the conclusions of the European Commission's statements of July 1997 with the Swedish objectives to date, can be noted that, with the exception of the promotion of a security community, there is a significant degree of consistency. (Regeringens proposition 1997/98-70: 8)

The main difference, in terms of content, was that Sweden prioritised security objectives, while the EU did not assign security the same level of importance. This owed partly to the EU's lack of defence cooperation at that time, and partly to the fact that the membership debate itself had different motives, whereby security became a consequence of cooperating with the EU. As soon as the Baltic countries and Poland were close to attaining EU membership, Sweden's development cooperation was phased out (Regeringens proposition 2000/01: 119). In Swedish politics, great care was taken to avoid a divided Europe, an ideological orientation that ultimately became a component of the ENP. Therefore, both Russia and Ukraine assumed the status of priority countries in Sweden's eastward politics, modelling the post-2003 new eastern neighbourhood policy adopted by the EU, for similar underlying motives (see Regeringens proposition 1997/98-70: 17). In addition, between 1991 and 2008, Sweden supported the Russian reform process in Russia, motivated by an ambition to bolster security and democracy, as well as the economy and the environment. This occurred at a time characterised by an optimistic hope that Russia would voluntarily integrate with the West. The cooperation was terminated when there was no further need to pursue such a course (Sida 2009: 91–92).

In terms of security policy cooperation, in 1995, the Swedish Social Democratic government articulated a more active policy, with regard to the Baltic countries. This meant, among other things, that the relevant foreign policy declarations reflected the Swedish opinion that the Baltic's freedom and security was important for Sweden's own security. Sweden also aimed to facilitate the integration of countries into the policy objectives identified by both the EU and NATO, which would represent a contribution to increased security for the Baltic States, as well as Sweden. Moreover, Sweden assisted with civilian aspects of the new defence forces, including formal mining instruction and the establishment of the Baltic peace force, BALTRON/BALTBAT. The early 2000s brought the Baltic States expanded military cooperation, including training efforts (focused on producing officers), military exercises that involved multiple states at once, as well as contributions to military equipment, such as arms, ammunition and technical aids (Regeringens proposition 2000/01: 119). Military and security cooperation focused mainly on organisational assistance at building a defence force, providing education and counselling, as well as furnishing material support. Additional support aimed at developing border controls, related to maritime boundaries as well as airspace restrictions. These areas were regarded as important for future EU membership, and also included certain measures to limit cross-border crime.

Sweden also actively engaged in providing assistance related to development cooperation, to develop democracy in the Baltic States, at both local and national levels (Regeringens proposition 2000/01: 119). This would operate mainly by supporting the development of democratic institutions. Thematically, Sweden gave support that was primarily aimed at developing the rule of law and promoting gender equality, local cooperation and civil society. Even issues related to the role of media and citizenship in countries with a large Russian minority were included in the cooperation. In addition to supporting the development of democracy and security policy, there was, for example, less extensive support for environmental issues related to the Baltic Sea. In the case of Poland, from 1989 to 1995, Sweden had rendered aid, which was limited, relative to the size of the Polish economy. In this instance, the aid was focused primarily on the environment, where Sweden played a role in the development of a more sustainable society, especially with regard to sewage emissions. Sweden's assistance, as in the case of the Baltic countries, also focused on tax legislation, property issues and the labour market and on providing some democratic support, particularly for civil society. Assistance efforts related to integrating Poland into a new European security community were also available (Roman & Königson 1999).

From 1995 through 2004, Sweden clearly coordinated its policy concerning the Baltic Sea in accordance to the ongoing enlargement process that the EU was pursuing (see Sida 2004: Regeringens proposition 2000/01:119). Swedish policy was thereby directly Europeanised. This was even stated explicitly in Swedish policy strategy. Moreover, unlike that of the EU, Swedish cooperation had a clear and explicit security policy dimension in cooperation. Sweden also increasingly shifted its focus toward the future EU member countries around the Baltic Sea as member negotiations progressed. At the same time, Sweden assumed an active role in helping neighbouring countries become new members of the EU. This trend manifested with particular clarity in 2001, in connection with the Swedish Presidency of the EU (see, for example, *DN*, 2001-06-13).

However, it should here be emphasised that, despite its EU membership, Sweden decided to organise its own unilateral policy towards the Baltic Sea. Sweden was one among all EU member states that needed to approve the entire procedure of considering membership applications. In addition to the fact that the Commission, after careful examination of the candidate countries, had to ensure they met the membership requirements, both the Council of Ministers and European Parliament had to approve the admission of new members. Further, each candidate country and member country had to ratify agreements within their own respective parliaments or equivalent political bodies (European Commission 2018).

After the Eastern Enlargement: Sweden, the 2004 Eastern Partnership and Beyond

When Poland and the Baltic States became EU members, Sweden's attitude toward these countries changed, to acknowledge their equal status as members of the EU. Sweden's independent policy regarding the Baltic Sea also disappeared. The EU also jointly established its own eastward neighbourhood policy, with regard to the older post-Soviet states in Moldova, the Ukraine, Georgia, Belarus, Armenia and Azerbaijan. Sweden's previous eastward policy was then, in principle, replaced with the new neighbourhood policy adopted by the EU. For Sweden's part, this reflected a direct Europeanisation of the entire policy previously adopted toward different countries around the Baltic Sea and Eastern Europe.

The background of the neighbourhood policy was a December 2002 meeting of the European Council in Copenhagen marking the EU's official opening of a debate on future enlargements integrating post-communist countries. Offered as an alternative solution to future enlargements in an already-enlarged EU, the Neighbourhood Policy was proposed as a way of averting divisions between the EU and its non-members (European Union 2015b). It was also suggested as a way of encouraging cooperation with countries to the south and southeast of the EU border, in the Mediterranean region. For this reason and for the first time, in 2002, the EU launched the idea of 'widening Europe,' beyond the future member countries of Eastern and Central Europe (Emerson 2003; ab. Commission of the European Communities 2003). That same year, the idea of expanding Europe was emphasised further, by the president of the European Commission, Romano Prodi (Prodi, 2002). Prodi stated how supporting states with geographical proximity to the Union would also protect EU member states. By spreading democracy through the use of free and fair elections, the rule of law, human rights, reduced corruption and support for civil society, the EU neighbourhood would become more democratic and less authoritarian, thereby amplifying European security. The ENP was thereby established to avoid generating new division lines between the EU and its neighbours (Emerson 2003; Landaburu 2006). Sweden's own foreign policy toward the Baltic countries, in the 1990s, had been guided by the same vision.

The ENP procedure was rooted in the method relied on during the EU enlargement strategy integrating Eastern and Central Europe, namely, conditional cooperation (see Schmitter 2001). The EU imposes certain requirements, related to democracy and market economy, in exchange for cooperation or different trade agreements. Although the neighbourhood policy, in principle, has similarities to the enlargement policy, the ENP does not offer membership. Instead, countries offered the chance of association agreements with the EU are selected with the aim of deepening general political cooperation and a comprehensive trade agreement rather than membership. In 2014, the EU formalised relations with its first neighbours, signing association agreements with Moldova, Georgia and the Ukraine. Approved by the European Council and European Parliament, these agreements came into force when the legislative bodies of all member states and partner countries ratified their respective bilateral agreements. Both substantively and organisationally, this is an EU-level issue, as opposed to an issue that should be decided on at the national level.

The neighbourhood policy revolves around bilateral action plans, between the EU and a given partner country (European Union 2018b). Each respective action plan identifies short- and medium-term reforms deemed necessary for each state. The action plans consist of political and economic reforms, recommended on the basis of developments in the so-called country reports, which summarise the political, economic, institutional and social issues that should be addressed by the EU and the partner state. Action plans are developed by the Commission and supported by the European Council and the individual state. An action plan includes the reforms to be taken and made individually, for each partner state, although some areas are always considered, like political and socioeconomic reforms, security and trade policy cooperation, and sectoral issues related to energy, transport, education, health, etc. However, out of the six partner-states, only one of the former Soviet republics, Belarus, has not yet concluded any bilateral action plans with the EU. On the other hand, the EU has written special memoranda applicable to domestic development in Belarus. The EU monitors action plans, which articulate reforms intended for implementation within three to five years, via the European External Action Service and the Commission, generate annual follow-up reports. Since the period from 2010 to 2011, the reforms undertaken in individual states have been assessed according to the 'more to more' principle (European Union 2018). Generally, this refers to the idea that the more interest that a single state shows in implementing reforms, the stronger will be the partnerships to the EU. Since 2011, democracy development also became a formal requirement for qualification to the entire partnership (European Commission 2011).

While the ENP is primarily a bilateral agreement, between the EU and individual partner countries, regional and multilateral partnerships also exist. For example, there is an Eastern Partnership, comprising Armenia, Azerbaijan, Belarus, Georgia, Moldova, and the Ukraine (European Union 2018a). Belarus only participates in a few such multilateral programs with the EU (Council of the European Union 2012). Launched in 2009, the Eastern Partnership was devised as a mode of developing even closer collective ties to the EU's eastern neighbours. In particular, it emphasises the importance of regional democratic reforms, the rule of law, human rights, market economy and security. Given the enormity of Russia and the legacy of the Soviet Union, the EU initially sought to establish its own cooperation strategy for cooperating with Russia, aimed at engendering closer links between Russia and the EU, but as with Sweden's various efforts at cooperation with Russia, the EU has abandoned this optimistic goal, as the authoritarian rule of Russia's political regime has consolidated since the turn of the 21st century. Russia's military intervention in Georgia (2008) and also its later intrusion into the Ukraine (2014), which prompted the EU to issue economic sanctions, generated more friction and resulted in even worse diplomatic relations between the EU and Russia (European Union 2018a). Despite the objectives driving it, the Eastern Partnership appears to be affected by the geopolitical tension between the EU and Russia, but the European Commission has not abandoned its targets for the partnership; the 2020 Partnership agenda includes targets related to economic development, institutional democratic reforms, corruption, trade and climate change (European Commission 2017). However, in practice, due to the geo-political setting and EU's internal agenda, with Brexit and other emerging issues to handle such as refugees- and migration policies, the ENP seems to be a low priority area, at least in practice.

Sweden was an active advocate, in the early 2000s, for the establishment of the neighbourhood policy. At the same time, the Swedish government and parliament regarded the outcome, in part, as a disappointment, given its inclusion of eastern and southern perspectives that, to some extent, stripped the meaning of the original conception of a 'wider Europe' created to avoid dividing lines between Europe and formerly Soviet countries (Utrikesutskottets betänkande 2004/05: UU10). Sweden regarded the differences between the EU and the countries to its east and south, around the Mediterranean, as simply too big, with regard to issues of democracy and human rights. Therefore, Sweden and Poland, during the Polish and then Swedish Presidency of the European Council in 2008, jointly launched the Eastern Partnership, to impose a clearer focus on those countries between the EU and Russia, and the goals of strengthening democracy, the market economy and security in the neighbourhood (Regeringskansliets faktapromemoria 2008/09).

In recent years, the whole neighbourhood policy has been discussed, in relation to both the Eastern and Southern Partnerships. In November 2015, the European Commission issued a report, paving the way for a modified neighbourhood policy (European Commission2018b). Broadly speaking, this may mean that the EU must account for the fact that the different partner countries are characterized by significantly different conditions and acknowledge the disparities between nations to prompt proposals that vary, in terms of requirements and content. At the same time, partner countries have very different ambitions with the partnership. For example, Georgia wants to become a member of the EU and currently has association agreements with the EU, while Belarus does not aspire to become a EU member state nor to establish bilateral cooperation with the EU. Further, the report asserts that the EU should, in several cases, articulate fewer priorities. As it currently stands, cooperation is covered, at least partly, by all policy areas, and partly by the overall objectives of democracy, human rights, market economy and a functional state. At the same time, the EU must impose greater restrictions on partner participation, or risk rendering such partnerships ineffective partnership and producing a bad outcome for the ENP. In addition, as was mentioned, above, the entire somewhat old but new geopolitical setting with Russia affects the entire ENP as well.

To conclude, it bears emphasising that (see, for example, Government Bill 2013/14: 249) Sweden's formal influence resembles that of other member states. This is to say strategies are being pursued by the European Council and the Council, together with the European Parliament, in terms of approving the agreements. Moreover, each member state and respective association country must approve the agreement. For Sweden, this means that agreements must be ratified by the Swedish Parliament (Svenska Riksdagen 2015a-b). However, in practical terms, the Commission operates through, among other modes, the Enlargement Commissioner and the EU External Action Service, which is responsible for the developing policy, as well as doing the daily work and follow-ups on all neighbouring countries.

The Europeanisation of Sweden's Neighbourhood Policy 1995–2015

The EU's neighbourhood policy is currently a part of the EU's Common Foreign and Security Policy (CFSP), wherein the EU *de facto* has a common, comprehensive and relatively long-term policy. Although the Commission is the driving force of cooperation and represents the EU, the member states are involved in the discussion on long-term neighbourhood policy strategies by the European Council and on negotiations related to association agreements or other types of agreements. The European Parliament also has an active role, as the Parliament must be kept informed on a regular basis, and both the Parliament and all the Member States must approve new cooperation agreements, such as the New and Comprehensive Free Trade Area with Georgia, Ukraine and Moldova. Neighbourhood policy and, in particular, the neighbourhood policy includes all possible dimensions of EU foreign and security policy, such as increasing security through diplomacy and international cooperation, developing democracy, the rule of law and human rights, and establishing trade agreements with the outside world. It also covers a multitude of other policy areas, such as agricultural and rural policy, climate issues, education and culture, entrepreneurship, relations with Russia, legal issues, marine biology and fisheries, as well as research and innovation (European Union 2018c).

Based on the Swedish perspective, and in light of historical Swedish policy toward the Baltic and Eastern European countries before Sweden's EU membership in 1995, this development means that the entire policy has evolved contentiously and organisationally, gradually transmitted from the Swedish national level into its own parallel policy in relation to the EU in the late 1990s, and finally shifted completely to the EU level. EU foreign relations can be identified with different types of policy models. The more traditional foreign policy, with different positions in the world matters such as the Iraq war (2003–), Afghanistan (2001–) or similar issues related to war and peace, intergovernmental cooperation. There is a consensus among the Council of Minsters, to enable conclusive decisions, but once such a decision is reached, the EU can speak to the world with one voice. The European Parliament can only comment on various issues but lacks a decisive role in the decision itself. This means that each member state is sovereign in this matter and has power, at the national level, to control its foreign and security policy. However, it may be so, in practice, that the EU can have a common policy if member states are agreed. However, in formal terms, it is not a question of sharing common powers between the EU and its member states. That being said, in the area of development aid and development cooperation, the EU has, through its decisions in the Council of the European Union and in European Parliament, its own budget policy running parallel to that of the member states, along with a national aid policy established in the national parliament of each member state. At the same time, this does not apply to trade agreements, where the EU currently has exclusive competence and thereby the legal right to sign different types of trade agreements, all of which certainly require approval from the European Union Council, the European Parliament and all member states. It is very clear that the EU Commission functions as a representative for the EU, and is, in principle, speaking with a single voice to the world.

The same exclusive competence attaches to the EU, in relation to the neighbourhood policy, which is governed by various agreements, and has objectives that include, among other things, association and trade agreements, over which the EU has exclusive domain. A member state, like Sweden, can therefore reject an agreement but, in practice, all member states have typically accepted the content of the agreement somewhere along the path to ratifying the agreement in its entirety. Nor can a member state impose a parallel national neighbourhood policy that does not correspond to the content of EU policies. Regarding agenda setting and policy formulation, the Commission is primarily charged with carrying out individual directives concerning today's neighbourhood policy; but where the European Council, through the member states, has decisive influence over the general strategy, such as which countries are to be covered, the appropriate objective (membership, association agreements or other agreement) and the timeframe within which different things should happen the entire neighbourhood policy, drawing up action plans describing what goals should be achieved in different areas, making recommendations, and monitoring the extent to which a country meets the established goals, etc. The Commission therefore seeks to implement and monitor everything, both on an annual basis and over a longer period. There are also financial resources allocated to the EU budget to facilitate its management of all of these things. However, the Council of the European Union, together with the European Parliament, approves new trade agreements under the ENP, and all the involved states must ratify the agreements. Finally, the Commission is also responsible for evaluating the neighbourhood policy and proposing any relevant changes. As such, the neighbourhood policy bears considerable resemblance to the so-called 'Community model', and also, to some extent, the regulatory model (see Chapter 2). This is so in the sense that it involves high levels of centralisation, an EU budget for policy, the member states, via the European Council, set the framework for neighbourhood policy and both the Council of Europe and the European Parliament must approve all new agreements. The Commission has a clear agenda-making role and, further, manages all relations with neighbouring countries and ensures that policies are developed, and that an entire policy is also implemented, evaluated and, if necessary, modified.

Conclusion

This chapter has demonstrated how the Swedish Neighbourhood Policy has gradually changed, both before and after Sweden's 1995 EU membership, partly as a response to the eastern expansion of the EU in the 21st century. Before the accession of the EU and after the end of the Cold War, Sweden began to pursue an active security and development policy, largely towards neighbouring Baltic countries – Estonia, Latvia, Lithuania, Poland and, somewhat, towards Russia. At that time, this was a Swedish policy toward neighbouring countries, aimed both at increasing security around the Baltic Sea, but also at integrating these countries into the Western democratic and market economy system. It was a Swedish policy purely in the substantive sense, which was organised organically by the Swedish government and supported by the Foreign Affairs Council and the parliament. When Sweden subsequently became a member of the EU in 1995 and eastern enlargement began to accelerate, Sweden and the EU introduced a parallel policy toward these countries. This produced a gradual Europeanisation in cases where Sweden could decide on its own policy, while Sweden was one of several EU countries to make a common decision regarding eastern enlargement. It was a mutual Europeanisation. When Estonia, Latvia, Lithuania and Poland also joined the EU in 2004, Swedish policy related to the Baltic region had already begun to phase itself out, as these countries had joined the same community of which Sweden was part.

When the EU, in the early 2000s, established its own neighbourhood policy against older post-Soviet states, to avoid a division in Europe, between the EU and its neighbours, this meant that the ENP, from a Swedish perspective, shifted, both geographically and philosophically, becoming further Europeanised – until it reached the EU-level. Therefore, Sweden actively contributed to the Europeanisation of parts of the policy content, regarding its Eastern politics. This meant that Sweden no longer had its own policy. Today, the EU's neighbourhood policy draws on both the Community model and the regulatory model, involving all actors, but where the Commission drives all policies forward, along with the European Council, where the influence of individual member states can be important, but also where the European Parliament must approve all new agreements. Moreover, all member states must approve all agreements under the ENP. In conclusion, as the EU enlarges the number of member states, the neighbourhood policy may, in future, continue to evolve, both geographically and substantively, although currently (2018), there are no new extensions eastward on the agenda.

References

Commission of the European Communities 2003a. 'Wider Europe: Neighbourhood, a new framework for relations with our eastern and Southern Neighbours'. Communication from the Commission, Brussels, COM 2003: 285.

Retrieved from: http://ec.europa.eu/world/enp/pdf/com03_104_en.pdf

Commission of the European Communities 2003b. 'Paving the Way for New Neighbourhood Instrument'. Communication from the Commission, Brussels, COM 2003: 393. Retrieved from: http://ec.europa.eu/world/enp/pdf/com03_393_en.pdf

Council of the European Union 2003. 'Presidency Conclusion: Copenhagen European Council 12 and 13 December 2002'. Brussels, 29 January 2003. 15917/02. Retrieved from: http://aei.pitt.edu/43349/

Council of the European Union 2012. 'Council conclusions on Belarus'. 3191st Foreign Affairs Council Meeting, Luxemburg, 15 October 2012. Retrieved from: http://eeas.europa.eu/belarus/index_en.htm

DN, 2001-06-23, 'Toppmötet: Persson får kämpa för östutvidgningen'. Hämtad via: http://www.dn.se/arkiv/nyheter/toppmotet-persson-far-kampa-for-ostutvidgningen.

Doeser, F. 2008. *In Search of Security After the Collapse of the Soviet Union: Foreign Policy Change in Denmark, Finland and Sweden, 1988–1993*. Stockholm: Stockholms universitet.

Emerson, M. 2003. 'The Shaping of a Policy Framework for the Wider Europe'. CEPS Policy Brief, No. 27, Brussels: Centre for European Policy Studies.

European Commission 2002. 'The Enlargement Process and the three Accession-instruments: Phare, ISPA, Sapard'. Enlargement Directorate General, Brussels, February 2002.

European Commission 2011. 'A new response to a changing Neighbourhood'. European Commission / High Representative of the European Union for Foreign Affairs and Security Policy, Brussels, COM 2011: 303 final. Retrieved from: http://ec.europa.eu/europeaid/where/neighbourhood/documents/communication_conjointe_mai_2011_en.pdf

— 2017. Eastern Partnership – 20 Deliverables for 2020

— 2018. European Neighbourhood Policy: What is it? Retrieved from: http://ec.europa.eu/enlargement/neighbourhood/overview/index_en.htm

Focusing on key priorities and tangible results. European Commission/High Representative of the European Union for Foreign Affairs and Security Policy, Brussels, 9.6.2017, SWD 2017: 300 final. Retrieved from: https://ec.europa.eu/neighbourhood-enlargement/sites/near/files/eap_20_deliverables_for_2020.pdf

European Union 2018a. External Action: EU Relations with Eastern Partnership.Retrieved from: http://eeas.europa.eu/eastern/index_en.htm

— 2018b. External Action: European Neighbourhood Policy. Retrieved

from: http://eeas.europa.eu/enp/about-us/index_en.htm
— 2018c. External Action: The ENP in various EU policy areas. Retrieved from: http://eeas.europa.eu/enp/eu-policy-areas/index_en.htm
— 2018d. European Neighbourhood Policy and Enlargement; Steps towards joining. Retrieved from: http://ec.europa.eu/enlargement/policy/steps-towards-joining/index_en.htm
Gustavsson, J. 1998. *The Politics of Foreign Policy Change. Explaining the Swedish Reorientation on EC Membership*. Lund: Lund University Press.
Hallenberg, J. 2002. *The demise of the Soviet union: analysing the collapse of a state* Aldershot: Ashgate.
Landaburu, E. 2006. 'From Neighbourhood to Integration Policy: Are there concrete alternatives to enlargement?' CEPS Policy Brief, 95, 1 March 2006.
Prodi, R. 2002. 'A Wider Europe – a proximity policy as the key to stability'. Key-note speech at the 6th ECSA-World Conference Peace, Security and Stability – International Dialogue and the Role of the EU, in Brussels, December 5–6 2002. Retrieved from: http://europa.eu/rapid/press-release_SPEECH-02-619_en.htm
Regeringens proposition 1991/92:142. Om godkännande av frihandelsavtal mellan Sverige och Lettland, m.m.
— 1992/93:100. Med förslag till statsbudget för budgetåret 1993/94: Bistånd till Östeuropa.
— 1992/93:146. Om godkännande av avtal mellan EFTA-stater och Polen, m.m.
— 1994/95:160. Sveriges samarbete med Central- och Östeuropa.
— 1997/98:70. Att utveckla ett grannlandssamarbete Sveriges utvecklingssamarbete med Central- och Östeuropa år 1999–2001.
— 2000/01:119. Europa i omvandling – Sveriges utvecklingssamarbete med Central- och Östeuropa.
— 2013/14:249. Associeringsavtal mellan Europeiska unionen, Europeiska atomenergigemenskapen och deras medlemsstater, å ena sidan, och Ukraina, å andra sidan.
Regeringskansliets faktapromemoria 2008/09: FPM85. Östliga partnerskapet – Utrikesdepartementet.
Róman L. & L. Königson 1999. *Resultatanalys – samarbetet med Polen*. Stockholm: Sida.
Schmitter, P.C. 2001. 'The Influence of International Context upon the Choice of national Institutions and policies in Neo-Democracies'. In: L. Whitehead (ed.) *The International Dimensions of democratization – Europe and the Americas*. Oxford: Oxford University Press.
Sida 2009. Det svenska stödet till reformprocessen i Ryssland 1991–2008. Stockholm: Sida.
— 2004. Sveriges stöd till de baltiska ländernas omvandling. Stockholm: Sida, mars 2004.
Svenska riksdagen 2015a. Så arbetar EU-nämnden. Retrieved from: https://www.riksdagen.se/sv/Sa-funkar-riksdagen/Sa-arbetar-EU-namnden/
— 2015b. Utrikespolitiken. Retrieved from: https://www.riksdagen.se/sv/Sa-funkar-riksdagen/Riksdagens-uppgifter/Utrikespolitiken/
Utrikesutskottets betänkande 2004/05: UU10. Verksamheten i Europeiska unionen 2004.

13. Aid Policy and Development Cooperation

Europeanisation, Norms, Structures and Instruments

Anne Haglund Morrissey[1] *& Daniel Silander*

Given the last years of refugee crisis in Europe, the large proportion of the global population living in poverty, widespread child labour and a wide income gap in developing countries, European Union (EU) and individual member-states' aid policy and development cooperation are very important (Sida 2015). Over the last years, the EU has faced waves of refugee inflows leading to EU debates over the limitations of the European open border approach, the increased security surveillance, societal strains and a rising populist movement, including nationalism, xenophobia and anti-immigrant political parties (Juncker 2018, 2017). Jean Claude Juncker, the former President of the European Commission, called in his State of the Union 2018 for common and intensified actions on migration. EU external borders had to be protected, support to Greece, Italy, Bulgaria, Spain had to persist and the on-going successful activities in the Mediterranean Sea would continue. Juncker also called upon internal burden-sharing of migration flows and how neighbouring countries, on the other side of the Mediterranean Sea, had to improve the protection and promotion of human rights standards on migration (Juncker 2018, 2017).

In 2014, at an EU-Africa Summit in Brussels, EU and African states agreed on the roadmap for 2014–2017 with five identified priorities and areas for collaboration in Peace and Security, Democracy, Good

1 The content of this chapter does not reflect the official opinion of the European Commission. Responsibility for the information and views expressed therein lies entirely with the author.

Governance and Human Rights, Human development, Sustainable and inclusive development and growth and continental integration and Global and emerging issues (EU-Africa Summit 2014). This was followed up on May 4, 2017, with a Joint Communication for a renewed impetus of the Africa-EU Partnership by the High Representative Federica Mogherini and the Commission. The Communication called for a stronger and intensified partnership for prosperity and stability in the two continents and set out key-objectives in increased cooperation in the international arena, based on common values and interests, security, on land and on sea, and sustainable and inclusive economic development in Africa (European Commission 2017).

The EU with its member-states is the largest development aid donor in the world. Sweden is considered as one of the leading EU countries in the aid sector. With a long experience of aid and an annual budget of 3 billion SEK donated to the EU, Sweden has since its membership in 1995 participated fully in the shaping and implementation of an EU development aid policy (Sida – Svenskt bidrag till EU:s utvecklingssamarbete 2018). This chapter focuses on Swedish aid policy and development cooperation in relation to its EU membership.[2] The aim of this chapter is to analyse how almost a quarter of a century of Swedish EU membership has influenced the content and direction of Swedish aid policy. The analysis focuses on the EU, Europeanisation (see Chapter 2) and the impact on Swedish aid policy and development cooperation over time. Europeanisation can be seen as both a top-down and bottom-up phenomenon, but also as a horizontal one. First, Europeanisation, as a 'top-down' phenomenon ('downloading'), refers to when elements of EU policy are embraced and implemented by the member-states, and where the EU influences the changes in national policy. Second, Europeanisation,

2 It should however be emphasised that Europeanisation is only one of a number of processes that can influence the development of an area of policy. The Bretton Woods Institutions – the International Monetary Fund (IMF) and World Bank together with the International Development Association, and the United Nations (UN), Organisation for Economic Cooperation and Development (OECD) and World Trade Organisation (WTO) – have come to play a large part in global development. A number of international declarations, above all those of the UN and OECD, have also had a far-reaching effect on the way donor countries including members of the EU cooperate with other countries and pursue their policies.

as a bottom-up phenomenon ('uploading'), refers to when elements of national policy are embraced and implemented by the EU. Finally, the influence of certain member-states with a shared approach, to others, so-called 'horizontal Europeanisation' ('cross-loading'), is a third dimension (*cf.* Zemanova 2012, Elgström & Delputte 2016:29, see also Lightfoot 2008, 2010).

The potential effect of Europeanisation, will be explored regarding:

(1) Norms and values (motives, objectives and the prioritisation of interim targets);
(2) Structure (aid volume; thematic and geographic focus); and
(3) Instruments and channelling (including multilateral and bilateral aid).

This chapter is divided into three parts. It begins by discussing Sweden's aid policy, followed by the policy and activities at EU level. It ends with an analysis of how we can characterise the Europeanisation of Swedish aid policy.

Swedish Aid Policy: Norms and Values

Swedish aid policy and the motives behind it have remained relatively unchanged over time. When the United Nations (UN) was created, Sweden began supporting the development of UN aid programmes in the form of annual grants. It began organising aid in 1952 when the partly state-owned Central Committee for Swedish Technical Aid to Less Developed Areas was set up. This Committee was replaced in 1962 by the Board for International Aid, which in 1965 gave birth to the Committee for International Development (Sida). In 1995, an umbrella authority for Swedish aid – the Committee for International Development Cooperation (Sida) – was created as a merger between Sida, the Swedish Agency for International Technical and Economic Cooperation (BITS), the Swedish International Enterprise Development Corporation (SwedeCorp), the Swedish Agency for Research Cooperation with Developing Countries (SAREC) and Sandö U-centrum.

The first government bill on aid in 1962 made clear that solidarity was the fundamental reason for Swedish aid, whereby altruism, a moral outlook and humanitarian considerations rather than material interests were key (Odén & Wohlgemuth 2006: 6–7, Prop. 2002/3: 122). The overall goal since then has been to reduce global poverty, even though the formulation of this goal has changed somewhat over time. The Bill also set out three interim targets: i) to help ensure an increase in production; ii) to help take social development in a direction that is more politically democratic and iii) to promote social equality (Prop. 1962:100). In 1968, these targets were supplemented by a fourth one: to help ensure greater political and economic independence (Prop. 1968:101). The Bill also set a volume target for Swedish aid; namely, one per cent of its gross domestic product (GDP) (Vikinge 1997: 31–35, Hveem & McNeill 1994: 39–40). In the mid-1980s, Swedish aid also came to focus on environmental issues, leading to a fifth target: to make efficient use of natural resources and protect the environment (Prop. 1987/88:100) and in the mid-1990s, a sixth target was identified in the equality between men and women (Prop. 1995/96:153).

In 2002, the 'Joint Responsibility' Bill stressed as main objective of aid policy to ensure 'fair and sustainable global development' and improve the conditions for those living in poverty. The Swedish Policy for Global Development (PGU), which is based on this Bill, has had the overall objective of helping to bring about fair and sustainable global development. Instead of the previous six targets, one single overall target was singled out. However, most of the previous targets remained in the form of key elements. In addition, two perspectives were formulated that aimed to embody the spirit of this policy: a rights perspective and the perspective of the poor on development. The overall target was further supported by eight key elements: Respect for human rights; Democracy and good governance; Equality; the Sustainable use of natural resources and protection of the environment; Economic growth; Social development and security; Conflict management and security, and the Sharing of global commodities (Prop. 2002/03-122: 22, Skr. 2007/08:89, Odén & Wohlgemuth 2006: 9).

The 'Joint Responsibility' Bill also stated that Sweden ought to pursue a coherent policy for global development and that such coherence between the different policy areas had to be stronger (Prop. 2002/3,122). A lack of coherence between the different policy areas would run the risk that measures taken in one policy area could counter efforts to promote development and reduce poverty in another area (Skr. 2007/08:89, Odén & Wohlgemuth 2006: 21–22). In 2008, the focus of the coherence policy addressed six global challenges: Oppression, Financial exclusion, Climate change and environmental impact, Migration flows, Infectious diseases and other health hazards, and Conflict and fragile situations (Skr. 2007/08:89, Skr. 2013/14:154). Sweden was the first country to have formally introduced a coherence policy for development (see Odén 2011: 8, 30, 46). Furthermore, Sweden has been at the forefront in terms of the organisation and follow-up of such a coherent policy. In 2013, Sweden was ranked second in the international 'coherence index', which carries out annual assessments of the OECD countries, and has since then been ranked among the top countries (Skr. 2013/14:154, Skr. 2007/08:89, Skr. 2011/12:167, Skr. 2013/14:154, Regeringskansliet 2010: 18).

Besides the principle of coherence, the principles of ownership, efficiency and transparency have become important. Ever since 1962, one cornerstone has been the ownership of the recipient country. Chief responsibility for combating poverty and promoting development rests with the government of the developing country, whereby the recipient country 'owns' its project, programme or economic/political reform, and aid must be adapted to the procedures, systems and regulations in force in the country (Skr. 2007/08:89). This adaptation to the system applied in the cooperation country was adopted by the PGU three years before the OECD Paris Declaration, and demonstrates that Sweden was ahead of the international trend in these issues (Odén & Wohlgemuth 2006: 14–15, 22, DAC Development Cooperation Report 2015).

The PGU also seeks to streamline the work of development cooperation while focusing on achieving measurable results through better coordination, simpler procedures and more painstaking follow-up (Skr. 2007/08:89, DAC Development Cooperation Report 2015). Sweden has been the first country to adopt a Strategy for Multilateral Development Cooperation to take coherent, strategic and effective action (Regeringskansliet 2007: 9–11). There has also been an emphasis on transparency to give the public greater insight into the aid results. In this area too – results-based aid administration – Sweden can be seen as a pioneering country. There is also the desire to see a more general untying of aid. This can be linked to developments in the OECD Development Assistance Committee (DAC), which as of 2002 has been recommending the general untying of aid (Skr. 2002/03:122, 19). Here we can clearly see the way Swedish policy has been influenced by international trends in multilateral organisations.

There has been an overview of the direction of aid policy in order to develop a new policy framework, which resulted in a Government Communication to the Riksdag in the summer of 2016. The objective of aid and development remained the same, but focus would also be on those groups that come under the poverty line in middle-income countries (Interview 2).

In December 2016, Sweden developed a new Policy Framework for development and humanitarian aid aiming at promoting the work on poverty reduction globally based on socioeconomic, environmentally sustainable and equal development activities. It was defined that development cooperation would focus on the conflict, gender equality and environment and climate perspectives. The new Policy also identified thematic directions of development cooperation in Human rights, democracy and the principles of the rule of law; Global gender equality; Environmentally and climate-related sustainable; Development and sustainable use of natural resources; Peaceful and inclusive societies; Inclusive economic development; Migration and development; Equal health and Education and research. In addition, the Policy Framework also identified five priorities on humanitarian assistance in Greater respect for humanitarian principles and international humanitarian law (IHL); A stronger, more efficient and coordinated humanitarian system; Greater cooperation with civil society; Greater cooperation and increased synergies between humanitarian initiatives and long-term development cooperation to reduce the risk of recurring humanitarian crises; and New and innovative forms of financing (Government Communication 2016). This policy was a replacement of the former platform for aid and development (Sida September 18, 2018). In 2016, Sweden's humanitarian aid summed up to about 6.5 billion SEK making Sweden the seventh largest humanitarian donor in the world after USA, Germany, Great Britain, Japan, Norway and United Arab Emirates (Sida How we work 2018).

Swedish Aid Policy: Structure

In 1970, a UN goal was introduced whereby all industrialised countries would contribute a minimum of 0.7 per cent of their GDP to development aid. Since the mid-1970s, Sweden, along with Norway, Denmark and the Netherlands, has been among those OECD countries with the greatest aid volume in relation to gross domestic product (GDP). The one per cent goal of Swedish aid was included in Bill 1968:101 with the intention that the aid budget would gradually increase so that the 1974/75 fiscal year would correspond to one per cent of estimated GDP. This goal was later changed to constitute one per cent of GDI, as this was what the international goal of 0.7 per cent related to (see Odén & Wohlgemuth 2006: 9–10). Sweden achieved the 0.7 per cent goal in 1975 and has since then never fallen below this level. Most of the world's richer countries still lie far below the UN goal of contributing 0.7 per cent of GDI in aid. In 2017, by contributing 1.1 per cent of its GDI in aid, Sweden gives more in relative terms than any other country in the world (Regeringskansliet 2015: 4, Sida September 18 2018).

When Sida was established in 1965, the number of cooperation countries was seven, but this figure has increased over time. Today, Sida has bilateral agreements with 35 recipient countries (Sida Where we work 2018), roughly half of which lie in Sub-Saharan Africa (SSA). Sweden has, however, some form of development cooperation with over 120 countries – cooperation which has to some extent been influenced by the EU membership (Odén & Wohlgemuth 2006: 11–13).

Among Sida's activities (see Sida Reporting & Results 2018, Sida 2017), the following areas are prioritised:

Table 13.1: Sida's activities 2017

Humanitarian	Provide assistance to refugees from armed conflicts, environment and climate-related crises, natural disasters and epidemics.
Democracy and human rights	Support for democratic participation, civil society and rights and liberties.
Health	Reduction of maternal and child mortality, Sexual and reproductive health and rights (SRHR) and Health systems strengthening.
Water and sanitation	Promotes efficient, fair and sustainable water use and management and improved access to safe drinking water, basic sanitation and hygiene facilities.
Education	Promote equitable and inclusive education of good quality and support national education systems throughout life.
Trade	Promote trade agenda, including trade-related infrastructure, building productive capacity (private sector, financial sector, agriculture) and trade policy and regulations.
Peace and security	Support to transparent, inclusive and responsive institutions; strengthened resilience against conflict-related crises and capacity for peaceful conflict management; dialogue and mediation processes; participation of youth, women and girls in conflict prevention and peace and state-building processes and protection of children in armed conflict.
Environment and Climate Change	Support greater resilience to environmental and climate change; improved institutional capacity for environmental management; sustainable management and use of biodiversity and ecosystem services; sustainable cities; food security and sustainable agriculture; water and sanitation and improved access to sustainable energy.
Food Security and Agriculture	Promote eradication of hunger and poverty through the support to technological development and agricultural extension services, improved policy administration and research and support to land policy reforms and land administration, efforts for mitigation and adaptation to climate change.
Employment	Promote productive jobs, the rights, dignity and safe working conditions of the employed and improved living conditions for the poor.
Gender Equality	Promote equal rights for women and men, girls and boys, to life prospects and opportunities and power to shape their own lives and engage and contribute to their society.

Based on OECD-DAC sector codes, the statistics found on amount spent on different thematic areas where Sida is highly active, show the following (in Million SEK):Education and Research 1591, Health

Equality 2076; Peaceful and Inclusive Societies 991, Human Rights, Democracy and the Rule of Law 5843, Humanitarian Aid 4026, Economic Development 3207, and other 3779 (Sida 2017: 43).

Swedish Aid Policy: Instruments and Channelling

In general, there are two kinds of aid: i) *humanitarian aid* and ii) *long-term development cooperation*. Humanitarian aid means emergency assistance in saving lives, alleviating suffering and upholding human dignity in assisting those in need. Development cooperation activities are run in two ways: bilaterally (from state to state) and multilaterally (participation in multilateral cooperation via the UN Development Programme and its bodies, the World Health Organisation and the OECD, and via EU Development Cooperation). The aid is channelled via public administrations, voluntary organisations or multilateral organisations. (Odén & Wohlgemuth 2006: 13–14, DAC Development Cooperation Report 2015).

In 2017, Swedish Development aid was approximately SEK 47 billion of the Gross National Income (GNI). The distribution of Swedish development assistance in 2017 (MSEK) were to Sida 22,545, the Foreign Ministry 16,300, asylum seekers in Sweden 7,078 and other 1,183. Some of the most targeted countries in terms of MSEK were Tanzania, Afghanistan, Somalia, Ethiopia, Palestine, DR Congo, and Zambia. The support to multilateral organisations (in MSEK) was in 2017 distributed in the following way: UN 5,734, EU 3,448, World Bank 2,922, Regional Development Banks 1080 and other multinational organisations 1,759 (Sida – Some results of Swedish development cooperation 2017).

The multilateral aid is managed by the Department for International Development Cooperation under the Minister for Development Cooperation at the Ministry for Foreign Affairs, while the bilateral aid is primarily organised through Sida (SOU 2001: 96, Vikinge 1997: 39). Besides being distributed directly to the cooperation partners in these countries, bilateral aid can also be channelled through Swedish framework organisations (grass-roots movements and private organisations), agencies and companies. A few countries receive budget support (support that goes directly towards the cooperation country's national budget). The aid is based on long-term strategies and cooperation agreements. The bilateral aid can sometimes be managed by multilateral organisations where this is judged to be most effective (*e.g.* disaster aid to UN bodies) – so-called 'multi-bi' support (Regeringen 2007:19, 30, DAC Development Cooperation Report 2015). In 2017, the total funding for aid operations were 34,150 million SEK. Out of this total sum, about 21,448 million SEK was channelled through Sida's identified strategic activities, and about 12,692 SEK was channelled through Sida to multilateral organisations. In addition, Sida had earmarked 68 million SEK for specific operations in the Baltic Sea region (see Sida 2017).

EU Aid Policy: Norms and Values

The EU and its member-states are the world's biggest donors in terms of public/state-funded development aid. In 2014, they jointly contributed with EUR 58.2 billion (0.42 per cent of the EU's GDI), which represented 52% of all state-funded development aid in the world (European Commission 2015, ip/15/4747). Today, the member-states together with the Commission account for more than half of all global aid. In 2014–2020, the EU will provide about EUR 80 billion to 150 countries around the world to address poverty, democracy, human rights, socioeconomic and sustainable development (Sida September 26, 2018).

Although the EU's joint aid policy had no legal basis until the Maastricht Treaty (TEU), development cooperation has been a part of the integration process right from the start and has resulted in the Europeanisation of member-state policies. Already the Schuman Declaration (1950), stated the intention that the Coal and Steel Community would contribute to the development in Africa, but it was the Treaty of Rome (1957) that established the European Development Fund (EDF) to supplement the member-states' aid programmes for supporting colonies and extra-European territories. The aid was based on the provisions for 'Dependent territories and countries', which were associated to the Community and the common trade policy. The aim was to promote socio-economic development, guarantee trade advantages and provide support for investment in their development (White 2001: 50). From the start, these provisions applied to the (former) colonies held by Belgium, France and the Netherlands, but were extended to include the Anglophone developing countries in the Pacific region and the Caribbean once the United Kingdom joined the EC. These countries enjoyed good relations with their (former) colonies and wished to maintain their economic and political ties with them within the framework of the EC, which can be seen as a determining factor in the shaping of the developing aid policy at EC level. In the early stages, France was successful in its attempts to leave its mark on this policy ('bottom-up' Europeanisation).

The Maastricht Treaty of 1993 (TEU) ushered in development cooperation with all the developing countries. That said, 'special relations' were retained with the dependent territories and developing countries geographically situated in Sub-Saharan Africa, the Caribbean region and the Pacific region (the so-called ACP countries) – first through the Yaoundé Convention, and then the Lomé Convention. Aid was also provided for the transition processes in Eastern Europe. Development aid policy came under the first supranational pillar with a 'shared competence' between the EU and its member-states, and the Commission was given a stronger coordinating role. The targets were to promote sustainable economic and social development; support the gradual integration of the developing countries into the global economy; support a campaign against poverty; help foster and consolidate democracy, the principle of law and order and respect for human rights within the framework of political stability; and to achieve coherence by meeting the international targets (such as those set by the UN). A number of principles were also established:

- The measures taken by the EU and its member-states shall *complement* and reinforce each other.
- The member-states' and Community's aid programmes shall be *coordinated* (including in international organisations and at conferences).
- The EU shall take into account the targets for aid policy in other areas of policy that could affect the developing countries – *coherence*.
- The least developed countries (LCDS) are given priority – *geographic weighting*.

- *Political terms and conditions* – aid is provided in return for the recipient countries developing democratic structures.
- The member-states have an obligation where necessary to contribute to the *implementation* of the Community's development aid programme.

Over time, the principles of the so-called '3 C's' – coordination, complementarity, coherence – have formed a key part of the EU development aid architecture and have, at least in theory, made room for a 'top-down' dimension of Europeanisation, where the 'bottom-up' dimension characterised the Europeanisation process in development aid before TEU. However, this opportunity for top-down Europeanisation was never explored in the 1990s as member-states were continuing with their attempts to 'upload' their preferences at Community level and influence the policy under development ('bottom-up'). That said, the 'horizontal' dimension was reinforced when Sweden and Finland became EU members in 1995, as consultancy and consultation prior to Council meetings now were being initiated within a group of aid-donor and like-minded countries: Sweden, Denmark, Finland and the Netherlands (*cf.* Zemanova 2012:36). The principles of the 3 C's were also included in the Cotonou Agreement (2000), which was adopted when the last Lomé Convention expired. The Cotonou Agreement is a comprehensive partnership agreement in the area of trade and aid and covers a total of 77 ACP countries, and it is valid until 2020.

In the new millennium, the 'top-down' perspective in the Europeanisation process was reinforced when aid policy underwent further development as a result of ever more EU initiatives (especially those of the Commission) (Zemanova 2012:37). In 2000, the Council adopted the 'Statement on Development Policy', where poverty reduction was identified as the main objective and the focus was on the LCDs; the same objective as that being pursued by Swedish aid policy since the 1960s (Dearden 2008:116). The Treaty of Nice (2003) took a new direction in development policy, whereby the overall objective was to reduce and in the long term eradicate global poverty and bring about sustainable development. The Lisbon Treaty (2009) gave it a more robust legal basis, and development cooperation now became a policy area of its own right (European Commission 2014: 3). This also meant a transfer of certain competencies from the Commission to the European External Action Service (EEAS), giving the policy more of an intergovernmental dimension.

Policy coherence was introduced into EU law in 1993 (TEU), reinforced by the *European Consensus on Development* (2005) and clearly set out in the Lisbon Treaty. This has given the EU the role of advocate in this area (Dearden 2008:122). Coherence is seen as a guiding concept where all policy areas that might have an impact on the developing countries are to take into account the development cooperation targets. A coherent aid policy (*Policy Coherence for Development* – PCD) is once again emphasised in the *Agenda for Change* strategy (2012), where the target is to set up an overall work programme embracing all areas of development cooperation, including the policies of the member-states (European Commission 2014:4–5). *Agenda for Change* can also be seen from the bearing Sweden has had in terms of its focus on soft values, and this agenda was pursued together with other like-minded countries (Interview 1, Interview 2). Progress in terms of PCD is in line with 12 policy areas (trade, environment, climate change, security, agriculture, fisheries, the social dimension of globalization, employment, migration, research and innovation, the information society, transport and energy).that come under five strategic challenges and guiding principles regarding PCD: 1) Trade and finance, 2) Managing climate change, 3) Ensuring global food security, 4) Linking migration to development, and 5) Improving the synergy and relationship between security and development in order to promote global peace (Council of the European Union 2005, 9266/05, Council of the European Union 2013). The Commission monitors progress in PCD both at EU level and in the member-states by regular reports, where Sweden is often seen as a pioneering country (European Commission 2015, SWD (2015) 159 final).

Through the *European Consensus on Development* the EU and its member-states commit to certain norms in all areas of development, including greater aid efficiency and improved coordination between the aid donors in the field (European Parliament, Council and Commission (2006/C 46/01). This is where Sweden, in collaboration with other like-minded countries (Denmark, Finland, the UK, the Netherlands and Ireland) played a substantial role in setting the agenda (*cf.* Riksdagen 2006/07:rfr7, Prop. 2002/3:122). In order to streamline the aid, emphasis is placed on the importance of regular evaluations with the use of progress indicators, and on aid being made results-oriented and more predictable. Aid efficiency was even further brought into focus during the Swedish Presidency of the Council in 2009, with a clearer allocation of responsibility, and a concentration on three prioritised sectors per country. It is also based on the Code of Conduct on Complementarity and Division of Labour (2007) where the member-states are encouraged to change their respective aid policies and focus on aid in geographic terms and to cooperate at local level by their own and through EU delegations/offices in the developing countries (European Commission 2007). This can be seen as 'top-down' pressure to adapt (Dearden 2008: 120–122). A greater division of tasks (between sectors and countries) and coordination between the EU and its members' delegations/offices in the recipient countries by way of joint actions (in particular joint programming) is intended to improve aid efficiency (European Commission 2011: 10–11). In this process, the Commission, EEAS and member-states identify a joint strategy for assisting different recipient countries and compiling a joint country strategy document that is to replace bilateral country strategies. However, despite all the EU countries supporting joint programming, it can take time for authorities at national level to hand over prioritised sectors and countries that are in their national interest to others. There are also signs that Europeanisation is taking place faster in the EU-15 countries than in the EU-13, meaning that the first group is introducing changes faster than the second (Zemanova 2012: 41–43).

EU Development Aid Policy: Structure

The structure of EU development aid is divided into two levels: national and supranational. The Commission, which is a key actor through its Directorate-General for International Cooperation and Development (DG DEVCO), formulates and implements policy, and the European External Action Service (EEAS), is since 2010 focusing on the strategic and overall design of European aid policy. Together, they manage, plan and implement the EU development aid policy. The Commission's humanitarian aid department (ECHO) manages humanitarian aid, and in addition the EU has 160 delegations and offices throughout the world which run the aid programmes (Haglund 2001: 162, European Commission 2014: 8).The *European Consensus for Development* was an agreement reached between the EU countries on the aid volume; namely, to reach by 2015 the UN goal of 0.7 per cent of GNI by focusing on LCDs, whereby half would go to Africa (in particular failing states) (European Parliament, Council and Commission (2006/C 46/01)). The leading aid donors in the EU (Sweden, Denmark, the Netherlands and Luxembourg) had already reached and exceeded the UN goal, thus meaning no 'top-down' Europeanisation in their case. However, other countries in the group of like-minded countries increased their amount of aid gradually and either reached (in the case of the UK) or came close to the volume target set (here we can see 'top-down' Europeanisation). The volume target for countries that joined the EU after 2004 was set at 0.33 per cent, and here too we see a 'top-down' Europeanisation (Zemanova 2012: 37–38). What has been shown, however, is that many of the EU member states are not reaching these aid volume targets, which is in part the result of the years of the global financial crisis.

The EU operates in 140 countries, and one of its tasks is to coordinate the measures of different donors. Its development funding applies to either a geographic or a thematic area. There are three geographic financing instruments for the period 2014–2020: the EDF, the Development Cooperation Instrument, and the European Neighbourhood Instrument. The EU's aid activities are financed either directly or indirectly by the member-states. Most of it goes directly to the EDF, and a small part of it indirectly by way of the EU membership fee, as a share of the EU budget is spent on development aid. There are also three thematic instruments: The Instrument for Democracy and Human Rights, the Instrument for Stability and Peace, and the Instrument for Nuclear Safety Cooperation. The EU thematic programme encourages civil society organisations and local authorities to participate in development cooperation projects. The funding is allocated via projects, grants and contracts and also via sector-specific support and budget support (European Commission 2014:3–6).

The EU and Swedish Aid Policy: Europeanisation?

As we have already seen, EU member-states are to coordinate their aid policy at EU level. It is therefore essential that Sweden's aid policy is formulated in accordance with EU development cooperation. At the same time, the EU development aid policy serves only to supplement that being pursued at national level given the shared competence between the EU and the member-states. Complementarity and the division of tasks (not a complete harmonisation) are the two aspects upheld as key ingredients, not least in ensuring that the aid going to the recipient countries is more results-oriented and is provided more efficiently (Interview 2). The fact that Sweden is generally seen as a country which is scrupulous in complying with and implementing EU Directives (will and capacity) would suggest there is a greater likelihood of 'top-down' Europeanisation of Swedish policy compared to countries where this is not the case. This assumption seems not, however, to apply to development aid. Swedish aid policy has been relatively stable with only minor differences in nuance. It is therefore interesting to see whether instead of 'top-down' Europeanisation we can see a 'bottom-up' and a 'horizontal' effect whereby Sweden, either on its own or together with other like-minded EU countries, has influence on the shaping of EU aid policy ('bottom-up') and on the policies being pursued in less progressive countries ('horizontal'). For this to be the case there need to be changes in EU policy in line with the policy in Sweden's after it has been implemented at national level.

Sweden has long had a progressive policy supported by a well-establish aid administration. Many view Swedish aid policy – as part of the broader 'Nordic aid model' – as a pioneer in this area whereby it runs generous and altruistic programmes and a large number of multilateral aid programmes. In comparison, EU aid policy has been viewed as less progressive and more bureaucratic and as representing a compromise between the policies of the member-states that reflect their different backgrounds and interests (Elgström & Delputte 2016: 1–2). This has often led to the perception that the EU has much to learn from the Swedish policy – especially given the shorter history of EU aid policy – and that Swedish influence on EU aid policy is striking. Swedish representatives do find that other countries listen to Sweden on aid issues (Interview 2). We might therefore expect the influence of the EU (and other member countries) on Swedish aid policy to be more limited.

EU aid policy has undergone huge changes in recent years. Compared to other areas of EU policymaking, there is a strong consensus today between member-states and the Commission regarding development aid, especially among those member-states providing aid. Only minor differences in nuance on factual matters (different sectors and geographic priorities) set the countries apart from each other (Interview 1). Of the EU-28 member-states, those in Central and Eastern Europe have introduced an entirely new form of aid policy and administration, which they did not have before. At the same time, older member-states have introduced reforms in the way they provide aid. These reforms have helped bring about a broader group of countries with a more like-minded aid policy – resembling the Swedish and the traditional 'Nordic aid model'. This convergence is evident in the *Agenda for Change*. This informal group of progressive, like-minded EU countries consists of Sweden, Denmark, Finland, the Netherlands and the UK. They consult each other on a frequent basis and have in recent years had a powerful influence on the shaping and direction of EU aid policy (*cf.* Odén 2011:9, 21). This core group is joined by other like-minded countries (such as France, Germany, Ireland, Belgium, Portugal, Spain and Poland) on different factual matters. At the same time, the Commission is an important progressive actor, which drives development forward (Interview 1, Interview 2).

Norms and Values

The motivation for Swedish aid has remained more or less unchanged in over sixty years; namely, international solidarity. In this context, other EU countries have pointed to their historic ties (*e.g.* Spain's ties to Latin America) or the security dilemma (*e.g.* the focus of the Mediterranean countries on the migrant flow from North Africa) and EU development cooperation activities were initially based on the former colonial ties of some of its member states (Dearden 2008: 115). However, solidarity has now become the main motivation for the EU development aid policy. This can be seen as the result of the impact to a certain extent of the Swedish/Nordic aid model at EU level ('bottom-up' Europeanisation).

The main objective of Swedish aid has been to combating poverty and providing assistance to LCDs – where the key elements of economic growth, the equal distribution of resources and support for the recipient countries to ensure their ownership with time have been supplemented with a focus on good social governance, human rights, the environment and equality (Elgström & Delputte 2016: 5–6). As we have seen, this differs somewhat from EU development cooperation in the past. Before aid policy was institutionalised in the 1990s, it had headed in a 'geographic' direction: instead of focusing on the LCDs, it had bestowed greater advantages on former colonies than on other developing countries in regions such as Latin America and Asia which had no association with the EU. Sweden adapted to the 'special relations' that still exist between the EU and the ACP countries and the territories dependent on a member-state, while at the same time and in collaboration with the other Nordic countries and the UK seeking to combat poverty and focus mainly on the LCDs. Today combating poverty is another main target of EU policy even though the ACP countries still enjoy certain advantages through the Cotonou Agreement. The EU has also begun focusing more on the LCDs (70 per cent of EU aid currently goes to the LCDs), in particular the SSA countries and failing states (Interview 1).

The prioritising of different interim targets in Swedish aid policy has changed somewhat over time. In recent years, Sweden has highlighted the role of the private sector in global development and the importance of integrating the developing countries into the global economy. Since these aspects have long been part of EU development cooperation activities (from the Lomé Convention to the *Agenda for Change*) and since Sweden was initially fairly sceptical about the role of private actors in the aid sector, this could be a sign of the 'top-down' Europeanisation of Swedish policy. At the same time, this change could also be explained by international trends in the past 15–20 years within multilateral organisations outside the EU, where the role of private actors in development and trade patterns has come increasingly to the fore. This has probably had an impact on both EU and Swedish policy (see also Elgström & Delputte 2016:6, Interview 1, Interview 2).

Sweden has also started prioritising a coherent development policy. At the time it joined the EU, the coherence between the different areas of EU policy that had an impact on the developing countries was less evolved than it is today, especially given the coordination that now exists between aid policy and trade and agricultural policy. This lack of coherence can be said to have indirectly brought about the Europeanisation of Swedish policy. In the years leading up to its entry into the EU Sweden had ushered in reforms and the deregulation of its agricultural policy (although these measures were not to reach fruition) at the same time that the restrictions on textile and clothing had been brought to an end. EU membership meant that Sweden reintroduced some of these protective measures, which meant repressive conditions for economic growth in the developing countries (see Haglund 2004, see also SOU 96: 256–257).

Sweden has been one of the countries that has been a driving force for greater coherence in the EU (Interview 2). Although the less developed coherence that existed between the areas of EU policy affected Swedish policy at the start, the EU's coherence policy today is in line with the Swedish (Skr. 2007/08: 89). In this area too, therefore, one can draw the conclusion that 'top-down' Europeanisation tends to be marginal, whereas both Swedish and EU policy seem to have been influenced by international trends in the aid sector.

One area where we see a change that was initiated at EU level and thereafter incorporated into Swedish policy is the stronger connection between security and development (see, for instance, *Agenda for Change*), which can be seen as a sign of a certain degree of Europeanisation ('top-down'). In recent times, more aid goes to countries experiencing conflict and where peacekeeping activities are ongoing. That said, this connection is being made not in the EU alone but also in international discourse, not least within the UN and in particular in the aftermath of the terrorist attacks in the US in 2001 (Interview 1, Interview 2). Any form of direct EU influence on the change in Swedish policy is therefore hard to prove.

Nevertheless, there are areas where it seems Sweden has had influence on EU policy and on policy in less progressive countries ('bottom-up' and 'horizontal' Europeanisation). The issue of equality is regularly brought up by Sweden in different aid contexts to give it greater clout. This issue is now given priority in like-minded countries and by the European Commission. Another area in which Sweden is a strong driving force is human rights (the rights perspective), and significant progress has been made in this area within the EU. One important issue for Sweden is SRHR (*Sexual Reproductive Health and Rights*) regarding human rights in the area of reproductive health and rights (such as abortion). This is perhaps one of the few areas where the active aid donors in the EU do not share the same outlook – a couple of countries have diverging views from the rest – but it is still one where Sweden is seen to have influence over other member states. Democracy is another key issue for Sweden; it was highlighted during the Swedish Presidency of the EU in 2009 and is now also a priority on the EU's aid agenda (Interview 1, Interview 2).

Structure

In contrast to the EU's eastward expansion (2004/2007), whereby the new member-states were largely forced to implement an entirely new development aid administration ('top-down' Europeanisation), Sweden already had an established policy with a well-developed administration and institutional structure for aid. On joining the EU, Sweden embraced all the EU regulations in the aid sector, and one direct effect of membership is that it now takes an active part in the EU decision-making apparatus and institutional structure, which means it has a say in the shaping of policy at EU level. Thus, since 1995, the EU with its organisational system has wielded institutional influence on the way decisions on policy are made.

Since 2006, Sweden has changed the way it works in relation to the EU in the aid sector. In particular since the Lisbon Treaty and the establishment of the EEAS, it has been taking a more active role in influencing the development and implementation of EU policy. Prior to that, the Commission had been regarded as a more independent actor in the aid sector (Interview 2). Today, Sweden contributes to the shaping of EU development aid at meetings of the Council of the European Union, Council working parties, implementation committees and groups of experts who are involved in the preparation and implementation of EU aid, and through the embassies/offices in the field

(Regeringskansliet 2015. Prop. 2015/16:1, p. 11). Swedish involvement in relation to the Commission's initiatives is evident in such matters as the wording of policy documents, and Swedish perspectives are seen as having great impact (Riksdagen 2006/07:rfr7). The formulation of targets and the content of Commission policy documents often closely resemble those of Sweden, albeit that the methods of implementation and follow-up can differ (Odén & Wohlgemuth 2006, Regeringskansliet 2007: 29–30).

A striking consequence of membership is that a significant part of the annual Swedish aid budget is now being channelled via the EU, partly in the form of contributions to its joint budget and the EDF (Riksdagen 2006/07: rfr7). The total Swedish contribution to EU aid has, as stated before, been about 3 per cent of the total EU aid budget (Regeringskansliet 2015. Prop. 2015/16-1: 16). However, despite this sum the proportion of the total aid budget making up multilateral aid has not increased as a result of EU membership and a large part is still channelled via the UN and the Bretton Woods Institutions.

Sweden's aid volume is far above the average for the DAC countries. The other core countries in the like-minded group have also reached the 0.7 per cent target (albeit that in 2013 the Netherlands fell just short of this level – the first time since 1975). Together with the other like-minded countries, Sweden gives more in multilateral aid than do other aid donors (25–30 per cent) and a large part to the LCDs (approx. 60 per cent of total aid), whereby the SSA countries receive the greatest share (40–50 per cent). Despite the global financial crisis in recent years, Swedish aid has come top. Instead of 'top-down' Europeanisation of the aid volume, we may instead be seeing 'horizontal' Europeanisation in the less progressive EU countries with a more limited aid volume. Greater influence of this kind on the less progressive countries will, however, be determined by such factors as the overall state of the EU economy (*cf.* Zemanova 2012: 38).

Instruments and Channelling

Prior to the EU membership, Sweden had had special country strategies in place for several countries in Central and Eastern Europe. These were replaced when Sweden joined the EU by structural support for regional development within the framework of EU regional policy. That said, Sweden believes it has had a strong influence on developments in the EU whereby programme planning is now based on country strategies in line with the Swedish model (the Riksdag 2006/07: rfr7). As regards aid allocation to different sectors under Swedish policy, this has generally been in line with international trends. While areas such as healthcare, education, infrastructure and rural development have always been part of the aid programmes, we can see that over the past 15 years there has been more focus on conflict prevention measures, democracy and private-sector initiatives.

One distinctive feature at national level is the Swedish doctrine of ownership, which remains intact and unaffected by EU membership. This runs counter to the idea of Europeanisation. Sweden has pursued the issue of ownership both within the EU and at international level generally, and this issue is now coming increasingly to the fore in EU policy (in the Agenda for Change) (*cf.* Odén & Wohlgemuth 2006:2). The Commission pioneered the use of the term budget support and during 2003–2004 encouraged Sweden to make greater use of budget support. Sweden, together with the other Nordic countries, came to provide more budget support than the average amount provided by the other DAC countries. This can be interpreted as representing EU influence on Swedish policy. The amount of budget support has, however, decreased in recent years, and a shift from general budget support to sector support is now taking place (Elgström & Delputte 2016: 6, Interview 1).

When the EU adopted the Policy Framework for Aid Efficiency (2009), Sweden already had a well-developed system of aid coordination that had been in place for several years. Swedish aid implementation is largely decentralised to the actors out in the field (as is the decision-making) and Sweden's aid offices and embassies in developing countries are seen as important sources of knowledge among other donors thanks to the broad experience. This would suggest there is no 'top-down' Europeanisation. The view is that Sweden is able to pass on its experiences of operational donor coordination in the field to ensure greater aid efficiency, and together with other Nordic and like-minded countries (which often coordinate the activities of their embassies/offices in the recipient countries) provide inspiration to other EU countries (Interview 1, Riksdagen 2006/07:rfr7, Prop. 2002/3:122). The decentralisation of decision-making, including accountability for both decision-making and funding, is an issue being pursued by both Sweden and the Commission, and such decentralisation has now increased (Interview 1). It is possible that over time there may be greater coordination to boost EU influence in relation to other, more recent aid donors (*e.g.* China and India) in the developing countries. The setting up of the EEAS may also lead to greater aid coordination in the recipient countries (*cf.* Elgström & Delputte 2016:39). Joint programming is one sign of greater coordination of this kind between the member- states and the EU in order to improve aid efficiency.

Conclusion

When Sweden joined the EU, development aid policy was a relatively new policy-area at EU level, and it brought in its long tradition of international development cooperation under the EU umbrella. We have seen that the extent of 'top-down' Europeanisation is relatively limited in Swedish aid policy. What characterises Swedish aid policy today is largely that pursued by progressive, like-minded states and promoted by the European Commission. Although we see fewer changes in prioritised areas of aid and instruments since Sweden joined the EU, we see no clear evidence for change in relation to motive, main objective, aid volume or implementation out in the field. The change that has taken place as a result of EU membership, is more about adding further elements to a structure of goals and instruments that is already in place, rather than a change in the nature of the policy as such. The shared competence between the EU and the member-states in development cooperation can in part explain the limited 'top-down' Europeanisation.

With its broad experience and leading position in terms of aid volume, Sweden is one of the core countries in a group of progressive, like-minded countries, which constitute a driving force for development and for the shaping of a more coherent aid policy in the EU ('bottom-up' Europeanisation). As discussed, this group consists not only of the Nordic countries, but also of a broader representation of countries. This can also be seen as the spread of Nordic norms to other EU countries, where certain Nordic countries have acted as norm entrepreneurs within the EU (horizontal Europeanisation). We have seen that EU aid policy is now largely synchronised with the direction of Swedish policy.

References

Council of the European Union and the European Commission. 2000. The European Union's development Policy, Statement by the Council and the Commission, 20 November 2000, Brussels.

Council of the European Union. 2005. Millennium Development Goals: EU Contribution to the Review of the MDGs at the UN 2005 High Level Event – Conclusions of the Council and the Representatives of the Governments of the Member States Meeting within the Council, 9266/05, 24 May 2005.

— 2009. Council Conclusions on Policy Coherence for Development (PCD).

— 2013. Council Conclusions on Policy Coherence for Development.

Dearden, S. 2008. 'Delivering the EU's development policy: policy evolution and administrative reform', *Perspectives on European Politics and Society*, 9(2).

Development Assistance Committee. 2000. Development Cooperation Review of Sweden, Main Findings and Recommendations. OECD, www.oecd. org/dac/htm/sweden00.htm

— 2015. Development Cooperation Report 2015: Making Partnerships Effective Coalitions for Action – Sweden. http://www. keepeek.com/Digital-Asset-Management/oecd/development/ development-co-operation- report-2015/sweden_dcr-2015-51-en#page1

Elgström, O. & S. Delputte 2016. 'An end to Nordic exceptionalism? Europeanisation and Nordic development policies'. *European Politics and Society* 17(1).

EU-African Summit 2014. Fourth EU-Africa Summit, 2–3 April 2014, Brussels Roadmap 2014–2017. Accessed October 27, 2018 at https://www.consilium.europa.eu/media/21520/142094.pdf

European Commission 2000. Communication from the Commission to the Council and the European Parliament, The European Community's Development Policy, com(2000) 212 final.

— 2001. Commission Communication of 2 May 2001 on building an effective partnership with the United Nations in the fields of Development and Humanitarian Affairs, com(2001) 231 final.

— 2011. Communication from the Commission to the European Parliament, the Council, the European Economic and Social Committee and the Committee of the Regions – Increasing the

impact of EU Development Policy: An Agenda for Change, com(2011) 637 final.
– 2013. Communication from the Commission to the European Parliament, the Council, the European Economic and Social Committee and the Committee of the Regions – A Decent Life for All: Ending poverty and giving the world a sustainable future, com/2013/092 final
– 2014. Communication from the Commission to the European Parliament, the Council, the European Economic and Social Committee and the Committee of the Regions – A decent life for all: From vision to collective action.
– 2015. European Commission calls for renewed commitments to reach targets on official development assistance, Press Release, 08 April 2015, ip/15/4747.
– 2015. Communication from the Commission to the European Parliament, the Council, the European Economic and Social Committee and the Committee of the Regions: A Global Partnership for Poverty Eradication and Sustainable Development after 2015, com(2015) 44 final.
– 2015. Annex to the Communication from the Commission to the European Parliament, the Council, the European Economic and Social Committee and the Committee of the Regions: A Global Partnership for Poverty Eradication and Sustainable Development after 2015, com(2015) 44 final.
– 2015. Policy Coherence for Development, 2015 EU Report, swd(2015) 159 final
– 2017. Joint Communication to the European Parliament and the Council – for a Renewed Impetus of the Africa-EU Partnership 2017, com(2017) 17 final
Europeiska Kommissionen 2014. Internationellt samarbete och utveckling: Tillsammans mot fattigdomen i världen, November 2014.
European Parliament, Council and Commission 2006. Joint statement by the Council and the representatives of the governments of the Member States meeting within the Council, the European Parliament and the Commission on European Development Policy:'The European Consensus'. *The European Consensus on Development*, (2006/C 46/01)
Förenta Nationerna 2000. Förenta Nationernas Millenniedeklaration, The Millennium Summit, New York
Globkom 2002 *En ny svensk politik för global utveckling, rapport från Globkom.* Kommittén om Sveriges politik för global utveckling, SOU 2001:96
Government Communication 2016. Policy framework for Swedish development cooperation and humanitarian assistance. Com(2016) 17:60.
Haglund, A. 2001. 'The European Union and Humanitarian Assistance: Definition, International Context and Developments', In: C. Cosgrove-Sacks (ed.) *Europe, Diplomacy and Development. New Issues in EU Relations with Developing Countries*, Basingstoke: Palgrave.
– 2004. 'Biståndspolitik' I: T. Bryder, D. Silander & C. Wallin

(ed.), *Svensk politik och den Europeiska unionen.* Malmö: Liber.

Hveem, H. & D. McNeill *1994. Is Swedish Aid Rational? A Critical Study of Swedish Aid Policy in the Period 1968–1993.* Ds 1994:75, Report 2. Stockholm: Fritzes.

Horký-Hlucháň, O. & S. Lightfoot (ed.) 2013. *Development Policies of Central and Eastern European States: From Aid Recipients to Aid Donors.* New York & London: Routledge

Juncker, J-C., September 13, 2017. State of the Union Address 2017. European Brussels: Commission. Accessed at http://europa.eu/rapid/press-release_SPEECH-17-3165_en.htm Retrieved November 3rd, 2017.

— 2018. State of the Union 2018 – The Hour of European Sovereignty. Accessed October 13, 2018 at https://ec.europa.eu/commission/news/state-union-2018-hour-european-sovereignty-2018-sep-12_en

Lightfoot, S. 2008. 'Enlargement and the challenge of EU development policy'. *Perspectives on European Politics and Society* 9(2).

— 2010. 'The Europeanisation of International Development Policies: The Case of Central and Eastern European States'. *Europe-Asia Studies* 62(2).

Nyman-Metcalf, K. 2001. 'The Future of Swedish Development Cooperation seen in an EU perspective, rapport på uppdrag av den parlamentariska kommittén'. *Sveriges politik för global utveckling – Globkom.*

Odén, B. 2011. 'The Africa Policies of Nordic Countries and the Erosion of the Nordic Aid Model' – Discussion Paper 55. Uppsala: Nordiska Afrikainstitutet.

Odén, B. & L. Wohlgemuth 2006. 'Svensk bistandspolitik i ett internationellt perspektiv'. *Perspectives* No 1, University of Gothenburg.

OECD 2005. Paris Declaration on Aid Effectiveness.

— 2008. Accra Agenda for Action.

Regeringen 2003. Regeringens proposition 2002/03:122. Gemensamt ansvar: Sveriges politik för global utveckling.

Regeringskansliet 2007. Strategi för multilateralt utvecklingssamarbete. Stockholm, April 2007.

— 2008. Globala utmaningar – vårt ansvar: Skrivelse om Sveriges politik för global utveckling. Stockholm, Skr. 2007/08:89

— 2010. Gemensamt ansvar för global utveckling. Stockholm: Utrikesdepartementet.

— 2013. Den globala utmaningen migrationsströmmar, Skrivelse om samstämmighet för utveckling 2014, Skr. 201314:154.

— 2015. Regeringens deklaration vid 2015 års utrikespolitiska debatt i riksdagen.

— 2015. Nytt ramverk för det svenska utvecklingssamarbetet, http://www. regeringen.se/regeringens-politik/hallbar-utvecklingspolitik/utveckling2016/

— 2015. Förslag till statens budget för 2016, Internationellt bistånd, prop. 2015/16:1 utgiftsområde 7

Riksdagen 2007. Sveriges deltagande i EU:s biståndspolitik, 2006/07:rfr7, Stockholm, June 2007.

Sida 2015. Svenskt utvecklingssamarbete och dess resultat i siffror 2014, www.sida.se

— 2015. Strukturella orsaker till fattigdom och ojämlikhet samt förutsättningar for en rättvis och hållbar utveckling, Skrivelse 15/000595

– 2017. Some results of Swedish development cooperation. Swedish development cooperation and its results in figures. Stockholm: Sida.
– 2017. The Year in Review – Sida's Activities in 2017. Stockholm: Sida.
– 2018. How we work. *Sida's humanitarian aid in 2016*. Accessed October 4 2018 at https://www.sida.se/English/how-we-work/our-fields-of-work/humanitarian-aid1/sidas-humanitarian-aid/
– 2018. Reporting & Result. Portfolio overview. Accessed October 2 2018 at https://www.sida.se/English/how-we-work/Reporting-and-results/
– 2018. September 18. Det här är svenskt bistånd. Accessed October 5 2018 at www.sida.se/Svenska/sa-arbetar-vi/Detta-ar-svenskt-bistand/Bistand-via-EU/
– 2018. September 26. Svenskt bistånd via EU. Accessed October 5 2018 at www.sida.se/Svenska/sa-arbetar-vi/Internationellt-samarbete-/
– 2018. Where we work. *Where Sida works*. Accessed October 4 2018 at https://www.sida.se/English/where-we-work/
Steinglass, S. 2015. *The EU'S role in development cooperation: Promoting aid harmonisation in times of crisis*. EUSA Biennial Conference, Boston, March 5–7, 2015
United Nations 2001. Road map towards the implementation of the United Nations Millennium Declaration, Report of the Secretary-General, United Nations General Assembly, 6 September 2001, A/56/326, Fifty-sixth session, Item 40 of the provisional agenda, Follow-up to the outcome of the Millennium Summit.
– 2015. Draft outcome document of the United Nations summit for the adoption of the post-2015 development agenda. General Assembly, 12 August 2015, A/69/L.85, including the Annex: Transforming our world: The 2030 Agenda for Sustainable Development.
– 2015. Addis Ababa Action Agenda of the Third International Conference on Financing for Development (Addis Ababa Action Agenda), 13–16 July 2015.
Usherwood, S. 1998. 'Development Cooperation', In: G. Glöckler, L. Junius, S. Usherwood and J. Vassallo. *Guide to EU Policies*. London: Blackstone Press Limited.
Vikinge, L. 1997. *Etik och biståndspolitik. En konstruktion av etisk bedömningsgrund för inriktningen av svensk biståndspolitik*. Acta Universitatis Upsaliensis, Uppsala Studies in Social Ethics 19, Uppsala University.
Wong, R. 2007. 'Foreign Policy', In: P. Graziano & M. Vink (eds.). *Europeanization. New Research Agendas*. Basingstoke: Palgrave Macmillan.
White, B. 2001. *Understanding European Foreign Policy*. Basingstoke: Palgrave.
Zemanova, S. 2012. 'The Europeanisation of official development assistance: EU governance by cooperation – communication and domestic change'. *Eastern Journal of European Studies* 3(1).

Interviews

Interview 1: Minister Counsellor, Development Policy, Head of Development Cooperation Coordination Division, humanitärt samarbete och mänskliga rättigheter/demokrati, horisontell biståndspolitik, Sveriges ständiga representation vid den Europeiska unionen, Brussels, 20 November 2015.

Interview 2: Group Manager, the Ministry for Foreign Affairs' EU Unit, Stockholm. 26 November 2015.

14. Lessons Learned

Swedish Politics and the EU

Daniel Silander & Mats Öhlén

With this book, we hope to raise the general level of knowledge about the impact of EU membership on national politics. In Sweden, which is the focus of this book, knowledge is still limited as to how the two systems – the European and the national – are linked to one another, and how politics is shaped in a continuous interplay between them (see Swedish Government Official Report 2016:10). This low level of knowledge is especially alarming today, since more and more issues are being discussed and decided at the European level. We hope to provide new insights on how the Union and a member state – in this case Sweden – work and influence each other, and how specific policy areas which affect our daily lives are shaped and changed in the interplay between the two levels.

The EU is a complex organisation. For decades, it has expanded with the successive admission of new member states. As it has expanded it has also deepened, thereby increasing its influence over various policy areas in Sweden. It is becoming more and more difficult to separate national and international politics – to distinguish Swedish politics on the one hand from European politics on the other. This makes it particularly important to help citizens gain greater knowledge about the Union and its impact on concrete policy. However, the lack of knowledge seen in Sweden in this regard is also evident among central actors such as journalists, teachers, politicians, and even academics – people who are expected to inform the public about political affairs. This book is therefore not just for students and citizens, but also for politicians, civil servants, journalists, and teachers. Greater knowledge in this area may encourage a more enlightened debate on how Sweden both affects and is affected by the multi-level governance system of which the country has been a part since 1995, when it joined the EU.

The aim of this anthology has been to analyse the impact of EU membership on Sweden, both over time and across policy areas. The core questions have been: What are the implications for Sweden's polity (form) and policies (content) of deepening integration into the EU's political system? We focus on the multilevel linkage between institutions at the local, regional, and national levels in Sweden on the one hand, and Union institutions and legislation on the other. In chapter 2, in an effort to cast light on the dynamics involved, we introduced the concepts of *Europeanisation, governance*, and *policy processes*. This conceptual framework, we believe, can be helpful for attaining a deeper understanding of how and why Swedish politics is influenced by the EU. We then examined eleven different policy areas: economic policy, agricultural policy, environmental policy, social policy, educational policy, gender-equality policy, asylum-and-migration policy, crime-prevention policy, foreign and security policy, neighbourhood policy, and finally foreign-aid policy. We covered the period since 1995, when Sweden joined the EU.

Our point of departure was that the Union is a well-developed and institutionalised system of European cooperation, which over time – with its increasing number of member states and its progressively denser cooperation in a number of policy areas – has had a significant impact on both the outcomes and the organisation of Swedish politics. As we underscore in chapter 1 the EU is an important power factor. It is not unreasonable to describe it as the most significant actor shaping national and continental politics in Europe today. It is a dominant actor in this part of the world, and it has grown stronger in global affairs as well (mainly on questions of trade, but also on issues of security). The Union today is far more than a traditional international organisation. A complex political system, it can be described as a hybrid between an intergovernmental and a supranational organisation.

In chapter 1, we mentioned the 'catalogue of competencies', in which three different categories of EU competence are set out: exclusive, shared, and supportive. *Exclusive competence* refers to policy areas where the Union has the exclusive right to promulgate legal acts, which the member states are then bound to implement. When *shared competence* is in question, both the Union and its member states can legislate. In policy areas marked by *supportive competence*, finally, the EU has merely a supporting role – in the form of consultation and coordination – in the processes by which the member states enact legislation (see chapter 1). It bears mentioning, moreover, that any policy area not regulated in the EU treaties falls within the exclusive purview of each member state. The policy areas examined by the authors in this book vary in the kinds of competencies that apply.

One important tool for enhancing our understanding of the interplay between Swedish politics and the EU is the concept of Europeanisation. In chapter 2, we defined Europeanisation as the process whereby the institutions and policies of the Union influence those of the member states. This process can be direct or indirect. Direct Europeanisation takes place when the Union requires that new regulations be implemented. Indirect Europeanisation, by contrast, does not take the form of specific EU decisions; but it is still connected to political discussions, events, or ideas at the Union level. Formal Europeanisation consists of legislation and regulations from the EU, with resulting legal obligations for the member states to adapt their rules and institutions thereto. Informal Europeanisation involves influence on the behaviour expected of the member states. Upon becoming a member in 1995, Sweden incorporated the full set of EU regulations (*acquis communautaire*) into its laws; since then, moreover, it has adopted various new treaties, regulations, and goals in order to function within the Union. It has also undergone informal Europeanisation, whereby it has assumed the norms, values, and ideas that prevail in the Union. This can be seen in the substance and organisation of Swedish politics, as well as in the way Swedish politicians consult with their counterparts in other member states and take their views into account before making decisions for Sweden.

The treatment of economic policy in chapter 3 illustrates this adaptation, whereby Swedish policy has been influenced by the Union through the latter's exclusive competence in matters of competition regulation, and through shared competence between the two levels in matters relating to the single market. The analysis in that chapter points out how the EU has shaped the framework for Swedish economic policy, even as the Swedish government has kept strong influence over the content of policy. Swedish policy in this area has been subject to direct Europeanisation by the Union's regulations on competition, as well as its requirements regarding state subsidies to specific enterprises. Chapter 4, on agricultural policy, shows the strong influence of the EU in that area. This is evident above all in the subsidies dispensed, which for the most part are financed directly out of the EU budget. It is also seen in the fact that the member states may not pursue any policy in this area which might undermine the principle of equal competition on the single market. At the same time, agricultural policy in the Union is a matter of shared competence. Swedish proposals for agriculture must accordingly be approved by the Commission before they can be implemented. Chapter 5 underlines the shared competence applying in the area of environmental policy, whereby Sweden can make its own decisions on some issues but not others. This policy area is furthermore intertwined with several others, complicating conditions for governing – a complexity reflected in the variable nature of the fit between Sweden and the EU on different issues within this policy area.

Chapter 6 deals with social policy, an area where Sweden is internationally renowned for its unique welfare-state model. On most issues of this kind, the EU has only a supporting role. This means that, in practice, Sweden alone has the right to legislate on national issues like taxes, health care, pensions, housing, education, and family-related matters. However, competence is shared on some issues in this policy area – such as the work environment or the coordination of social-security systems – due to their close association with the single market and the free movement of employees. Indeed, Swedish regulations are becoming increasingly Europeanised on a number of issues, including health care, labour law, gender equality, discrimination, public procurement, the work environment, and the rules governing access to social support. These developments all point to reduced national sovereignty in this policy area.

Chapter 7 takes up educational policy, an area relatively uninfluenced by the EU until the early 2000s. However, with the elaboration of more extensive EU policies on education – as seen in the Bologna and Lisbon processes especially – the Union has become increasingly important in this area too. Indirect Europeanisation has been evident here, among other things in the way Sweden has started applying the methods for evaluating higher education for which these processes have called, despite the limited competence of the EU in this area. However, elements of direct Europeanisation are also present, as seen in the adoption of an action programme for policy development in education and the recognition of foreign degrees. Chapter 8 looks at policy for gender equality. The EU has no formal policy here, but the area falls *de facto* within the Union's purview, and equality between men and women constitutes a fundamental value for its member states (see article I-2, article I-58, and article I-59). There is thus a certain lack of clarity about what kind of competence applies in this area. On some social-policy issues, for example, competence is shared; but the Union has only a supporting role when it comes to health. In fact, on one central topic for gender equality – violence against women – it has no competence at all. On the other hand, it has shared competence on several questions related indirectly to gender equality, like freedom, security, justice, and the single market. Moreover, the EU has exclusive competence on the customs union. EU regulations may thus apply for cross-border business operations and for some forms of violence against women. The chapter does point to some adjustment on Sweden's part to EU norms and policies in this area, both institutionally and substantively, but it also shows how Sweden has influenced the EU in turn.

The subject of chapter 9 is asylum-and-migration policy, an area closely connected to such matters as foreign aid and internal and external security. As a consequence of EU membership and the Schengen Convention, a somewhat complicated overlap between internal and external security is found in this area. Thus, responsibility for controlling territory and the movement of people is now shared between the EU and its member states. In a clear break with the typical Swedish preference for intergovernmental decision-making in the Union, Sweden has pushed for increased supranational decision-making on asylum-related issues. The refugee crisis of recent years has also laid bare the inability of the member states to arrive at a common position. As a consequence, several member states have taken increasingly restrictive measures. When the refugee crisis was at its worst, in 2015, the Commission pushed for both political and judicial reforms in this area, in an attempt among other things to strengthen external border controls and to make the processing of asylum applications more efficient. Nevertheless, the Commission has met with but limited success in its attempt to solve the main problem by introducing a new quota system, in which member states share the refugee burden. The EU's influence has also been limited when it comes to labour immigration to Sweden. There is one issue in this area on which Sweden has been pressured to change its policy – on the equal-treatment principle in connection with the right of third-country nationals to social security. According to the Treaty of Lisbon, competence in this area is shared. This means the EU has the authority to regulate immigration and the issuance of residence permits for third-country nationals, but that Sweden still decides the number of persons admitted. Chapter 10 deals with a policy area closely related to asylum and migration: crime prevention. The object of policy in this area – to control immigration and to combat cross-border criminal activities – assumes particular importance as a consequence of the four freedoms and the operation of the single market without internal border controls. The member states have thus decided to coordinate asylum policy, to institute intelligence cooperation, to take compensatory measures within the Schengen Area, and to set up a European public prosecutor. Taken together, these developments have resulted in a Europeanisation of crime prevention in Sweden. No longer a strictly national activity, it is now an area of shared competence and increased intergovernmental cooperation. This Europeanisation is reflected in the creation of new organisational units, the emergence of new policy content, and the appearance of a new political discourse in Sweden. (It is important to note, however, that the maintenance of order and security in Sweden remains a national matter.)

Chapter 11 takes up foreign and security policy. This area is marked by rather obvious Europeanisation, in that Sweden must now consider the positions taken by other member states when making its own decisions. By coordinating its policies in this area with those of the other member states, Sweden is able to strengthen its influence over the common foreign and security policy, and over the common security and defence policy as well. Formally speaking, policy in this area is conducted by the member states themselves. Issues are discussed and decided in forums that include several cooperating member states, with the EU playing a supporting and coordinating role. Chapter 12 examines the neighbourhood policy, which is closely connected to the common foreign and security policy. Policy in this area forms an integral part of the Union's external relations, and member states are expected not to pursue their own policies independently of EU influence here. For Sweden's part, the neighbourhood policy has shifted from being a strictly national matter (concerned with the post-communist countries in the Baltic Sea region) to forming an integral part of the Union's relations with the countries which now – after eastern enlargement in 2004 and 2007 – are its eastern neighbours. Since the early 2000s, the EU has stressed the importance of the neighbourhood policy. It is the member states which have the formal authority to sign agreements or enter partnerships with the countries in question. Chapter 13, finally, examines foreign-aid policy, an area where Sweden has long had a prominent international role. Still, the EU has furnished an additional platform for Swedish policy in this area. Competence here is shared between the EU and its member states. This means that, parallel with EU policy, each member state has the right to conduct its own policy in this area, as long as it does not undermine the pursuit of the basic goals of EU policy. Sweden has long experience with foreign aid, where it has strong organisation, far-reaching networks, and substantial expertise. Accordingly, it has been a significant actor in formulating the Union's foreign-aid policies. Like several other progressive countries within the Union, Sweden has kept control over the bulk of policy in this area. Together, moreover, these countries exert substantial influence over the Commission's activities in this regard. Europeanisation in this area consists, then, in a broadening of aims and instruments, but not in any change of the established policy itself. Still, the common foreign policy does play an important role as a forum for discussion in this area – between member states, EU institutions, and foreign-aid agencies – and it has contributed to a general improvement in foreign aid.

Our point of departure in this book, like that in earlier research on this matter, is that the degree of Europeanisation reflects the closeness of fit between the Union's demands and expectations on the one hand, and the norms, routines, and institutions of the member states on the other. Europeanisation thus finds varying expression – both in organisational form and in policy content – in different policy areas.

Finally, it is important to mention that Sweden today forms an integral part of a uniting Europe. The difference in this regard is substantial compared to the situation that prevailed shortly after the country's accession to the Union in 1995, when the discussion was still dominated by the pro and cons of membership as such. Two decades of Europeanisation, in the context of an expanding and deepening EU, has resulted in a Sweden which is naturally linked together with the other member states in a common project of improving Europe through cooperation and coordinated action. The European project has met with both successes and failures, but it is both broader and deeper now than ever before. Furthermore, current challenges demonstrate the need for even more cooperation between the member states and within the EU's institutions. As this book is being finalised, the Union and its member states are still struggling with the consequences of Brexit; with a drawn-out economic crisis; with the rise of right-wing populist parties in several member states that question not only the EU as a project, but also some of democracy's core principles; with a refugee crisis which has not only challenged but even incapacitated earlier agreements on the asylum process within the Union; and finally with serious tensions with Russia, which in its rhetoric and its foreign and security policies has confronted Europe with a possible 'return of the cold war'. These challenges affect all of the member states, and they touch on most of the policy areas directly or indirectly discussed in this book. The question is not whether the Union and its individual member states will deal with these challenges, but rather how they can do so within the framework of the EU. The manner in which they do this, and the degree of success they achieve in so doing, will have great importance to European integration.

References

Swedish Government Official Report 2016:10 *EU på hemmaplan* [*The EU at home*]. Stockholm.

About the Authors

Therese Bjärstig is Associate Professor at the Department of Political Science at Umeå University. Her research includes political steering and implementation on local-, regional-, national- and EU-level with focus on natural resource policy and rural development policy.

Tobias Bromander is Senior Lecturer of Political Science and Head of Pedagogy and Learning at Linnaeus University. His main research areas are Europeanization of Swedish and EU economic policy, entrepreneurship and political/economic scandals.

Fredrik Bynander is Associate Professor and the Director of the Centre for Societal Security at the Department of Security, Strategy and Leadership at the Swedish Defense University. His main research focus concerns international security, crisis management and leadership.

Katarina Eckerberg is Professor of Political Science at Umeå University. Her expertise comprises environmental, climate and natural resource policy and politics at global, national and local level.

Camilla Eriksson is Researcher at the Swedish Defense Research Agency. Her research explores the relationship between agriculture, the state and society with specific interest in underlying rationales of agricultural policy and defense policy.

Ingrid Grosse is Senior Lecturer of Sociology at Dalarna University. Her main expertise is in the areas of social policy, rural and urban social development and human welfare.

Anne Haglund Morrissey is Associate Professor of Political Science and works as Acting Head of Horizon Europe Association Unit – DG Research and Innovation, European Commission.

Martin Nilsson is Senior Lecturer of Political Science at Linnaeus University. His research focuses on European politics, the European Neighborhood Policy and prerequisites to sustainable democracy.

Anna Parkhouse is Senior Lecturer of Political Science at Dalarna University. Her research interests include the European Union as regional and global actor, the impact of the EU membership incentive on rule adoption in minority rights legislation and European policies on asylum-seekers and refugees.

Charlotte Silander is Associate Professor of Political Science and Deputy Head of Department of Education and Teachers' Practice Pedagogy and Learning at Linnaeus University. Her research focus is on gender equality in higher education, systems of higher education and research policy.

Daniel Silander (ed.) is Associate Professor and Research Leader of European Studies at the Department of Political Science, Linnaeus University. He is conducting research on international security, democratization and European integration.

Sofia Strid is Associate Professor and Senior Lecturer of Gender Studies at Örebro University. Strid's research departs from feminist social theory and focuses on intersectional violence, violence as a post-disciplinary research field, gender (in)equality architectures and policy.

Rebecka Villanueva Ulfgard is Researcher at the José María Luis Mora Research Institute, Mexico. Her research focuses on theories of international relations and international cooperation for development and the policies and institutions of the EU.

Mats Öhlén (ed.) is Senior Lecturer of Political Science at Dalarna University. His research includes EU institutions and transnational European parties.